Burning Down the House

SUNY series

FRONTIERS IN EDUCATION

Philip G. Altbach, Editor

The Frontiers in Education Series draws upon a range of disciplines and approaches in the analysis of contemporary educational issues and concerns. Books in the series help to reinterpret established fields of scholarship in education by encouraging the latest synthesis and research. A special focus highlights educational policy issues from a multidisciplinary perspective. The series is published in cooperation with the School of Education, Boston College. A complete listing of books in the series can be found at the end of this volume.

Burning Down the House

Politics, Governance, and Affirmative Action at the University of California

Brian Pusser

State University of New York Press

Published by
State University of New York Press, Albany

© 2004 State University of New York

All rights reserved

Printed in the United States of America

No part of this book may be used or reproduced in any manner whatsoever without written permission. No part of this book may be stored in a retrieval system or transmitted in any form or by any means including electronic, electrostatic, magnetic tape, mechanical, photocopying, recording, or otherwise without the prior permission in writing of the publisher.

For information, address State University of New York Press,
90 State Street, Suite 700, Albany, NY 12207

Production by Judith Block
Marketing by Anne Valentine

Library of Congress Cataloging-in-Publication Data

Pusser, Brian
    Burning down the house : politics, governance, and affirmative action at the University of California / Brian Pusser.
       p. cm.—(SUNY series, frontiers in education)
    Includes bibliographical references and index.
    ISBN 0-7914-6057-6 (alk. paper)
    1. University of California (System)—Admission. 2. Education, Higher—Political aspects—California. 3. Minorities—Education (Higher)—California. I. Title. II. Series.

LD729.8.P87 2004
378.1'18'09794—dc21
                                                                      2003052619

10 9 8 7 6 5 4 3 2 1

Contents

Figures and Tables	vii
Acknowledgments	ix
1. Burning Down the House: The Politics of Higher Education Policy	1
2. The UC Governance and Decision-Making Structure: History and Context	13
3. The Context Shaping the Affirmative Action Contest at UC	25
4. Interest Articulation and the Illusion of Control	45
5. The New Politics of Governance	83
6. National Contest and Conflict	119
7. Contest, Resistance, and Decision	143
8. Aftermath	197
9. The End and the Beginning	211
Appendix 1. SP-1 as Amended and Passed	229
Appendix 2. SP-2 as Amended and Passed	231
Notes	233
Bibliography	253
Index	263
List of Titles, SUNY series: Frontiers in Education	279

Figures and Tables

Figure 3.1. California SAT Scores	31
Figure 3.2. Eligibility Rates	33
Figure 3.3. UC Berkeley Freshman Applications and Admissions, Fall 1980–Fall 1994	35
Figure 3.4. Number of Applicants to UC San Diego, Berkeley, and Santa Cruz by Academic Index: 1994	35
Figure 3.5. Number of Admits to UC San Diego, Berkeley, and Santa Cruz by Academic Index: 1994	36
Figure 6.1. Fall 1992 Freshman Admissions at Berkeley	139
Figure 8.1. UC Berkeley Enrollment	202
Table 3.1. Parental Income, Occupation, and Education Level: UC In-State Freshman Applicants, Fall 1994	32
Table 3.2. UC Board of Regents: Backgrounds and Appointments	37
Table 3.3. Confirmation Dynamics for UC Regents (1972–2002)	39

Acknowledgments

Every project imparts a number of lessons. One that I take from this endeavor is that you can never have too much assistance, nor can you be too grateful for that support. This book was made possible with the cooperation of students, staff, faculty, administrators, and Regents of the University of California who lent their voices, experiences, and energy to its creation. I am grateful to the Office of the Secretary of the Regents of the University, and to the University of California Office of the President. Special thanks are also due to the Secretary of the Board of Regents, Leigh Trivette, and the Associate Secretary of the Board of Regents, Anne Shaw.

I am also very grateful for the guidance I received from Patricia Gumport, who has been a mentor from the beginning, and to Henry Levin, Michael Kirst, and Martin Carnoy, who deserve recognition for providing direction at the earliest stages of the work.

Special thanks are due to Sheila Slaughter and Estela Bensimon for their extensive comments on the manuscript, and for the example they have set in their intellectual and professional endeavors. Carter Wilson has been a teacher and friend from the day we met. His wisdom and good counsel are a treasure, and did much to shape this project.

A number of scholars have welcomed me into collaborations that have helped immensely in the preparation of this book. Among these, Sylvia Hurtado, Charles Schwartz, Jeffrey Milem, Mitchell Chang, Joseph Berger, Eric Dey, John Levin, Jim Hearn, David Kirp, Scott Thomas, and Don Heller deserve special recognition. I have also been fortunate to work with a unique group of international scholars. Simon Marginson, Barbara Sporn, Jussi Vaalima, Marcela Mollis, and Humberto Munoz have been essential in helping me to expand my intellectual horizons.

I owe a debt of gratitude to Annette Gibbs, Jennings Wagoner, and Alton Taylor, my colleagues at the Center for the Study of Higher Education at the University of Virginia. It has been a privilege to work alongside such exemplary colleagues. I have also benefited greatly from conversation and collaboration with David Breneman, Sarah Turner, Hal Burbach, and Marcia Invernizzi.

I am very grateful to Ken Kempner and Gary Rhoades for lessons in balance, and for creating a unique series of seminars that were invaluable to the preparation of this book. I am greatly indebted to Imanol Ordorika for sharing his vision, his family, and an office at Stanford. His good humor, innumerable talents, and dedication to progress have proved invaluable from the first days of this project.

A number of people were instrumental in stewarding this project. Philip Altbach and Priscilla Ross at SUNY Press have offered exceptional editorial support. Terry Fierer read many iterations of this manuscript and improved each one with his thoughtful comments.

This book has also been shaped by those most dear to me: my parents, Portia and Gordon, my brothers Kevin and Craig, Jane and Gene Foster, Tim Taylor, and Steve Levintow. There are many others who are in my thoughts and in my heart. I trust they know how I feel.

For her creativity, patience, and irrepressible spirit, this book is dedicated to Rebecca Hart Foster, the love of my life.

1

Burning Down the House: The Politics of Higher Education Policy

There is a story that blacksmiths tell. It seems that when the pioneers headed west from the territories, as they left a settlement behind, their final act was to set fire to their homes. When the blaze had cooled, the pioneers would sift through the ashes, and collect the nails to begin again.

INTRODUCTION

On July 20, 1995, in the culmination of twelve months of rising organizational and political economic conflict, the University of California (UC) Board of Regents voted 14–10 to end race and gender preferences in university admissions, and 15–10 to do so for employment and contracting.[1] The votes, having been delayed by a bomb threat, were taken at the end of more than twelve hours of deliberation. The Regents' votes on proposals SP-1 and SP-2 marked a historic reversal of nearly thirty years of UC affirmative action efforts, and made UC the first public university in America to eliminate the use of race and gender in admissions and employment. The Regents' actions were all the more remarkable coming from a university that, as the defendant in the landmark 1978 U.S. Supreme Court case *UC Regents v. Bakke*, had done much to preserve and codify existing national affirmative action policies in higher education.

The fall of affirmative action at UC challenged a number of prevalent understandings of the nature of policymaking and governance in higher education. An impressive array of institutional factions had urged the Regents to preserve UC's existing policies on affirmative action. Supporters included the president of the system, the university provost, all nine chancellors, representatives of the nine campus academic senates, representatives of all nine UC student associations, representatives of the system's major staff organizations, representatives of the university alumni association, and the faculty representatives to the Board of Regents.

There was also considerable support for UC's affirmative action policies beyond the campus borders. The Clinton White House and its Chief of Staff, Leon Panetta, showed considerable support, as did the California State Senate and Assembly Democratic caucuses and a number of elected state officials. They were joined by a significant cohort of organizations devoted to an end to discrimination and the redress of historical economic and social inequalities in America. The Reverend Jesse Jackson representing the Rainbow Coalition, the Reverend Cecil Williams and other church leaders, the NAACP, MALDEF, the ACLU, national student organizations, labor organizations including UPTE and AAUW, and such activist community organizations as the Grey Panthers all came to the defense of affirmative action at UC. Through a number of social and political actions, these groups worked to resist the effort to end affirmative action, and to link the struggle at UC to a broader struggle over access and equality.

Powerful forces were also arrayed in pursuit of an end to affirmative action at UC, including California Governor Pete Wilson, the State Assembly and Senate Republican caucuses, several candidates for the Republican presidential nomination, and a number of conservative legal foundations and interest groups. Despite nearly a year of public deliberation, a barrage of state and national attention directed at the Regents' deliberations, and the active involvement of the university's administrative leadership in the contest, the outcome came as a profound shock to institutional leaders at UC and across the country.[2]

That many in academe were surprised by the outcome of the affirmative action policy contest at UC points to the lack of theoretical and empirical work on contemporary university policymaking in a rapidly shifting political and economic context. Scholars of higher education have rarely addressed the role of public and private universities in broader state and national political contests, nor have they generally linked research on university policies to broader questions of race, gender, and power in the academy. As public universities increasingly become sites of contest over the allocation of scarce public resources, it is imperative to understand the uses of the university as an instrument in broader political contests, and the role of the State in the provision of public higher education.[3]

Intensified global economic competition has led to demands for increased contributions from higher education to state and federal economic development, and has also heightened the competition for access to both the most prestigious institutions and their most prestigious disciplines. At the same time, institutions are faced with competing demands for expanded access to higher education on the part of groups historically underrepresented in the academy, and for a broader distribution of the benefits of higher education throughout society.[4] These essentially contradictory demands have refocused attention on the importance of postsecondary policy as part of broader national and international policy contests, and have brought to the fore questions of institutional purpose and locus of control.

The contest over affirmative action policy at UC provides a particularly useful lens for understanding contemporary governance and policymaking. Since World War II, the University of California has been a highly salient site of conflict over public policies affecting academic research with military applications, the right to free speech and assembly on campuses, institutional investment practices, and admissions policies.[5] Over the past two decades affirmative action policies have also played a pivotal role in state and national electoral and interest group contests,[6] as these policies have been key factors in State efforts to redistribute access to postsecondary educational opportunity and the private and public benefits generated by higher levels of education.[7] Another unique aspect of this case is that the intensity and personal character of this contest induced policymakers within and outside of the university to reveal their preferences in public.

This contest also offers considerable insight into the nature of contemporary organizational decision making in higher education. Making sense of the Regents' votes entails reconsidering the role of bureaucratic rationality in decision making, the effect of institutional culture on administrative behavior, the concept of collegiality, the extent of faculty authority, and the limits on interest articulation. While each of those approaches to understanding higher education organizations has utility, they are not what define this case. Comprehending the outcome of the contest over affirmative action at UC requires an understanding of the university as a democratic political institution, as an institution with both symbolic and instrumental political value in broader contests for State power and authority. It is a way of understanding public universities that scholars of higher education organizations have rarely adopted.

This is also a story of race and gender. To understand the struggle for affirmative action at the University of California, one must understand the role of public higher education in the redress of racial and gender inequality in America and the ways in which interest groups coalesce politically around those issues. Fundamentally, this is a story of politics and power. It details the long-term efforts of political leaders in one of the nation's key political battlegrounds to gain control of an important public institution and to use that institution's policies on access as levers in broader political contests.

For researchers and scholars of the organization and governance of higher education, this case is ultimately a window into how we understand our own institutions. It offers both a powerful reminder of what is useful about existing models of organizational behavior in higher education, and a challenge to improve our understanding of the political dimension of those models. The case reveals the influence of the university administrative leadership in the unfolding contest, the collegial, consensus-driven approach taken by the university faculty,[8] the symbolic power of UC's historical commitment to access and affirmative action, and the influence of internal interests in the shaping of the contest. Yet taken together, these frameworks fail to explain the decision reached in this contest.

The decision-making contest over affirmative action at UC was decided both slowly, through nearly twenty years of political action on gubernatorial appointments to the Board of Regents and senate confirmation of those appointments, and all of a sudden in July 1995, by a 15-10 vote of the board. It was also decided both near at hand, by the unsuccessful efforts of the Office of the President to articulate the various interests weighing in on the contest, and at some distance, by the efforts of a powerful governor in the state capitol and his political allies across the country.

Each of these dichotomies serves as a useful reminder of the many ways we have conceptualized decision making in public higher education, and of the fundamental arena in which we have failed to conceptualize that process. The routine description of the mission of a public university encompasses teaching, research, and service, but very rarely addresses the larger role of a university as a political institution, and the political value of a university's mission. More often than not, we have treated political challenges to a university as unfortunate anomalies and have moved forward with existing theoretical lenses and frameworks intact.

The data from this case study suggest that a new framework is necessary for understanding contemporary higher education decision making. That we need new ways of conceptualizing the politics of higher education is due in large measure to a historical separation of political theory and the study of organizations.

UNDERSTANDING HIGHER EDUCATION ORGANIZATIONS

Understanding the politics of postsecondary organizational behavior has been an enduring challenge for researchers in higher education. While models of behavior in other types of organizations and institutions have been transformed over the past four decades by an infusion of research and theoretical perspectives grounded in political science (Weingast and Marshall, 1988; Wilson, 1973) and economics (Arrow, 1974; Stigler, 1971; Williamson, 1985), research on university organization and governance has generally utilized multidimensional models (MDMs) with little connection to contemporary political or economic theory (Berger and Milem, 2000; Pusser,

2003). This anomaly emerges from some key distinctions between the disciplines. Research in higher education has focused on the institutions themselves, complex organizations with myriad missions that are not easily illuminated by the rational modeling favored in contemporary economics and political science. Further, institutional decision making in higher education has been understood as a consensual process that often avoids the declaration of individual preferences central to political models of organizational behavior. In this case, the public, pitched battle over affirmative action at the University of California offers a rare opportunity to revisit our existing frameworks for understanding organization and governance in higher education (Pusser, 2001).

THE PREVALENT MODEL OF ORGANIZATIONAL BEHAVIOR IN HIGHER EDUCATION

The multidimensional model of organizational behavior is one of the key analytical frameworks in higher education research on organization and governance (Bensimon, 1989; Berger and Milem, 2000). Although the model varies in the number of elements incorporated and their relative importance, nearly all permutations incorporate the political dimension developed by J. Victor Baldridge (1971). Baldridge's political dimension has been recognized as one of the essential elements of MDMs (Berger and Milem, 2000) and as the analytical frame most in need of revision (Ordorika, 2003; Pusser, 2003). The political dimension of the MDMs can be traced to Baldridge's (1971) *Power and Conflict in the University*, a study of organizational contest at New York University during the student protests of the sixties. Baldridge presented decision-making dynamics through an interest-articulation model, one that portrayed organizational "authorities" who made decisions for the whole, and "partisans" who were affected by those decisions (Baldridge, 1971, p. 136). The authorities served as "boundary spanners," key actors who mediated, or articulated, between internal and external constituencies.

Over time, scholars of organizations and higher education have revised the political frame to turn attention to external context, agenda control, interest groups, and legitimate authority in the higher education decision-making process, yet, until quite recently, research in higher education has treated institutional organization and governance as a largely endogenous process.[9] As a result, there is relatively little that a political theorist would recognize in the contemporary political model for research on higher education organizations.

POLITICAL THEORY AND ORGANIZATION STUDIES

The separation of political theory from the study of organizations has been particularly problematic for the evolution of a political theory of higher education.[10] Terry Moe (1991) has suggested that this differentiation is due to the historical structure of the study of public administration. Since the early part of the twentieth century, administration and politics have been treated as quite separate entities in the study of public sector institutions. Over time, the study of effective administration and organization became the domain of organizational theorists, while political scientists turned attention to the dynamics of Congress and the executive branch.[11]

More recently, an emerging perspective in political science research in the United States, the positive theory of institutions (PTI), has turned attention to institutions as instruments in a broader political process. PTI has been applied to research on the organization and governance of public institutions, combining elements of political and economic theory to address the structuring of political institutions for partisan gain. Moving beyond its original application to regulatory agencies, congressional committees, and bureaucratic structures, the PTI model has been usefully applied to the study of the organization and governance of the elementary-secondary system and to specific structures and processes within postsecondary institutions.[12]

Positive theories have emerged from work on social choice. Kenneth Arrow and other social choice theorists pointed out that although majority rule policymaking is unstable and leaves a great deal undetermined, the political process and political institutions are relatively stable. PTI offered an explanation: the structure of political institutions brought stability to majority rule decision making and offered a mechanism for successfully implementing gains from those decisions. The exercise of public authority through majority rule voting demanded particular structures and processes to ensure that political bargains and contracts could be enforced under conditions of uncertainty. That is, few individuals or interest groups would "contract" to allow a majority rule body to decide gains or losses on a particular issue. Since in a democratic process many policy decisions are made in precisely this fashion, interest groups have an increased incentive to organize such political institutions as legislatures and governing boards in order to make it more difficult to overturn status quo bargains.[13]

The new economics of organization proved a quite useful component of PTI, as it added insights from economic theory, particularly agency theory and transaction cost economics, to the analysis of the structural form of political institutions. Principal-agent contracts between individuals are a staple of modern life, and within the PTI framework the relationship between institutions, state legislatures, and state universities, for example, is conceptualized as a principal-agent problem.[14]

POSITIVE THEORIES OF INSTITUTIONS AND HIGHER EDUCATION

Initial applications of positive theories of institutions to postsecondary governance have conceptualized the university as a site of struggle between competing interest groups within the institution and have focused on efforts to build institutional structures, such as the tenure system, that help enforce bargains.[15] Like J. Victor Baldridge's early work and the subsequent application of the political frame of multidimensional models of organizational behavior, PTI has until quite recently been applied only to the endogenous articulation process in higher education. While useful, this approach does not go far enough.

A political theory of higher education decision making needs to encompass more than external interest pressure on the internal formulation of institutional policy. It also needs to account for a far more exogenous process, the efforts of external actors and interest groups who intervene in postsecondary policy struggles to gain influence over public benefits and to use public institutions as instruments in a broader political process.

The central elements of external efforts to gain influence over any political institutions are delineated in the PTI model. These factors include efforts to control the agenda for organizational action; ex ante legislative design of institutional governance structures; personal relationships between policy actors apart from any formal relationships; and the control of the allocation of costs and benefits from institutional policy.[16]

PUBLIC HIGHER EDUCATION INSTITUTIONS AS POLITICAL INSTITUTIONS

Developing a contemporary political theory of higher education entails conceptualizing public higher education institutions as political institutions, entities that control significant public resources, possess the authority to allocate public costs and benefits, implement policies with significant political salience such as conditions of labor or standards of credentialing, and that stand as particularly visible sites of public contest. A number of researchers have argued that these conditions describe public higher education institutions in the United Sates, that public higher education institutions are political institutions, and that higher education can be seen as a key commodity in its own right.[17] Consequently, the postsecondary policy formation process may be characterized as an interest group struggle for that commodity value.

There is a significant limitation on prevalent models of higher education decision making that must also be addressed in order to build an effective political theory of higher education. Positive theories in political science rely on pluralist[18] assumptions about the governance of public institutions. The pluralist, "common good" assumption suggests that the political system allows for representative expression of the general will. PTI and interest articulation models have conceptualized decision making as an essentially pluralist process, as they examine, for example, the role of political parties in state and national policymaking. While that is one aspect of political contest, there are many levels of access to a given decision process, and many groups that do not necessarily have meaningful representation. The ways in which their interests are brought to the attention of decision makers and the ways in which the disenfranchised shape public policy contests are unlikely to be made clear under pluralist frameworks. To get beyond the limitation of pluralist processes requires an analysis of the role of political institutions within theories of the State.[19]

A STATE THEORETICAL VIEW OF HIGHER EDUCATION

A class view of the State suggested that the State is an instrument for perpetuating and reproducing dominant formations. Subsequently a variety of State theoretical perspectives emerged, including Antonio Gramsci's (1971) vision of hegemony as key to understanding class conflict and contest. Gramsci's work brought attention to the role of the State and its institutions, including education, as sites of contest. Bowles and Gintis (1976, 1990) presented a rather static, reproductivist view of the function of the education system, arguing that "the educational system, basically, neither adds to nor subtracts from the degree of inequality and repression originating in the economic sphere. Rather, it reproduces and legitimates a preexisting pattern in the process of training and stratifying the work force" (1976, p. 265). Resistance theorists challenged the reproductivist view by restoring a strong degree of agency to the process. Resistance theory suggests that schools are contested sites characterized by structural and ideological contradictions and student resistance, where subordinate cultures both reproduce and resist the dominant formations.[20] A number of researchers have extended this proposition to suggest that the education system holds the potential for equalization and democratization as well.[21]

Carnoy and Levin (1985) argued that contests over the provision of education can be seen as one part of a broader societal conflict rooted in the inequalities of income, access, opportunity, and power. Labaree (1997) conceptualizes the conflict pointed to by Carnoy and Levin as an essentially political dynamic. Labaree characterizes the tension as one between democratic politics (public rights) and markets (private rights) and suggests that these inherently contradictory forces have been expressed as three essential and competing educational goals: democratic equality, social efficiency, and social mobility. He suggests, "In an important way, all three of these goals are political, in that all are efforts to establish the purposes and functions of an essential social institution."[22]

The role of the State itself in civil society has been widely debated.[23] Building on Weber's insights on institutions, Mann proposed that State interest is expressed through State political institutions, which in turn constrain future struggles. As Mann puts it, "States are essentially sites in which dynamic social relations become authoritatively institutionalized, they readily lend themselves to a kind of 'political lag' theory. States institutionalize present social conflicts, but institutionalized historical conflicts then exert considerable power over new conflicts." Within this process, the creation and control of public institutions is essential. Mann concludes, "Degrees of success in achieving political goals, including the enactment of social legislation, depend on the relative opportunities that existing political institutions offer to the group or movement in question, and simultaneously deny to its opponents and competitors."[24]

THEORIES OF THE STATE AND HIGHER EDUCATION RESEARCH

A problematic aspect of research on higher education policymaking is that very little work has invoked State theoretical standpoints. As Wirt and Kirst suggested nearly thirty years ago, scholars of the State and scholars of the school have been "temporarily separated brethren."[25] That "temporary" separation has continued to the present day. As noted, research in higher education has generally been based in pluralist paradigms that conceptualize the university as distinct from the State, and that conceive of the State as a political actor operating independent of higher education institutions (Rhoades, 1992). This rather limited view of the role of higher education in a social welfare context also significantly constrains research on the role of postsecondary institutions as political institutions and sites of contest. Perhaps the foremost exception to the general treatment of the State in higher education is the work of Sheila Slaughter, individually and in collaborations.[26]

In her pioneering work on academic freedom and the state, Slaughter (1988) traced the growth of higher education as both outcome and catalyst for the larger growth of the American State in the post–World War II era. Following Carnoy and Levin's conceptualization of these tensions in education institutions generally, Slaughter (1988) concluded that "it may be necessary to conceive of the State and higher education as engaged in multiple and sometimes conflicting functions simultaneously. For example, the State and higher education are both the subject and object of struggle. They are arenas of conflict in which various groups try to win ideological hegemony, yet at the same time they are resources for members of contending groups intent on political mobilization in external arenas" (p. 245).

Taken together, State theoretical perspectives effectively challenge endogenous models of higher education governance, as they suggest that powerful external forces, operating within a context of historical developments and conditions, shape political action and decision making at the institutional level.

RESEARCH DESIGN AND DATA

Two fundamental strands of data collection were used in this research. The first entailed building a historical record of this case using archival records and documents from the Bancroft Library of the University of California, the Office of the Secretary of the Regents of the University of California, and the UC Office of the President. Primary source documents included minutes of meetings of the Regents, documents and reports produced for the Regents during the period under study, as well as system-wide and campus-based reports and publications. These institutional documents were supplemented by state level data, including material from the Office of the Governor, legislative hearing transcripts and reports from members of the legislature, as well as such national data as Office of Civil Rights investigative summaries relating to the University of California, and Federal Court rulings. Another key portion of the documentation of this case was the transcription of the entire Regents' meeting of July 20, 1995. That transcript, compiled from nearly twelve hours of audio and videotape, is a verbatim record of the Regents' deliberations on the day of their votes to eliminate affirmative action.

The second avenue of data collection centered on semi-structured interviews with individuals central to the decision making contest. Those interviewed included individual Regents of the University, administrators on the individual campuses and in the Office of the President, state policymakers, students, representatives of the UC staff associations, alumni representatives to the Board of Regents, faculty Senate representatives to the board, and community activists. These interviews were transcribed, coded, and analyzed for linkages to the core analytical categories framing the study of this case (Strauss and Corbin, 1994). The presentation of this case includes a range of voices, perspectives, and data sources in order to illuminate the individual and institutional processes of education, negotiation and decision making that shaped the contest.

THE UNIVERSITY OF CALIFORNIA

Chartered in 1868, the University of California was created as a public land grant university and is administered under the authority of a constitutionally empowered Board of Regents. At the time of the Regents' deliberations over affirmative action in 1994-95, the university consisted of nine campuses: Berkeley, Davis, Irvine, Los Angeles, Riverside, San Diego, San Francisco, Santa Barbara, and Santa Cruz. Eight of the campuses provided broad undergraduate, graduate, and professional education, while UC San Francisco has been dedicated to the health sciences. A tenth campus, the University of California at Merced, is expected to open in 2004.

The University of California is one of the most complex postsecondary enterprises in the world, encompassing the ten campuses, a number of academic medical centers, research institutes, and national laboratories operated under contract with the federal government. National Science Foundation data indicate that at the time of the votes on affirmative action in 1995, five UC campuses (Berkeley, Los Angeles, San Diego, San Francisco, and Davis) ranked among the top 25 universities nationally for total research and development revenues. At that time, three UC campuses (Berkeley, Los Angeles, and San Diego) were members of the Association of American Universities, and UC had more academic programs ranked among the top 10 in the nation than any other public or private institution. The university had a total budget for 1994/95 of nearly $10 million. A measure of the centrality of the university to the state of California is that UC received over $2 billion in appropriations from the state for fiscal year 1995. Enrollment for fall 1994 was over 150,000 students with roughly one-quarter of those graduate and professional students.[27] The university is based in an equally large and diverse state. The total population of California in 1995 was over 32 million, with some 45% of the population White, 35% Hispanic, 12% Asian/Pacific Islander, and 6% Black.[28] California has the largest state economy in the nation, accounting for nearly 12% of the national GDP, and UC has long played a key role in the economic development of the state.[29]

The prominence of the University of California, its central role in the political economy of the nation's most populous state, and the prolonged public character of the challenge to affirmative action provide a unique insight into the contemporary politics of postsecondary organization and governance. The making of postsecondary policy is a dynamic, path-dependent process, one that is best understood in light of historical formations and precedents. For that reason, the struggle over affirmative action has its roots in the founding of the university, and it is there that the analysis of the case appropriately begins.

2

The UC Governance and Decision-Making Structure: History and Context

The context for policymaking at the University of California at the time of the Regents' votes was shaped by four key historical factors: (1) UC's constitutional autonomy under the Organic Act and the California constitution; (2) a state constitutional provision calling for the majority of the board to be appointed by the governor, subject, after 1972, to State Senate confirmation; (3) the enactment of Regents' bylaws and standing orders allocating responsibility for curricula and admissions policies to the academic senates; and (4) the California Master Plan of 1960 (Douglass, 2000, 2001).

THE FIRST CALIFORNIA CONSTITUTION AND THE ORGANIC ACT

The origin of the University of California governance and policymaking structure can be traced to the California Constitutional Convention of 1849. At the convention, article IX of the constitution was adopted, providing that funds received from the sale of federal land grants under the Morrill Act would be used for the funding of schools and the establishment of a common university. In 1868 the California legislature passed the Organic Act, authorizing the creation of a single state public university, the University of California. According to UC historian Verne Stadtman, the Organic Act was crafted so as to "qualify the University for federal agricultural-college land grants, while permitting the immediate introduction of courses in letters and pure sciences" (Stadtman, 1970, p. 32).

The Organic Act also delineated the structure of the first UC Board of Regents, a structure that would remain remarkably unchanged for the next 130 years. The Organic Act called for a board with eight members appointed by the governor, serving sixteen-year terms with staggered appointments. The appointed Regents were joined on the board by six ex officio members: the governor, lieutenant governor, Speaker of the Assembly, superintendent of public instruction, and the presidents of the State Agriculture Society and the Mechanics Institute. The appointed and exofficio Regents were responsible for jointly appointing eight additional Regents, bringing the total on the board to twenty-four.

The power to choose a president was vested in the board and, even before appointing the first president, the Regents selected a core faculty. From that point the Act clearly prescribed the following:

> The immediate government and discipline of the several colleges shall be entrusted to their respective Faculties... for approval by the Regents.... All the faculties and instructors of the University shall be combined into a body which shall be known as the Academic Senate, which shall have stated meetings at regular intervals, and be presided over by the president... and which is created for the purpose of conducting the general administration of the University. (California Statutes of 1867–68, 248, in Douglass, 2000, p. 368, note 71)

In 1869 the university enrolled its first class. The essential governance and policymaking structure then defined was much as it is today, with general education policy set by the Regents. Over time a significant shift in structure has occurred. At the founding, faculty members were responsible for serving as both instructors and the university's general administrators. The president served as the liaison between the Regents and the faculty, empowered to sit on both the Board of Regents and the Academic Senate. Today a bureaucracy has emerged on each campus to handle university administration in consultation with the academic senates. The chancellors and their administrative cohorts serve as a link between the campuses and the University of California Office of the President (UCOP). The Office of the President, which is located in Oakland, California, apart from all campuses, is the contemporary liaison between the Regents and the Academic Senate (Gumport and Pusser, 1995).

THE SECOND CALIFORNIA CONSTITUTION

At the time of the second California Constitutional Convention, held in Sacramento in 1879, the university was under political siege. A coalition of delegates was attempting to disband the Regents and place the university under the control of a legislative board (Douglass, 2000). One of their complaints was that the land grant university had become the captive of California's elite and that it was created out of collusion between bankers, railroad owners, and business interests for their own benefit, at the expense of farmers and other workers.[1] The coalition also complained about the appointed members of the Board of Regents, noting that its membership consisted of "merchants, lawyers, physicians and devines, devoid of one practical and experienced educator" (Schulte, in Douglass, 2000, p. 48). A bill was introduced into the California Senate in 1874 to reorganize the Regents so that the board would consist of seven ex officio Regents and eight elected Regents, one from each of the state's eight congressional districts. Although the legislature resisted efforts to revise the university governance structure, Gilman, an early believer in academic freedom, left in disgust to take the job as first president of Johns Hopkins. In his resignation letter he wrote, "However well we may build up the University of California, its foundations are unstable, because it is dependent on legislative control and popular clamor."[2]

The struggle at the convention was essentially between Grange members and Workingmen's Party delegates on the one hand, who favored placing the university under direct electoral control, and California Whig Republicans who represented the state's business class and major financial interests. At that time in California there was tremendous concern on the part of the populist political parties about the growing power of the railroads and banks, the lack of proportional representation in state government, and legislative corruption.[3] Their apprehension was made manifest in the question of whether Regents should be appointed or elected, a debate essentially over whether the university should be autonomous, or under direct legislative and electoral control.

As Douglass (2000) has chronicled, a key figure at the convention was Joseph Winans, a Regent of the university and chairman of the convention's Education Committee. Winans led the committee in presenting a recommendation for constitutional language that included these words: "The University of California shall constitute a public trust, and its organization and government shall be perpetually continued in their existing form and character, subject only to such legislative control as may be necessary to insure compliance with the terms of its endowments, and of the Legislature of this State, and of the Congress of the United States, donating lands and money for its support."[4] The committee further recommended that the constitution incorporate language ensuring that "the University would be entirely independent from all political or sectarian influences, and kept free therefrom in the appointment of its Regents and in the administration of its affairs."[5]

When the issue came before the convention for a vote, it was presented in the form of a constitutional amendment supported by the Workingmen that would have removed the words "public trust" from the university's charter and placed both the university and the Regents under direct legislative control, with Regents' terms and responsibilities dictated by legislative statute.

Floor debate was ended and the amendment passed by a vote of 68–49. Its sponsor returned home, as did a number of other delegates (Douglass, 2000).

According to Douglass (2000), six days before the convention adjourned, the issue was brought up again by supporters of the university. A new amendment was proposed, restoring the status of the Regents and the university as a public trust under the Organic Act. It also included language ensuring that no persons would be excluded from the university on account of their sex and incorporated language that provided the university remarkable insulation, subject only to "such legislative control as may be necessary to insure compliance with the terms of its endowment and the proper investment of and security of its funds."[6] This time the amendment passed, and thus the university's autonomous status was established in the constitution.[7] The importance of that status can hardly be overstated. The conceptualization of the university as an institution belonging to, and under the control of, the people of California rather than the legislature has been an essential part of the state's social and political culture. UC's autonomous status has been cited throughout the years in research on academic freedom and institutional control.[8] Former California Governor Edmund G. Brown described the university as "virtually a fourth branch of state government, equal and coordinate with the legislature, the judiciary and the executive."[9]

THE REGENTS UNDER THE CONSTITUTION

As a consequence of the codification of the university's status at the 1879 convention, subsequent changes in the structure of university governance have required constitutional amendments. Over the years, there have been four significant amendments. In 1918 two additional ex officio Regents were added. In 1970 the legislature passed, and the electorate ratified, a constitutional amendment requiring that Regents' meetings be open to the public.[10] In 1972 the constitution was amended by a statewide ballot initiative, Measure 5, which required that the governor's nominations to the Board of Regents be ratified by a majority vote of the State Senate Rules Committee for consideration by the full Senate (Scully, 1987).

In 1974 a number of significant changes were introduced. Regents' terms were reduced from sixteen years to twelve. In a nod to changes in the state's political economy, the ex officio seats provided to the president of the State Board of Agriculture and the president of the Mechanics Institute of San Francisco were deleted, and an ex officio seat for the vice president of the university's alumni association was added. More significantly, the number of appointed board seats was increased from sixteen to eighteen, and an advisory board was created to consult with the governor prior to making nominations to the Board of Regents. The advisory board consists of the legislative leadership and six members of the public appointed to four-year terms by that leadership, and representatives of students, alumni, and faculty. This board seems to have had relatively little influence over the years. The amendment also added language stating that the appointed Regents be "broadly reflective of the economic, cultural, and social diversity of the state, including ethnic minorities and women."[11]

THE REGENTS AS CALIFORNIA'S ELITE GOVERNING BOARD

Despite the intentions of the framers, since the founding of the university, the Regents have been an elite group. Many of the appointed Regents have been wealthy and throughout its history the board has resembled a Who's Who of California's political and economic elites. Their names are often found on buildings, businesses and monuments throughout the state. The bankers have included A.P. Giannini, founder of the Bank of America, William H. Crocker, founder of Crocker Bank, as well as I. W. Hellman, a principal of Wells Fargo Bank. Regents Leland Stanford and Charles Crocker helped create the state's transportation infrastructure. Business leaders turned Regents include Edward Carter, chief executive of the Broadway-Hale Corporation, William Roth, chairman of Matson Lines, and industrialist Norton Simon. Since founding, few of the appointed Regents have been women, among them Phoebe Hearst and Dorothy Chandler, one of the principals of the *Los Angeles Times*.[12] At the time of the votes on affirmative action, it was estimated that the median net worth of the eighteen appointed Regents was close to $1 million. It may be that the wealth of the Regents was significantly higher, as the public reporting limit for any single type of Regent's personal investment was simply "over $100,000 dollars" (Schwartz, 1996).[13]

In 1976, the language of the constitution was again amended to add an aspect that would be invoked often in the deliberations over affirmative action. The 1879 language ensuring that women would not be excluded from the university was amended to read, "no person shall be debarred admission to any department of the University on account of race, religion, ethnic heritage or sex."[14]

HISTORICAL GOVERNANCE CONTESTS

In addition to the changes in university governance structure enacted over the years, a number of shifts have also occurred in the process of making policy and in the allocation of authority for making policy at the university. Many of these shifts have occurred as the result of broader institutional and national struggles over university autonomy and shared governance.

The executive branch of the state government and the courts at both the state and the federal levels have had significant influence over the UC policymaking process.[15] UC's constitutional autonomy has been particularly circumscribed by the courts. Gardner (1967) noted in his discussion of the California Supreme Court ruling on the UC Regents loyalty oath of 1949, "On the point of the University's constitutional rights, the decision continued: 'Laws passed by the legislature under its general police powers will prevail over regulations made by the Regents with regard to matters which are not exclusively university affairs.'"[16] Despite the exceptional degree of constitutional autonomy that UC possesses, and the power of the Regents, a shared system of governance over academic and administrative affairs has been enacted out of a series of confrontations between various internal and external constituencies of the university. One of the earliest and most influential episodes has become known as the Berkeley Revolution of 1920 (Fitzgibbon, 1968).

The Berkeley Revolution of 1920

The Berkeley Revolution of 1920 codified a number of the relationships and responsibilities that have formed the basis for what has been generally understood as shared governance in the UC system to this day.[17] The revolution was inspired in part by the publication of the *1915 General Declaration of Principles* prepared by the American Association of University Professors. The General Declaration of Principles spoke to academic freedom on three dimensions: "freedom of inquiry and research; freedom of teaching within the university or college; and freedom of extra-mural utterance and action."[18] The declaration went on to point to the importance of delineating "1) the scope and basis of the power exercised by those bodies having ultimate legal authority in academic affairs; 2) the nature of the academic calling; 3) the function of the academic institution or university."

The UC Academic Senate met in October 1919 and produced a proposal that was later described as possibly "the most important memorial ever sent forward to the Board of Regents."[19] The senate requested a modification of the Regents' Standing Orders in order to clearly delineate a number of procedures and structures that addressed academic freedom and the conduct of the university. The revised orders, approved by the Regents in June 1920, assigned the university president the responsibility of recommending personnel changes to the Regents, but specified that such action could only be taken after consultation with faculty advisory boards. The orders further required the president to consult with the Academic Senate before making changes in educational policy, and enhanced communications through the creation of a joint Regent-senate conference committee. Perhaps most germane to the university's affirmative action contest, the revised Standing Orders gave unprecedented authority to the senate in the area of admissions policy, stating that "The Academic Senate, subject to the approval of the Board of Regents shall determine the conditions for admission, for certificates, and for degrees other than honorary degrees."[20] This portion of the Standing Orders formed a key rationale for faculty authority over admissions in arguments presented to the Regents by faculty and Academic Senate members during the affirmative action debate (Karabel, 1996; Schwartz, 1996).

The Loyalty Oath

Despite the careful structuring of roles and responsibilities in the 1920 revision of the Standing Orders, just over thirty years later the system would again be rocked by conflict over authority, in the loyalty oath controversy of 1949–1952. The loyalty oath crisis revolved around three primary issues: a Regents' proposal that all faculty and staff prepare affidavits disavowing membership in the Communist Party; a Regents policy prohibiting appointment to the faculty of members of the Communist Party; and a struggle within the university for authority over appointment, promotion, and dismissal of faculty members (Gardner, 1967). The Regents' move to require the signing of the loyalty oath was prompted in part by legislative efforts that were seen by the university as an attempt to usurp some of the institution's constitutional autonomy. Bills were introduced into the State Assembly in 1949 to amend the university's constitutional status, in order to assign to the legislature the power to ensure the loyalty of UC employees.

The first two issues were resolved by the Supreme Court of the State of California, which ruled that the Regents could not demand an oath of its employees that superseded the existing oath required by the state. In that ruling, *Tolman v. Underhill*, the court held that "It is well settled that laws passed by the Legislature under its general police power will prevail over regulations made by the Regents with regard to matters which are not exclusively University affairs."[21] Elsewhere in the ruling, the court made it clear that matters of statewide concern are not exclusively university affairs, and that principle guided their ruling against the university (Scully, 1987). Neither the court nor the amendment spoke to the third issue, which continues to be debated to this day.

The Regents' actions in the face of legislative efforts to usurp UC's autonomy in 1949 point to the impact of external political considerations on UC governance. As Gardner (1967) makes clear, the Regents' actions at the time of the loyalty oath were shaped by a broader issue, the growing concern over world communism, and the efforts of key legislators to embroil the university in that broader ideological and political struggle.

With the loyalty oath controversy, a familiar pattern reemerged, one that had attended the founding of the university and the 1920 revolution, and that would return again during the Free Speech Movement of the mid-sixties and in the affirmative action debate of 1994–1995. It is a pattern of political context and political struggle shaping UC policy despite normative understandings of autonomy and academic freedom, and despite traditional procedures and structures of shared governance.

An Era of Campus Protests

The next major test of shared governance at UC came in the wake of the Free Speech Movement and campus protests at UC Berkeley in the mid-sixties. Shortly after the election of Governor Ronald Reagan, the Regents, at the urging of the new governor, voted early in 1967 to remove Dr. Kerr as president of the university. According to Fitzgibbon, "the very large majority of faculty members was virtually in a state of shock. All divisions of the Academic Senate adopted resolutions deploring the action."[22]

The Kerr episode demonstrates another interesting pattern in the enactment of shared governance procedures, a pattern of procedural and structural revisions that led to increased shared governance in the wake of political crisis. After firing President Kerr, the Regents encouraged the Academic Council to create a new and permanent faculty committee to advise the Regents on the selection of a new university president. Further, the Regents asked the advisory committee to draft a set of criteria governing the selection of a new president, and many of those criteria were incorporated in the Regents' published provisions for selecting presidents (Fitzgibbon, 1968). As Fitzgibbon describes it, "If the Senate's point of view had been ignored in the events related to the dismissal of President Kerr, that certainly was not the case in the choice of his successor" (p. 88).

It is worth noting that the procedures and structures that emerge from university conflicts have not simply been gains for a winning coalition imposed on a losing coalition. In the wake of the 1920 Revolution, the Academic Council codified gains for its own benefit. In the case of the loyalty oath, little procedural or structural change resulted but, as noted, in the wake of the firing of President Kerr, the Regents codified gains for the losing coalition of faculty.

At the foundation of the present system of policymaking at UC is the concept of shared governance.[23] That foundation relies on both legal and normative understandings of shared governance, academic freedom, and institutional autonomy in higher education. The legal and historical precedents that shape those central concepts further illuminate this case.

INSTITUTIONAL AUTONOMY AND THE LAW

In contemporary higher education research, institutional autonomy is generally conceptualized as the ability of a university or college to govern itself without outside controls. Autonomy and academic freedom may be, but are not inextricably, linked. Berdahl (1971) points to Oxford and Cambridge in the nineteenth century as examples of autonomous institutions that did not always protect academic freedom, and to nineteenth-century German universities as examples of institutions where norms of academic freedom prevailed in institutions that were not autonomous. In the case of UC, the granting and ensuring of funds, as with the confirmation of Regents, permits a significant legislative and executive influence on the conduct of the university, although hardly a defining one (Miller and Moe, 1983; Zusman, 1986; Gumport and Pusser, 1995).

The U.S. Supreme Court has also addressed in some detail the issue of institutional autonomy. Metzger (1990) points out that "although academic freedom is usually treated (as in the 1940 AAUP Statement of Principles on Academic Freedom and Tenure) as a matter of individual freedom, usually that of individual teachers to address matters of professional interest without threat to their jobs, some Court decisions apply a first amendment notion of academic freedom more corporately, that is, to the university or the college as an entity. The university, it is thought, may claim a certain corporate academic freedom to set its own institutional course—in curriculum, in admissions, in appointments—sheltered from government to some degree as a matter of constitutional right" (p. 81–82). Academic freedom remains an unenumerated first amendment right that is not particularly well defined. As one federal district court judge noted, there is a "fundamental tension between the academic freedom of the individual teacher to be free of restraints from the university administration, and the academic freedom of the university to be free of government, including judicial, interference."[24]

The legal tension between individual and institutional academic freedom is grounded in a question of who has the right to determine the limits of certain types of action and expression in the university. In similar fashion, the conflict that erupted over the affirmative action crisis at UC was grounded in part in the question of who had the right to determine admission and hiring policies at the university. In both cases, many of the fundamental principles that were being contested have been enumerated by the AAUP and with regard to institutional autonomy, the courts have affirmed many of the AAUP's principles.

SHARED GOVERNANCE

Shared governance has long been considered a key aspect of the administration of higher education.[25] Although the courts have not ruled definitively on the issue of shared governance, they have addressed some aspects of internal governance, and generally they have favored trustee or board authority. Courts have suggested that there is no compelling reason for trustees to refrain from intervening in university affairs, for example in teaching, research, or publication, if to fail to interfere would constitute an irresponsible neglect of their oversight duties (Van Alstyne, 1990). The Supreme Court, in *Minnesota State Board for Community Colleges v. Knight*, refused to recognize a "constitutional right of faculty to participate in policy-making in academic institutions," and concluded, "Faculty involvement in academic governance has much to recommend it as a matter of academic policy, but it finds no basis in the Constitution" (Rabban, 1990, p. 296).

This turns attention to the historical roots of the perceptions of what the appropriate point should be, if any, where the sharing of governance gives way to the exercise of ultimate authority. On the one hand, the Regents have argued at several critical junctures in the university's history that while they acknowledge the importance of consultation with internal and external constituencies of the university, they have the ultimate authority to establish policy in nearly every realm of the university. On the other hand, a number of those internal and external constituencies, though most frequently the faculty, have argued that there are historically enacted and well understood limits on the action that the Regents should take in exercising their authority.[26]

The assessment of where the limit on shared governance should be set, if it should be set at all, depends to a great extent on the perspective of the author. According to Clark Kerr and Marian Gade, "The appropriate sharing of governance, particularly with faculty, is crucially important." The basic rule is that "sharing should be 'enough' but not 'too much.' 'Enough' includes faculty control of the essentials of academic life—both teaching and research—subject to overall board policy and to review of performance, without which it becomes too much" (Kerr and Gade, 1989, p. 100).

John Douglass has written, "The second [major feature] is the University of California's tradition of shared governance: the concept that faculty and administration should share in the responsibility of guiding the operation of the University, while the right of final say on policy is reserved to the governing board, the Board of Regents" (1995, p. 1).

Louis Heilbron, former chair of the Board of Trustees of the California State College system, wrote, "The faculty is the continuing part of the institution and ultimately will spell its success or failure. The board, therefore, should seek, through the administration and otherwise, to cooperate with the faculty" (Heilbron, 1973, p. 74–75).

The AAUP, in its 1994 *Statement on the Relationship of Faculty Governance to Academic Freedom,* stated: "Being responsible for carrying out a task is one thing, however, and having authority over the way in which the task is carried out is quite another. The *Statement on Government* connects them in the following general principle, enunciated at the outset: 'differences in the weight of each voice, from one point to the next, should be determined by reference to the responsibility of each component for the particular matter at hand.' Thus degrees of authority should track degrees of responsibility" (AAUP, 1995, p.187).

A number of arguments advanced within UC over the years have suggested how governance should be shared. Eley (1964) noted that the Standing Orders of the Regents delegate "unlimited authority over the design and administration of the curriculum of instruction" (1964, p. 9). She also notes that the Academic Senate determines conditions for admission and the awarding of degrees, although that power "is subject to the approval of the Regents, and thus the Senate's power is less than complete, it is virtually unthinkable that the Regents would ever substitute their judgment for the Senate's" (Eley, 1964, p. 9).

What these arguments constitute in essence is a recommendation that the Regents, in some arenas, not simply consult with other internal constituencies but, in effect, yield their constitutionally mandated authority over policy at the university. As the historical record shows, they are not always willing to do this—there have been a few issues, at significant historical moments, that were sufficiently salient and contested to force a showdown between the Regents and other internal constituencies over policy. The affirmative action deliberations constituted one of those moments.

THE CALIFORNIA MASTER PLAN

Perhaps the greatest challenge to the UC policymaking structure and process in the twentieth century came during the deliberations over the California Master Plan for Higher Education.[27] In light of California's rapid population growth in the late fifties and the need for expansion of state higher educational capacity, a state legislative commission was convened to investigate the possibility of coordinating the various segments of the higher education system in California. More significant from UC's perspective was the challenge in the commission's charter to consider the creation of a "superboard" to govern all three public segments (community colleges, state universities, and UC campuses) of state higher education. After two years of study, lobbying, and political negotiation, the California Master Plan was approved as the Donahue Higher Education Act in the spring of 1960 and ratified on the November 1960 general election ballot.

The Master Plan left intact the University of California's governance structure and legislated a number of provisions quite favorable to the university. It left the planning for new UC campuses in the hands of the Regents and codified UC's virtual monopoly on granting the PhD among California public higher education institutions. The Plan was not without unintended consequences for the university, some of which would become manifest in the contest over affirmative action policy. Under the Master Plan, UC became essentially California's only public provider of doctorates, law, and medical degrees. UC also became the only public segment that would conduct large-scale research and doctoral training. UC's elite status has also garnered the University disproportionate state funding. On a per-student basis, UC has long received the lion's share of state general fund revenues for higher education. The Master Plan was also in many ways the first step on the university's road to its contemporary "zero sum" admissions challenges. The intense competition for spaces in the most desirable of this elite system's campuses, created in part by the Master Plan's access restrictions, did much to shape the context of the debate over the abolition of the university's affirmative action policies.

3

The Context Shaping the Affirmative Action Contest at UC

BROWN V. BOARD OF EDUCATION

Affirmative action policymaking at the University of California was shaped in myriad ways by the Supreme Court's 1954 ruling on public education in *Brown v. Board of Education*. In *Brown*, the Court held that racial distinctions at the core of segregationist education laws violated equal protection under the Fourteenth Amendment. As a result of *Brown*, so-called separate but equal educational facilities were ruled unconstitutional. *Brown* served not only to launch the battle over desegregation of public schools, but it also inspired a series of challenges to racial discrimination in education that continue to this day.

In *Brown*, the Court noted that racial classifications were divisive, and that individuals were to be judged independent of their racial heritage (Howard, 1997). *Brown* holds a special place in the UC affirmative action contest, as it was used as an integral reference for arguments both for and against affirmative action. That is, proponents of affirmative action cited the actions of Regents endeavoring to end existing policies as efforts to roll back a process of equalization that began with *Brown*. Proponents of ending UC affirmative action policies also cited *Brown*, except that in their view it was a ruling that sought to end precisely what UC affirmative action promoted, policies based on group racial affiliations.

In 1961, President Kennedy signed Executive Order 10925 establishing the Equal Employment Opportunity Commission (EEOC) to hear complaints of racial discrimination in the workforce. In 1963 the president signed the Equal Pay Act, which introduced the first federal prohibition on discrimination in wages on the basis of gender. Wage discrimination in contemporary society would be raised as a significant issue in the Regents' discussions over affirmative action in hiring and contracting. The contemporary argument was slightly different, not that the university or other public sector employers paid differential wages on the basis of gender, but rather that women were disproportionately located in lower-paying positions at the university and in other public sector organizations.[1]

THE CIVIL RIGHTS ACT OF 1964

Perhaps the most often cited precursor of contemporary affirmative action policy was the passage of the Civil Rights Act of 1964. The act stated, "It shall be unlawful to discriminate in employment or education against any individual because of such individual's race, color, religion, sex or national origin. While its contributions to ending various forms of overt discrimination were immediately apparent, so were its limitations with regard to more subtle forms of racial and gender-based discrimination. The rise of affirmative action programs reflected the rapid change in the conceptualization of antidisrimination efforts. The Civil Rights Act was designed to remedy intentional acts of racial discrimination. To redress other forms of discrimination, aggressive affirmative action would be necessary.

Howard (1997) conceptualizes the creation of affirmative action policies in the mid-sixties as the product of three key challenges. The first was that "Blacks were excluded from participation in society by intentional discrimination" and by "institutional racism." Institutional racism manifested as "disparate impact," where racial and gender discrimination was the product of hiring criteria or social circumstances that had "a disparate or negative impact on a 'protected class'"(p. 30). Second, it was necessary to act affirmatively to eliminate institutional barriers to equal participation, and third, eliminating those barriers would require new standards to ensure access to education and employment for groups that were disproportionately suffering the impact of discrimination and institutional racism.

NATIONAL AFFIRMATIVE ACTION

The move beyond nondiscrimination law to affirmative action policies generated an immediate and lasting controversy. The move to affirmative action was seen in many quarters as violating the "color-blind" provisions of the Fourteenth Amendment, and as a move away from both *Brown*'s call to end benign racial classification, and the Civil Rights Act's abolition of differential access on the basis of race (Mills, 1994). A decade after the passage of the Civil Rights Act, Alan Bakke, in his litigation against UC Davis's denial of his application to its medical school, would base a significant element of his complaint on his right to protection against discrimination in education under Title VI of the Civil Rights Act. Despite the controversy, the Supreme Court subsequently upheld a number of challenges to affirmative action. At the same time, the federal government was moving to implement landmark affirmative action programs, including the Philadelphia Plan in 1969 (one of the principal authors, Arthur Fletcher, would testify in favor of preserving UC affirmative action policies at the July 1995 meeting), which required that companies seeking federal contracts provide a portion of the work for minority employees. The Labor Department issued guidelines in 1970 and 1971 that required efforts to bring the racial composition of the federal workforce in line with the proportion of minorities in the population, and that women should be included in the "protected classes" under emerging affirmative action programs.

The University of California also initiated affirmative action programs at that time, with considerable prodding from then chair of the Assembly Ways and Means committee Willie Brown. Brown summed up his position in a 1973 letter to UC President Charles Hitch: "The University has some distance to go before it approaches a more equitable distribution of minorities and women within its work force, both academic and staff."[2] Brown was more forceful in a letter the same year to the chairman of the UC Black Caucus: "The issue of Affirmative Action and the University has been a very sore point between the University and me for some time, and it will continue to be a factor in my consideration of its budget proposals."[3] The University agreed to implement affirmative action policies shortly thereafter, including consideration of students' socioeconomic disadvantage as admissions criteria (Richardson, 1996).

Against this backdrop, in 1975 the nation was confronted with an unprecedented challenge to affirmative action programs in higher education, in the case of *Bakke v. Regents of the University of California.*

BAKKE V. REGENTS OF THE UNIVERSITY OF CALIFORNIA

Bakke represented the first national test of the use of affirmative action in higher education admissions. Alan Bakke, an engineer in his early thirties, had been denied admission to the medical school at the University of California at Davis in both 1972 and 1973, although his academic qualifications were superior on several measures to those of thirty-two other students who were admitted without being compared to Bakke (Ball, 2000). Bakke's lawsuit claimed that any consideration of race in the admissions process violated the equal protection provisions of state and national constitutions, and also violated Title VI of the Civil Rights Act. In 1976 the California Supreme Court held for Bakke, declaring by a 6–1 vote that any consideration of race did violate the equal protection clause of the constitution. The Regents voted to appeal and were joined by the Attorney General of the United States and a number of other public and private universities.

On June 28, 1978, the U.S. Supreme Court issued a complicated and conflicted ruling. By a 5–4 vote, the Court held that race could be a consideration in admissions consistent with the equal protection clause and the provisions of Title VI of the Civil Rights Act. Six separate opinions were issued by the Court. Four justices (Brennan, White, Marshall, and Blackmun) upheld the UC Davis policy as a remedy for past discrimination. Four other members of the Court (Stevens, Burger, Stewart, and Rehnquist) would have barred all race-attentive programs as contrary to Title VI. As a result, the majority judgment in the *Bakke* case was presented by Justice Powell, who cast the deciding vote in an opinion in which no other justice joined him. He concluded that race could be considered for the purpose of increasing diversity in the admissions class.[4]

In defending the use of race as a criterion, Powell suggested that the medical school faculty had used reasonable professional expertise in making admissions choices. Powell noted, however, that the faculty had erred in denying Bakke his Fourteenth Amendment right to be compared with all applicants on an equal basis, and Bakke was admitted to the medical school. Out of the six separate opinions, three fundamental guides emerged: (1) quotas, or admissions programs that set aside admissions slots or that separate applications for separate consideration on the basis of race or ethnicity were impermissible; (2) in order to achieve racial diversity in the admissions class, race could be used in admissions, even where there was no finding of past discrimination; and (3) race could only be one factor among many in evaluating all applicants against one another (Howard, 1997).

UC ADMISSIONS AFTER *BAKKE*

In the aftermath of *Bakke*, the University faced contradictory constitutional mandates. On the one hand, they were constrained in the degree to which they could use race as a factor in admissions by the *Bakke* ruling. On the other hand, they had clear language in the California constitution directing them to admit classes to the university that represented the state's ethnic, racial, and gender diversity. That clear intent was affirmed by a number of Senate and Assembly resolutions and the California Master Plan, all of which recommended that the racial, ethnic, gender, and economic diversity at UC reflect the patterns in the state as a whole.

The university response was to revise the admissions system over the next decade to continue using race and gender within the guidelines of *Bakke*. Campuses with specific set-asides or admissions tracks shifted their policies to incorporate a greater degree of flexibility in the use of supplemental criteria. The university as a whole increased the percentage of not fully eligible students who could be admitted by special action to 6%, triple the level provided for in the Master Plan. While the university's efforts were significant, until the end of the seventies they attracted little attention. Very few UC-eligible students were turned away from the system, as virtually all UC-eligible students could be admitted at one of the campuses. At the same time, UC-eligible underrepresented students were often admitted to the campus of their first choice, and significant numbers of underrepresented students were admitted to Berkeley through special action (Karabel, 1989). The program at Berkeley was so effective that from 1980 through 1987 the number of underrepresented students admitted to the Berkeley campus grew for nearly every group in nearly every year. Taken together, the underrepresented minorities (African American, Chicano/Latino and American Indian) students made up over 30% of the freshman class at UC Berkeley in 1988. Over the same period, from 1980 through 1987, the percentage of White students in the Berkeley freshman cohort decreased from 58% to 37%.[5]

The rapid growth in underrepresented admissions in general, and special action admission in particular, along with the increasing competition for admission to UC Berkeley, led to calls by a number of groups for review of Berkeley's admissions policies. National media accounts noted the increasingly zero-sum character of the admissions process and its disproportionate effect on Whites and Asian Americans. A *New York Times* article headlined, "College Admissions: Shaky Ethics,"[6] highlighted the Berkeley situation, and one chancellor testified before a legislative committee that the admissions process not only disproportionately impacted Asian American students, it had the potential to damage relations between Berkeley and the Asian American community. In response, a campuswide commission chaired by Berkeley professor Jerome Karabel released a comprehensive report on UC Berkeley admissions in 1989. It noted that "The various controversies that have surrounded the admissions process—among them, the at-times bitter conflicts over both Asian American admissions and affirmative action—cannot be understood without grasping that all policy decisions on admissions have taken on a zero-sum character" (Karabel, 1989, p. 18).

The commission proposed the end of numerical targets and guaranteed admissions for UC-eligible underrepresented students, both of which were arguably illegal under *Bakke*, and a decrease in the number of special action admits in a given freshman cohort. They also recommended increasing the percentage of students admitted on academic criteria alone from 40% to 50%. This would reverse a policy implemented in 1984 which had decreased the proportion by that same amount and raised the ire of groups not designated underrepresented. The commission recommendations were subsequently adopted, and the number of underrepresented students admitted to Berkeley began a steady decline.

As at UC Berkeley, there was significant disagreement throughout the UC system over just how much of a "plus factor" race actually was in admissions policy after *Bakke*. Nor were the disputes confined to undergraduate admissions. The UCLA law school convened a task force in the wake of *Bakke* to consider an alternative to their pre-*Bakke* program (known as LEOP) of setting aside a specified number of admissions spaces in each class for underrepresented students (Favish, 1996). The UCLA task force devised a plan that, according to one professor, was "pure litigation strategy" (Karst in Favish, 1996, p. 365). That strategy was to admit 60% of an entering cohort largely on the basis of GPA and LSAT scores, and up to 40% of the cohort on the basis of multiple factors.

In 1992, UCLA admissions policies were reviewed by the federal Office of Civil Rights, in response to allegations that the university was discriminating against Asian American student applicants to UCLA.[7] The OCR found no violations of Title VI of the Civil Rights Act of 1964, and the university continued to treat Asian American applicants as other than underrepresented.

RACE, INCOME, AND ADMISSIONS

An essential question that drove the political contest over the founding of the University of California was whether working-class citizens would be given equal access to the university with California's economic and social elites. The tension between distribution of the costs and benefits of the institution also drove the contest over the structure and composition of the university's Board of Regents. Members of the Workers Party argued at the convention in 1879 that if the Regents were appointed by the legislature, the university would soon fall under the control of the same economic elites that were seen by the workers as controlling the legislature: bankers, industrialists, and real estate speculators (Douglass, 2000). The Workers succeeded in keeping the control of Regental appointments out of the hands of the legislature, but they failed to keep the elites from dominating the membership of the Board of Regents.

That contest over UC's founding was nested in a political context shaped by economic insecurity and racial strife. At the constitutional convention of 1879, the delegates not only contended over UC, they struggled with the status of Chinese immigrants and efforts to regulate the violence directed by Anglos at those immigrants (Douglass, 2000). The conflicts over economic class and racial status that were prevalent at the founding persist to this day and point to the need to consider the intersection, and interrelation, of class and race in the contemporary contest over affirmative action. The struggle over affirmative action policies at the University of California in the period 1994–1996 embodied many of the same issues as were raised at the founding of the university. Issues of race and socioeconomic class conjoined in a contest over access and allocation of education and public resources. In both cases, the issues of redress of economic inequality and racial discrimination were deeply intertwined in the politics and discourse of the respective conflicts.

Figure 3.1 provides one example of the degree to which income, race, and test scores conjoined in the larger competition for admission to UC. While SAT scores are not direct proxies for admission, they are extremely significant in the competition for places at the most selective UC campuses. For all California SAT takers in 1995, within each racial/ethnic and income category, SAT scores increased with income. At the same time, Black SAT scores in the highest income category lagged behind White and Asian American SAT scores in the lowest income category, and Latino scores in the highest income category were comparable to scores of Whites in the lowest income cohort.[8]

Research on social class and access to higher education has focused on the intergenerational transmission of "cultural capital" (Bourdieu, 1977; Chang, 2002; McDonough, 1997). The cultural capital framework suggests that elite groups highly value college attainment for the intergenerational transmission of status and power. While not entirely linked to high income, there is a significant relationship between family income, parents' levels of college attainment, and high school students' college aspirations (Garcia, 1997; McDonough, 1997).

It is difficult to overstate the importance of family income and educational attainment in admissions to UC Berkeley at the time of the contest over affirmative action policy. While fewer than 20% of admits came from families

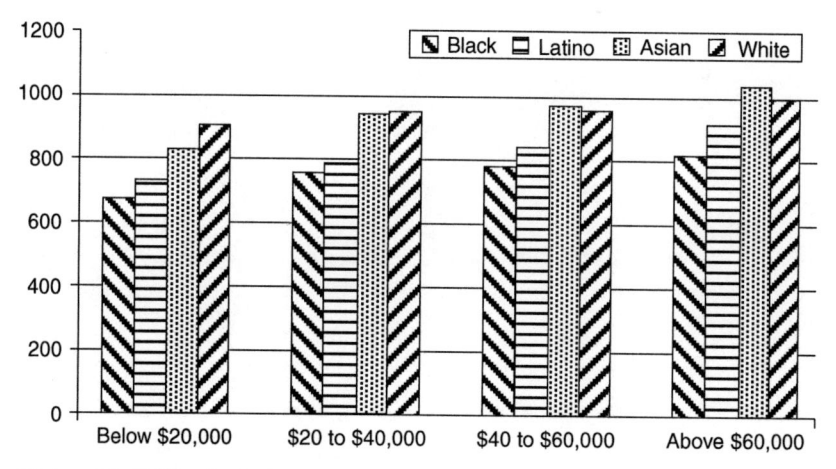

Figure 3.1 California SAT Scores. (Source: 1995 College Board Data and 1997 UC Outreach Task Force Report Data).

with income below $25,000 per year, over 40% of the admitted students came from families with income over $50,000 per year. Over 60% of the students admitted to UC Berkeley in 1994 came from families in which the father was a four-year college graduate or possessed a postgraduate degree, while fewer than 15% came from families in which the father had not attended college.

A presentation of family income and parents' educational achievement for all UC applicants in 1994 within racial/ethnic categories is shown in Table 3.1. Median income for White applicants was more than double that of either African American or Chicano applicants. The percentage of White applicants with parents who held at least a four-year degree was also twice as high as for either African American or Chicano applicants.[9]

The historian George Fredrickson (1997) has suggested that race and class can be seen as historical inventions, interpretations of ideological constructions that are powerful influences on human perceptions. He argued, "Class is as much a historical and social construct as race, which also builds on differences that actually exist, but are not meaningful until constructed into an ideology of differences that serves the purposes of a social group" (p. 83). Fredrickson also pointed to the use of racial and caste status arguments for dividing lower-income Blacks and Whites in political struggles, including

TABLE 3.1. Parental Income, Occupation, and Educational Level: UC In-State Freshman Applicants, Fall 1994

African American	American Indian	Asian American	Chicano	Latino	White/ Other	Total
\multicolumn{7}{c}{Median Parental Income}
$34,000	$51,000	$38,400	$30,000	$38,000	$70,000	$50,000
\multicolumn{7}{c}{Father's Occupation: Percent Professional or Management}
39.8	52.2	38.3	22.9	36.9	64.4	49.5
\multicolumn{7}{c}{Mother's Occupation: Percent Professional or Management}
44.8	44.9	21.8	20.5	28.4	48.7	37.4
\multicolumn{7}{c}{Father's Education: Percent 4 Year College Degree or Higher}
37.9	51.1	60.2	29.4	46.3	74.5	63.7
\multicolumn{7}{c}{Mother's Education: Percent 4 Year College Degree or Higher}
34.2	36.1	38.7	12.8	26.9	58.7	46.1

Source: Statistical Overview, Fall 1994, UCOP

contests over affirmative action, particularly in times of economic uncertainty. These issues would be invoked in myriad ways during the period preceding the Regents' votes on affirmative action.

Adding to the competitive pressure on UC admissions, and to the difficulty in admitting a diverse class, were a number of contextual shifts that rapidly changed the admissions dynamic. Four of these in particular deserve mention.

The first occurred as a result of Proposition 13, the 1978 ballot initiative that dramatically lowered state and local tax revenues, and established a "supermajority" requirement for the passage of any new taxes.[10] Proposition 13 became one of the leading contributors to the subsequent decline in per student expenditures in K–12 education in California, and indirectly to a decline in the number of UC-eligible students from underrepresented groups over the period 1981–1996.[11] By the time of the Regents' votes on affirmative action, African American, American Indian and Chicano/Latino students made up 46% of California's K–12 enrollments and 39% of California's high school graduates, but only 12% of the total pool of UC-eligible students.[12] As Figure 3.2 shows, Chicano/Latino eligibility rates appear to have increased slightly in the period 1990–1996, yet low eligibility rates and increasing competition were major factors in

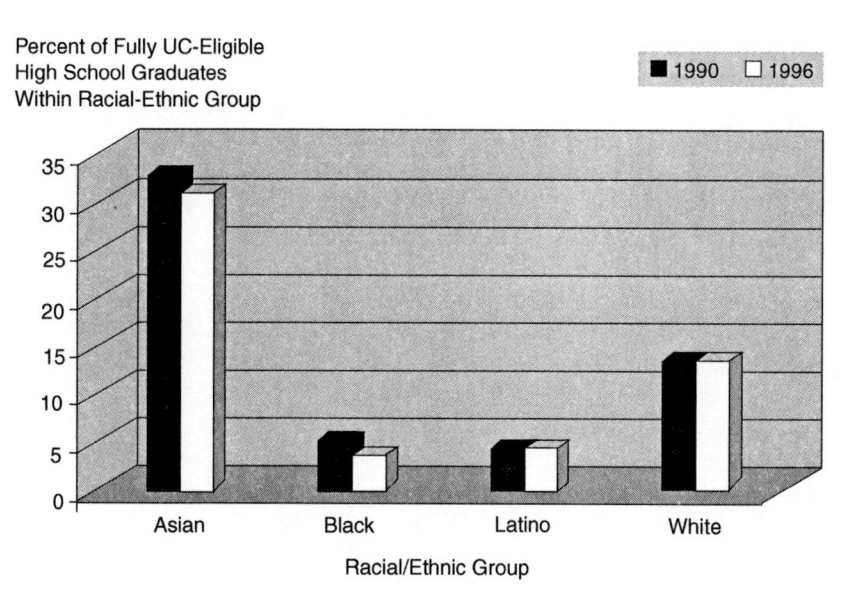

Figure 3.2 Eligibility Rates. (Source: California Postsecondary Education Commission).

shaping the access crisis that added urgency to the Regents' deliberations on affirmative action in 1994–1995.

The second shift in the policymaking context was prompted by the setting of university fees. During the state economic recession of 1988 to 1992, general fund appropriations to the university were declining, and the university implemented a series of rapid fee increases. Between 1989 and 1994, UC undergraduate fees rose nearly 150 percent to over $4,200 per year. The fee increases raised significant student protest and led to a number of legislative hearings on university fee policy. Democrats in the legislature threatened to cut the university's general fund appropriation if cost savings were not implemented in lieu of fee increases, and State Senator Tom Hayden cosponsored a full-page ad in major newspapers complaining about UC administrative salaries. When Regent Lester Lee, who had twice voted in 1993 to approve fee increases, appeared before the Senate Rules Committee for confirmation in February 1994, he became the first Regent to be rejected by the Rules Committee in the twentieth century (Pusser, 2003).

A third key factor was the rapid population growth in the state of California that had taken place over the previous quarter century, the change in its ethnic composition, and the attendant pressures on UC admissions. In 1970 the population of California was just under 20 million, of whom 78% were White. By 1996 the population was 32 million, of whom 52% were White, and increasingly in older age cohorts. The population had exploded, and become significantly more ethnically diverse and younger (Schrag, 1998b). Along with that population explosion came a similar surge in admissions applications to UC. As Figure 3.3 demonstrates, the number of applications to the Berkeley campus doubled from 1976 to 1985. For the fall of 1986 a new multiple filing system was introduced, but even after accounting for that change the number of applications increased by another 45% over the next ten years. Taken together, these shifts placed exceptional pressure on the most selective campuses.

While UC Berkeley led the other campuses in the number of applications, it also was the campus that received the greatest number of applications with high academic indexes. The disparity in the number and ranking of applications to the UC system's eight undergraduate campuses would play a key role in the contest over affirmative action.

Figure 3.4 presents applications to three UC campuses in 1994, the most recent admissions cohort at the time of the contest. The figure incorporates the "academic index" for each application received by UC Berkeley, UC San Diego, and UC Santa Cruz. The academic index was calculated under a formula that combines a multiple of an applicant's grade point average and SAT or ACT scores. The maximum academic index score at UC was 8000. As the figure shows, UC Berkeley received more applications from students with high

Context Shaping the Affirmative Action Contest 35

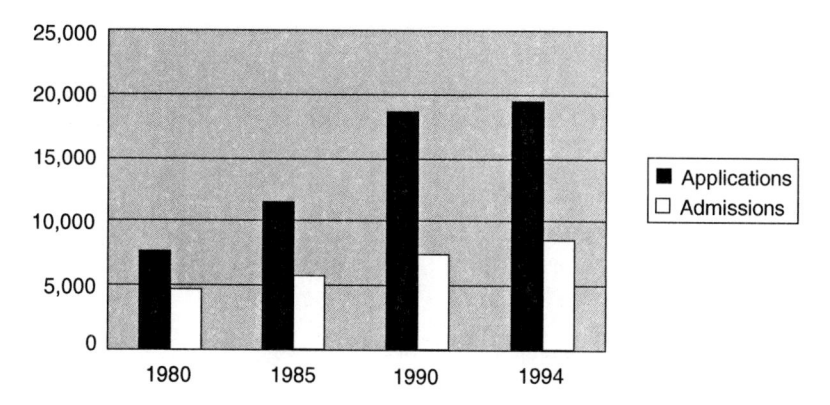

Figure 3.3 UC Berkeley Freshman Applications and Admissions, Fall 1980–Fall 1994. (Source: UC Berkeley Office of Student Research Data).

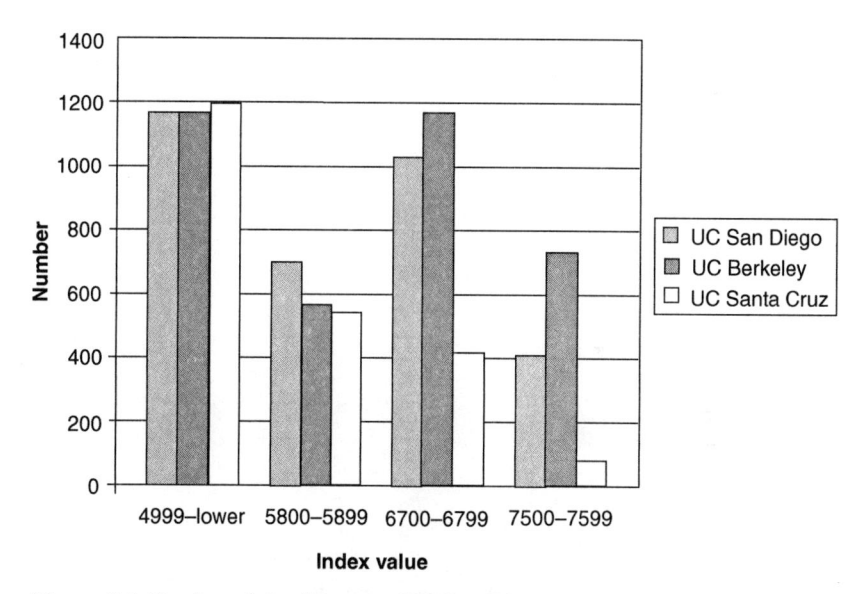

Figure 3.4 Number of Applicants to UC San Diego, Berkeley, and Santa Cruz by Academic Index: 1994. (Source: UCOP Data Tables).

academic indexes than did UC San Diego, while both campuses received far more applications with high academic indexes than did UC Santa Cruz.

Figure 3.5 presents data on the academic indexes of students actually admitted to the three campuses. While the pattern is similar to that displayed in Figure 3.4, it is notable that UC Berkeley admitted far more students with

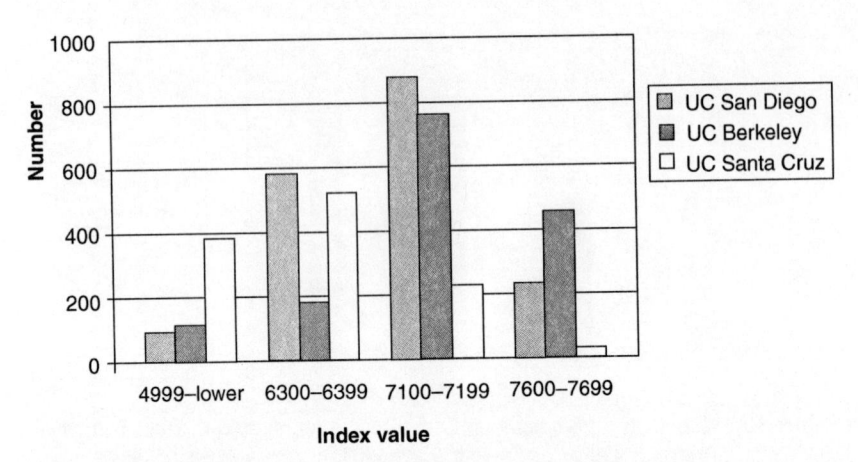

Figure 3.5 Number of Admits to UC San Diego, Berkeley, and Santa Cruz by Academic Index: 1994. (Source: UCOP Data tables).

academic indexes above 7300 than UC San Diego was able to admit, and San Diego admitted significantly more students above that level than were admitted to UC Santa Cruz. These figures illuminate an issue that emerged in the affirmative action contest, the difference between being "UC-eligible" per se, and being eligible for admission to one of the more selective campuses.

COMPOSITION OF THE BOARD OF REGENTS, 1994–1995

The most important contextual factor shaping the affirmative action contest was the composition of the board at the time of the contest. Table 3.2 presents the voting membership of the Board of Regents on the day of the Regents' votes on affirmative action, July 20, 1995.[13]

Regents' Confirmation Dynamics

The confirmation dynamic in the California state legislature over the prior two decades shaped the highly partisan composition of the board at the time of the Regents' deliberations over affirmative action. Under the California Constitution, after consulting with an advisory board, the governor nominates a candidate for the Board of Regents. A nominee serves one year on the board as a Regent Designate. At the end of that year, the Senate Rules Committee holds confirmation hearings on the nominee. If the nomination is approved by the Rules Committee, it moves to a vote of the full Senate. If approved by the full Senate, the Regent Designate becomes a Regent and continues serving on the

TABLE 3.2. UC Board of Regents: Backgrounds and Appointments[14]

Regents	Background	Appointed By	SP-1	SP-2
Ex Officio				
Pete Wilson	Governor		Yes	Yes
Gray Davis	Lieutenant Governor		No	No
Judith Levin	President, UC Alumni Association		No	No
Ralph Carmona	Vice President, UC Alumni Association		No	No
Delaine Eastin	State Superintendent of Public Instruction		No	No
Jack Peltason	President, University of California		No	No
Doris Allen	Speaker of the Assembly		NP	NP
Appointed				
Clair Burgener	Former Congressman, real estate	Deukmejian	Yes	Yes
Glenn Campbell	Economist	Deukmejian	Yes	Yes
Frank Clark	Attorney	Deukmejian	Yes	Yes
Ward Connerly	Consultant	Wilson	Yes	Yes
John Davies	Attorney	Wilson	Yes	Yes
Tirso del Junco	Surgeon	Deukmejian	Yes	Yes
S. Sue Johnson	Civic leader	Deukmejian	Yes	Yes
Meredith Khachigian	Civic leader	Deukmejian	Yes	Yes
Leo Kolligian	Attorney	Deukmejian	Yes	Yes
Howard Leach	Investor	Deukmejian	Yes	Yes
David Lee	Telecommunications Executive	Wilson	Yes	Yes
S. Stephen Nakashima	Attorney	Deukmejian	Yes	Yes
Dean Watkins	Chairman, Watkins Johnson Co.	Deukmejian	Yes	Yes
Roy Brophy	Construction	Deukmejian	No	No
Ed Gomez	UC Riverside graduate student		No	No
Alice Gonzales	Former director of State Employment Development Department	Deukmejian	No	No
Tom Sayles	Utility company executive	Wilson	No	No
William Bagley	Attorney	Deukmejian	Abstain	No
Velma Montoya	Former Commissioner, U.S. OSHRC	Wilson	No	Yes

board. As Table 3.2 demonstrates, of the eighteen appointed Regents on the board at the time of the affirmative action votes in July 1995, all but one, Frank Clark, were Republicans who had been appointed by Republican governors. Clark was appointed by a Democrat, Governor Jerry Brown, and reappointed by Republican Governor Deukmejian. Financial contributions to the governor and the governor's party have long been a strong predictor of gubernatorial appointments to the Board of Regents as have service to the state party and close personal ties to the governor (Schwartz, 1991). Among the members of the board at the time of the Regents' deliberations over affirmative action were Meredith Khachigian, the wife of a prominent political consultant, Dr. Tirso del Junco, a former chair of the state Republican Party, Howard Leach, one-time national fund-raising chair for the Republican Party,[15] and John Davies, a San Diego lawyer and an ally from Governor Wilson's college days. Regent Connerly lent some insight into the level of connection to the party apparatus expected of a Regent, in comments on Regent Roy Brophy. Brophy, a longtime Republican Party fund-raiser and activist, and former member of the statewide Republican central committee, found himself estranged from the party over affirmative action. Connerly suggested:

> If Brophy sees himself as not a good Republican, it's because maybe in the last three years Roy hasn't made any contributions, he hasn't gone to any fund-raisers, he hasn't gone out and tried to help any candidates get elected. I mean he talked about how close he was to the governor—Roy hasn't lifted a finger. So, you have to consistently pay your dues in politics. I've got a stack of invitations that high from people who want me to speak at events, raise money, and it's one thing to say well, jeez I gave 150,000 dollars five years ago. The question is, what have you done this year?[16]

A PATTERN OF DEFERENCE

One key to the partisan nature of the appointed Board of Regents is that prior to 1994 there was essentially no contest in the Senate Rules Committee over gubernatorial appointments.[17] For more than twenty years, the Democratic majority in the Senate had been almost entirely deferential to the governor on appointments to the Board of Regents. Table 3.3 presents the outcomes of the confirmation hearings held by the Senate Rules Committee from 1972 through 2002.

For the first twenty years of the period, the senators deferred completely to the governor, regardless of the governor's party affiliation, approving every single gubernatorial nominee to the board. A close analysis of the Senate votes on each nomination shows that from 1974 until 1992 there was only one instance when a "no" vote was cast. With that exception, every nomination was unanimously confirmed, despite a majority of Democrats on the Rules Committee (Pusser, 2003).

In the majority of the confirmation hearings, there was virtually no discussion. Nominees were generally asked the same opening question: "What are your qualifications for this position?" Most cited business experience or membership in service organizations or civic groups. Few had ever served on any sort of education governing board; fewer still on a postsecondary board.

TABLE 3.3. Confirmation Dynamics for UC Regents (1972–2002)

Governor	Governor's Party	Senate Majority	Nominees	Party of Nominees Democrats	Party of Nominees Republicans	Confirmation Outcomes Yes	Confirmation Outcomes No	Confirmation Outcomes Pending
R. Reagan (1967–1974)	Republican	Democrat	2	0	2	2	0	0
J. Brown (1975–1982)	Democrat	Democrat	13	13	0	13	0	0
G. Deukmejian (1983–1990)	Republican	Democrat	18	1	17	18	0	0
P. Wilson (1991–1998)	Republican	Democrat	15	0	15	9	6	0
G. Davis (1999–Pres.)	Democrat	Democrat	9	9	0	9	0	0
Total			57	23	34	51	6	0

Source: California State Senate Rules Committee Archives.

Some seemed not only to have little experience with higher education, but they also didn't seem to think it would matter to the committee. The response of one Regent nominee, Leo Kolligian, was representative of the general approach of nominees:

> MR. KOLLIGIAN: Well, I'm a Boalt Hall Law School graduate of the University of California, and I've been practicing in Fresno for, oh, something over 40 years. I feel I'm qualified because I've been involved in so many different business experiences and have had the opportunity to get into land development and go into different—different fields of law as well as law itself. I feel that I'm from the Valley. I am Armenian, but—and, I should say, and I do feel that there's a need for a representative on the Board from that area for geographical reasons.
>
> SENATOR PETRIS: Anything else? Anything about education?
>
> MR. KOLLIGIAN: No.[18]

That a state senate controlled by Democrats would confirm the appointment of nominees put forward by a Democratic governor is not surprising. This was the case for the period from 1974 to 1982. However, the data show that the process did not change significantly under conditions of divided governance. Beginning in 1982 with the consecutive elections of Republican Governors Deukmejian and Wilson, fifteen Republican nominees appeared before the Rules Committee (controlled by Democrats) before a senator in the Rules Committee, Nicholas Petris in 1990, actually cast the first vote against a nominee, Regent designate Howard Leach.

Regent Leach was confirmed by the committee on a 4–1 vote, and as was nearly always the case, the event was practically unnoticed. No witnesses appeared to testify either for or against Regent Leach. In the period 1974–1992, few witnesses ever testified against a gubernatorial appointee to the Board of Regents and it does not appear from the record that they were expected to. In a 1984 committee hearing on three gubernatorial nominees to the Board of Regents, only one witness, a representative of the UC student association, appeared to question the nominees. After a short testimony questioning confirmation of the first nominee, she returned to pose questions of the second nominee. The following exchange took place:

> VICE-CHAIRMAN JOHNSON: We have a motion [for confirmation]. Is there opposition? Are you opposing this nomination?
>
> MS. CAMPBELL: I have a number of questions. Is that possible?
>
> SENATOR CRAVEN: Are they different, Ms. Campbell, than the others [referring to her questions of the first nominee]?
>
> MS. CAMPBELL: Yes.
>
> VICE-CHAIRMAN JOHNSON: This is not a normal procedure. We've got a long agenda. We'll bring you up, come on. We've got a long agenda, and you realize that. So, the Committee will not ask any questions; we'll let you ask them and I'll try to redirect them as briefly as I can.[19]

A number of Regents on the board at the time of the affirmative action deliberations had been active supporters of state ballot Proposition 187, an initiative that was vigorously opposed by the Senate Democratic leadership. The board had also raised the ire of Democrats in the legislature who blamed the Regents for supporting UC fee increases and for failing to reign in university spending. Particularly galling to the Democratic leadership was the Regents' approval in 1989 of a generous severance package for outgoing system president David Gardner. Gardner's severance, which was arranged with limited disclosure, was approved by the Regents at a time when student fees were rapidly increasing. At the confirmation hearing of Regent Lester Lee in 1994, then State Senate Majority Leader Bill Lockyer expressed the State Senate majority's anger this way, as he cast the decisive vote against Lee's confirmation:

> CHAIRMAN LOCKYER: I'm mindful of the fact that the University routinely tells us how immune they are from our legislative and budgetary efforts, and that because of their unique constitutional status, that we can't affect or influence their affairs to the extent we might other state agencies. So, with that in mind, plus the fact that the consequences of today's vote would stretch to the year 2005, I'd like to, I guess, err on the

side of caution. And the reason I cast a no vote is that I think we need to tell the governor and the University that changes are needed, and not just tax increases for students, which has been their easy way of not confronting their management and budget problems.[20]

A similar rationale would accompany the rejection in 1997 of Regent Tirso del Junco. Senator Lockyer then summed up the Democrats' position on del Junco this way:

> CHAIRMAN LOCKYER: He was a Regent when he chose to be Chair of the California Republican Party, when he chose to sign a lot of questionable attack mail pieces sent against my colleagues. Now, that wasn't somebody who had much regard for the nonpolitical role of Regents. You know, I've had colleagues say to me in the Senate, "I've never met this guy. I don't know him. The only thing I know about him is when I was running for the Senate mail landed in my district, attacking me personally that was inaccurate, and it was signed by him as Chair of the Republican Party. So the point is this, sir. You come to us and say, don't be political. The politics started there, not here. That's the point. We don't need to debate it.[21]

By autumn 1993, the UC Regents were a highly partisan and conservative board, extremely loyal to their governor and mindful of broader state and national goals. Pete Wilson was not only a demanding and opportunistic governor, he was seated as president of the Regents. The context and the timing were perfect for a challenge to a policy that had long been fervently defended by the university and the state Democratic Party. That policy was affirmative action.

NATIONAL AND STATE POLITICAL CONTEXTS

While the actual board-level dynamics that led to placing a challenge to affirmative action on the board's agenda began late in 1993, three other political contests shaped the context and served as catalysts for subsequent action. Those three contests were the state and national midterm elections of 1994, the California ballot initiative known as Proposition 187, and the campaign to place an initiative known as the California Civil Rights Initiative (CCRI) on the California ballot for November 1996.

The Midterm Elections

The national midterm elections of 1994 represented the largest loss of congressional seats under an incumbent president in half a century. Not only did the Republican party take control of Congress after a forty-year reign by the

Democrats, the Republicans gained eleven governors and held a majority of state houses for the first time in a quarter century. While a number of social and economic issues drove the shift away from Democratic candidates, one group was identified as key to delivering votes for the "Gingrich revolution": White males. In the midterm voting, a majority of White males voted Republican, and that statistic sent Republican strategists in general, and more specifically those representing potential presidential candidates, looking for emerging issues that could secure those voters for the Republican camp.[22] One of the issues that had brought White voters to the fore in the 1994 midterm election in California was Proposition 187.[23]

Proposition 187

The year-long campaign to pass Proposition 187 waged from fall 1993 through fall 1994 by Governor Wilson and the California Republican Party had a significant effect on the evolution of SP-1 and SP-2. Proposition 187, the so-called Save Our State initiative, was a ballot initiative intended to restrict health benefits and education for undocumented immigrants. Proposition 187 not only touched on issues of diversity and access that would emerge again in the contest over UC affirmative action, but it also directly affected the university by limiting financial aid for students who were not legal residents of California, and by compelling university employees to report undocumented students to the Immigration and Naturalization Service (Tolbert and Hero, 1996; Chavez, 1998). When the campaign for Proposition 187 commenced in late fall 1993, Governor Wilson's popularity was at the lowest point of his tenure.[24] Given the continuing weakness of the California economy and his low approval ratings, Wilson sought an issue that could define a contrast between his own platform and that of his likely Democratic opponent in the general election, State Treasurer Kathleen Brown. He chose Proposition 187. Just as he would later link an effort to end affirmative action to his run for the Republican presidential nomination in 1996, Governor Wilson made support for Proposition 187 one of the defining issues of his 1994 campaign for reelection as governor.

The importance of Proposition 187 to Wilson's political fortunes can hardly be overstated. Shortly after the gubernatorial primaries in June 1994, Democratic nominee Kathleen Brown, a staunch opponent of Proposition 187, held a substantial lead over Wilson in opinion polls. By September 1994, Proposition 187 had become a national cause, Governor Wilson its leader. In November Wilson was reelected with 55% of the vote. Proposition 187 received even stronger support, 59% of the vote. Eighty-one percent of the total vote was cast by Whites, and of that group, 61% voted for Wilson and 63% voted for Proposition 187.[25] This pattern, which would be repeated in the votes on Proposition 209, has been conceptualized as policymaking in "bifurcated racial/ethnic contexts" (Tolbert and Hero, 1996, p. 816). Capitalizing on an issue designed to appeal to White voters had not only returned Wilson to the governorship, but it had also, according to the *Los Angeles Times*, "thrust Wilson firmly into the ranks of possible Republican contenders for the White House in 1996."[26]

The California Civil Rights Initiative (CCRI)

The California Civil Rights Initiative was drafted by Dr. Glynn Custred, a professor of anthropology at the California State University at Hayward, and Dr. Thomas Wood, executive director of the California Association of Scholars, a state branch of a national conservative research group. Custred and Wood had been working on various versions of the initiative, with little support from either political leaders or parties for nearly three years. Nor did they seem likely to succeed anytime soon. Placing a ballot initiative in California required collecting nearly seven hundred thousand signatures at a cost of well over a million dollars, Custred and Wood raised virtually no money. Second, the early drafts of their proposal were built on language proposing the elimination of "affirmative action," a politically difficult strategy.

Over the next two years, the pair revised the wording of the initiative until they arrived at a change in approach that not only improved their prospects for garnering funding and signatures, it subsequently shaped the debate at the Board of Regents over affirmative action as well. That change was to eliminate from the proposed language any reference to affirmative action, and to focus their campaign instead on the abolition of "preferences" on the basis of race and gender. When the concept of preferences was substituted for affirmative action, not only did the polling data on the proposed initiative shift significantly, the state Republican party leadership began to rally in support of the CCRI.[27] The 1994 version of the initiative was proposed as a constitutional amendment to prevent the state from "discriminating against or granting preferential treatment to, any individual or group on the basis of race, sex, ethnicity, or national origin, in the operation of public employment, public education, or public contracting." The proposed initiative was filed in October 1993, and its broader political significance became immediately apparent. In November 1993 an article on CCRI noted the following: "The dilemma into which this will plunge the whole national liberal establishment is obvious. It is a battle the liberals will be compelled to fight, and are doomed to lose."[28]

Presidential candidate Pat Buchanan noted the political value of a challenge to affirmative action this way: "To the point: If the GOP is casting about for a populist issue to reunite its old coalition and to slice Bill Clinton's new coalition asunder, that issue is at hand: the California Civil Rights Initiative."[29]

Despite the growing external awareness, there was still a significant division in California politics over efforts to reconsider existing affirmative action policies. California State Senator Bernie Richter introduced Assembly Bill 47 in June 1994, a measure that would have placed the precise language of CCRI on the ballot as a constitutional amendment. It failed to move out of the Assembly Judiciary Committee, as it received support from all the Republican members of the committee and none of the Democratic majority.

The Judiciary Committee hearings on the bill would ultimately be quite central to the shaping of Regents' proposals SP-1 and SP-2. Custred and Wood testified at the hearings, and for the first time they met UC Regent Ward Connerly, who also testified on behalf of the Richter bill. Custred and Wood were impressed by Connerly's presentation. In Wood's words, "He stole the show,"[30] and an alliance was made between the three. As Sacramento political consultant Wayne Johnson described it, "On that day the issue moved from the ivory tower and became a political issue."[31] In fact, while the academicians, Custred and Wood, had brought the CCRI to the political arena, Connerly would soon bring it to another level of the ivory tower.

4

Interest Articulation and the Illusion of Control

Regent Designate Ward Connerly had joined the Board of Regents in April 1993 and soon thereafter began testing the norms of board governance. He challenged the Office of the President's presentations, to such a degree that one longtime student of Regents' dynamics called it "a revolution."[1] When Connerly joined the Regents' Finance Committee, he made the following statement:

> We have a number of possibilities on the Committee and I want to outline three of them that I think are important for this Committee. The first is that we are to be involved in all matters relating to the business of the University, the University as a corporation, all matters relating to the business and management of the University. The second is the budgetary responsibility: we are to consider the budget prepared by the president; we are to be involved in presenting that budget to the Legislature. It becomes the Regents' budget and we have a responsibility, I think, to help the Office of the president to get that measure through. And the third one is an oversight responsibility on all appropriations. Now there are other things that we have to do as well, but those are the three major responsibilities that we have and I think that we all take those things seriously, I certainly do.[2]

Connerly's activist stance was somewhat surprising, given that his qualifications, like those of many other Regents, were essentially that he was a strong ally of the governor and had contributed money to the governor's campaigns over the years. It has been argued that Connerly's appointment had been part of an elaborate trade-off between the governor and the Senate Rules Committee leadership. Just prior to Connerly's appointment, one of Governor Wilson's appointments to the board from the prior year, Regent Designate[3] John Davies, a White male, was to come before the Rules Committee for a confirmation hearing. At the time there was a general concern in the Senate about a lack of diversity on the board. The concern was amplified by Davies's support for student fee increases and the generous severance package awarded outgoing President Gardner. A number of interest groups, including Common Cause, NOW, and the Latino Issues Forum were advocating a rejection of Regent Designate Davies (Chavez, 1998). In order to assure the confirmation of Davies, the governor agreed to make more "diversity" appointments, in exchange for the Democrats' support of Davies. Regent Designate Davies was confirmed, and Ward Connerly became the first of Governor Wilson's subsequent appointments.[4]

In December 1993, Regent Designate Connerly wrote an open letter to the board advocating that all Regents take a more proactive and demanding stance with regard to the university's Office of the President. In one paragraph he stated,

> The issue of effective governance is crucial to restoring public confidence in the University of California. "Effective governance" is more than voting to hire a president and voting "aye" on every issue placed before us by the president during his or her tenure. If we subscribe to this view, there is no reason for us to meet. This view might be appropriate for a corporate association. For the UC, however, the public expects a more assertive form of management than this. They expect us to exercise a greater degree of diligence than simply ascertaining the preference of the president and the administration on a given issue.[5]

President Peltason responded promptly, with a perspective on policymaking that would preview the Office of the President's approach to public conflict throughout the affirmative action contest: he wanted to avoid it. Further, he felt that the board should consider the Office of the President its primary agent. In an open letter to Regent Connerly and the rest of the board he wrote in part:

> I appreciate your recognition that the administration is to be entrusted with a "high degree of confidence in carrying out the policies adopted by the Board." But I am afraid that your letter could be interpreted to suggest that the administration's recommendations to the Regents are to be given much the same weight as those from any other constituency, and that is a point to which I feel obligated to respond. The Board of Regents is not an impartial judicial hearing body, a legislative committee, or a court of law. A meeting of the Board of Regents should not be conducted like a legislative hearing, a meeting of a city council, or a presentation before an impartial court in which various persons come before it to argue their cases. Although there are circumstances and issues in which the Board solicits a wide variety of comments and hears from a number of different constituencies, the Board is not there to balance among competing claims and pick and choose which it will support.
>
> The Board of Regents is the *governing* body of a great university, an incredibly complex multi-campus university. The administration—and this

is also true of the Academic Senate—is not just one of many constituencies, but is the Board of Regents' *chosen and publicly designated agent* in whom it has vested confidence and to whom it has delegated responsibility to manage the University. The Bylaws and Standing Orders of the Regents recognize this role in designating the president, Chancellors, Laboratory Directors, and several other senior administrators as Officers of the University.

The Board by its policies has instructed the president and the Chancellors to consult with constituencies—faculty, staff, student, alumni, and external publics—prior to bringing a recommendation to the Board. By the time a recommendation is presented to the Board it has been through an elaborate consultative process, appropriate for the particular recommendation at issue. Such a recommendation, appropriately, should come to the Board with a very strong presumption that it will be supported. Of course the Board should not be a rubber stamp. Of course it should ask tough questions. Of course it can turn down recommendations. I also agree with you that every time a Regent or the Board votes against a recommendation of the president, such action should not be construed as a vote of no confidence in the president.

Although I think you did not intend it, your comments could be interpreted as saying that the Board considers recommendations from the president and the Chancellors as merely one among several competing recommendations from various constituencies. For the Board to send such a signal would radically undermine the authority of its officers and make it extraordinarily difficult for them to bring tough or controversial recommendations. Such a method of governing would not work in the best of times. In times of budgetary stress, when painful decisions have to be made, it would be impossible.[6]

President Peltason had outlined a strong principle/agent relationship between the board and the Office of the President. As events unfolded, a key question would be to what degree the Regents would accept the UCOP as a primary agent, and to what degree they would trust that agent to advise them in the heat of a confrontation over policy with broad institutional and national implications. Connerly's audacious approach was noted in an editorial in the *Los Angeles Times*[7] and was elsewhere described as "astonishing."[8] It was also seen as opportunistic behavior, designed to insure Connerly's confirmation in a State Senate angry over fee increases and the generous severance package awarded to former UC President David Gardner.[9]

In March 1994, Regent Designate Connerly and Regent Designate Lester Lee reached the end of their initial year on the board and faced Senate confirmation hearings. Connerly was confirmed by the Senate, while Regent Designate Lee became the first Regent designate ever rejected by the Senate.[10] Shortly after the hearings concluded, the transcript of a closed meeting between UC President Peltason and the UC chancellors was leaked to the press and published around the state. A portion of the transcript revealed the extent of the anger in the UC administration over Connerly's activist stance. President Peltason was quoted as remarking, with apparent sarcasm, "He's the hero. He's the one who came in and is prepared to stand up and reform the place."[11]

If the UC administration thought Connerly had been an activist prior to spring 1994, they were in for a very rude awakening as spring gave way to summer, and a new challenge appeared on the horizon.

THE COOKS STRIKE A SPARK

In July 1994, UC Regent Clair Burgener, a former Congressman from San Diego, received a letter from Jerry Cook, a lecturer at the University of San Diego. The letter questioned the application of admissions standards at the medical school of the University of California at San Diego and was accompanied by an analysis of UC's medical school admissions prepared by Cook, a statistician, and his wife Ellen, a professor at the University of San Diego. The Cooks had a specific interest in the UC admissions process: their son James, a graduate of UC San Diego (UCSD), had been denied admission to several UC medical schools in 1992. James had then spent a year obtaining a master's degree at Cal Tech. Upon reapplication in 1993, he was again denied by some UC medical schools, although in that round he was admitted to the UC Davis medical school. Jerry Cook described the analysis of his son's initial rejection this way:

> I obtained a piece of paper that shows the application rate and the ethnic makeup of UC Davis' medical school. Chicano students, for example, were 5 percent of the applicants but 18 percent of the students offered admission. That's mathematically just not possible unless race was the overwhelming factor in deciding who gets in and who doesn't. Chicanos were offered admission at five times the rate of Whites and 19 times the rate of Japanese. Since the Hispanic applicants on average have lower test scores and grades than Whites or Asian Americans, their preferential treatment for admission under the *Bakke* requirements would have to depend on some special quality in addition to their ethnicity. Whatever quality they have, is it possible that they have it 19 times more often than Japanese and 5 times more often than Whites?[12]

The Cooks' analysis of medical school admissions argued many of these same themes, and used language that foreshadowed much of the debate to come. Referring to applicants accepted to the UCSD School of Medicine from 1987–1993, the Cooks wrote:

Affirmative Action students are about 32% of the total accepted, yet they were only 13% of those who applied. Even if we ignore the obvious disparity in academic qualifications, even if we assume that all applicants are equally qualified to become doctors, is it possible that this many Affirmative Action applicants could be chosen? Is this a system of "equal opportunity" for all races? The answer is no. In fact, the probability of 32% of the class being from the Affirmative Action group, given that they are only 13% of the applicants, is considerably less than one in a million. Applicants are being selected, and therefore others will be rejected, specifically because they are members of preferred racial groups.[13]

The Cooks focused on two other issues: merit (noting that the average GPA and test scores of accepted underrepresented applicants to UCSD's medical school were in the lowest 1% of the other accepted students) and the pitting of one ethnic group against another. To make this point, the Cooks chose to focus on Vietnamese applicants, a group not designated as underrepresented for UC admissions purposes. Using UC Irvine as an example, they noted that 89 UC Irvine graduates whom they characterized as "affirmative action applicants" applied for admission to UC medical schools, while 107 Vietnamese graduates from Irvine also applied. Of the 89 "affirmative action applicants,"[14] 21 were admitted. Of the 107 Vietnamese, only 9 were admitted. The average GPA of the "affirmative action" applicants was 3.24, while the average GPA of the Vietnamese applicants was 3.79. 66 Vietnamese students with GPAs over 3.24 were turned away, while only one member of the "affirmative action" group was turned away with a GPA higher than 3.24. The Cooks concluded, "The results of our research, only part of which is shared here, lead inexorably to the conclusion that race is not 'just one factor' considered in UC Medical school admissions, it is the major factor."[15] In essence the Cooks, in their letter and report to Regent Burgener, were raising the possibility that the University of California was violating the law as established by *Bakke*.

Regent Burgener's initial response to the Cooks' inquiry was to write to the Office of the General Counsel of the Regents asking for a review of the concerns raised by the Cooks. The reply from the Office of the General Counsel, dated July 12, 1994, and signed by University Deputy General Counsel Gary Morrison, was the first in a series of responses from the Office of the President designed to allay Regents' concerns. On that count it did not succeed with all of the Regents.

The Deputy General Counsel reported that he had met with directors of admissions and other officials at each of the medical schools to discuss admissions procedures and criteria in detail. He then stated,

> We have made a few suggestions for procedural changes which have been implemented or are in the process of being implemented. Overall, however,

we are very impressed with the sensitivity of schools toward legal constraints on affirmative action and with the overall fairness of the process at each school; especially so given the large numbers of qualified applicants competing for limited space.[16]

The Deputy General Counsel also stated a primary justification for the affirmative consideration of race that would reappear at a number of junctures in the contest over affirmative action. That rationale was that the university, as part of its service mission to the state, was compelled to provide medical training and services for underserved communities of the state, and that minority graduates of medical schools were more likely to provide service in traditionally underserved settings. Morrison wrote,

At the time the *Bakke* case was filed, there would have been virtually no minority students in our medical schools if grades and test scores alone had determined admission. (Indeed, the Davis Medical School opened in 1968 without an affirmative action program and its first class had no African American, Chicano/Latino, or Native American students.) Disparities in grades and test scores continue to make the affirmative consideration of race a necessity if we are to have more than token numbers of minorities in our medical schools. Moreover, our schools believe that minority students and physicians are contributing significantly to educational and social goals. Faculty at each school noted that minority students were responsible for increased research and teaching concerning health problems of poor and minority communities and indicated that minority graduates overwhelmingly choose to practice in medically under-served areas where the need for physicians is greatest.[17]

Morrison then went on to review the *Bakke* decision and its role in shaping UC medical school admissions policy. He concluded that section with the following assertion:

Each of our medical schools considers racial or ethnic minority status (i.e., status as African American, Chicano/Latino, and Native American) as a factor in choosing which applicants to accept for admission. Each school also considers other personal characteristics which may contribute to its educational and professional goals. No school has a set-aside or quota for minority students.[18]

The Deputy General Counsel also offered a number of "General Observations about the Cooks' concerns." These included his assertion that the university's various medical schools did treat applicants differently, and applications differently, on the basis of race. Although Morrison referenced the prior approvals of admissions policies developed in the wake of *Bakke*, he cited at least two instances, without judgment, of practices that could be interpreted as violations of *Bakke*. First he noted that at UCLA, "applicants who designated themselves as minorities were reviewed separately."[19] This assertion would later be cited by some Regents as evidence that UC campuses were indeed conducting admissions in a manner that violated the U.S. Supreme Court's holding in the *Bakke* decision.[20] From those Regents' perspectives, a key finding by the Court was that by considering minority applications separately from applications received from White students, UC had in effect operated two separate admissions programs for the Davis medical school. Deputy General Counsel Morrison, in his letter to Regent Burgener, also stated that at UCLA "In the future all applications will be considered together."[21] In similar fashion, he also predicted changes in the process at UC San Diego:

> Preliminary applications are screened on the basis of scores and grades. All applications are reviewed for other factors as well and, based upon this, some which fall below the normal cut off of grades/scores will also be asked to complete a secondary application. Minority and disadvantaged students are now screened separately and have a different cut off of scores and grades. We have recommended this be changed to require review of all preliminary applications above a particular cut off regardless of ethnicity.[22]

The Deputy General Counsel also pointed out that

> The Davis School of Medicine was reviewed by the Office of Civil Rights, which investigated a complaint by an applicant who alleged that she was denied admission because of her race (Asian). The OCR investigated the School of Medicine admission process in detail. Its report, issued in March 1994 finds that UCD is not in violation of Title VI of the Civil Rights Act of 1964.[23]

Morrison ended his letter with the following comment:

> Our conclusion is that the procedures and criteria at each school should pass legal muster under the *Bakke* case. Our review found nothing clearly unlawful. We have identified some vulnerabilities, and changes are being made, as discussed above.[24]

It is worth noting the exceptional attention paid to asserting the legality of university policy in the Deputy General Counsel's letter. On the other hand, the fundamental charge in the Cooks' letter to Regent Burgener was not that the university was breaking the law in its admissions practices. Rather, the explicit claim the Cooks made was that the university had set up a system of arbitrary preference. They described it this way:

In an effort to remedy this under-representation, the University of California has undertaken many forms of Affirmative Action for the last 28 years in order to bring four groups onto the medical profession. African Americans, American Indians, Mexican Americans and mainland Puerto Ricans. That there are other minority groups which are also underrepresented has been largely ignored. That there are disadvantaged and deserving people of every race and ethnicity seeking to become physicians has also been ignored.[25]

Deputy General Counsel Morrison did not directly address this claim. He wrote to Regent Burgener:

The Cooks have also expressed concern that minorities are admitted with lower grades and test scores than non-minorities. This is true, of course. There would be no need for affirmative action admissions programs but for the persistent disparity in grades and test scores.[26]

While Morrison acknowledged the disparity in test scores, he did not address another of the Cooks' arguments, that the university's definition of "minorities"[27] discriminated against various Asian American groups. The example the Cooks had used in their initial letter to Burgener juxtaposed admissions rates for Hispanic and Vietnamese applicants. They argued that Hispanics, a group representing nearly 40% of the state population at the time and defined as underrepresented by UC, were unfairly displacing Vietnamese applicants, who, although they represented less than 5% of the state population, were not defined by UC as underrepresented.

Regent Burgener shared the Deputy General Counsel's reply with the Cooks, and they in turn prepared a reply to Deputy General Counsel Morrison. They again pointed out the statistical improbability of the UC Davis medical school admissions outcomes. They estimated that if the underrepresented applicants had identical overall qualifications to applicants from the other fourteen races tracked by UC, the chances of the Davis medical school enrolling those underrepresented students in the numbers they did was less than 1 in 100 million.[28]

Jerry Cook later described his reaction to the General Counsel's response to the Cooks' initial letter to Regent Burgener this way:

It was a pure slap in the face. I called this guy Burgener and said this is all garbage, and he said, "What did you expect them to say?" He said, "You should meet Regent Connerly."[29]

BRINGING AFFIRMATIVE ACTION TO THE BOARD OF REGENTS

The response from the UCOP did nothing to allay the concerns of either the Cooks or Regent Burgener. Regent Connerly related what happened next:

I received a call from Clair Burgener who was the chair of the board, who said that he had met with the Cooks and that they had what he thought was a legitimate complaint. Clair and the Cooks lived in La Jolla, and he said, "Would you mind meeting with them?" At the time he was chair of the board and I was chair of the Finance Committee. Finance was the major oversight committee of the board, and I said, "Sure, just have them call my office and I'll meet with them." I'm pretty accessible and after meeting with them I was convinced that they had the goods on us. And so I called Clair back and said that I'd read their material carefully, I've done my own independent research, and I think that the data is really very compelling. And that we are not using race as one of many factors. It is the factor, and that's clearly unconstitutional. It's a violation of the *Bakke* decision.

Clair asked me, "Well what are you going to do?" I said, "I'm going to ask the president to look at this and tell us why the Cooks are wrong." And I said, "I think you as the chair ought to do the same thing," because at that point I'd only been on the board for a little over a year, and rookies don't rock the boat. You know there's a certain tradition on that board. It's a very traditional kind of institution and you aren't expected to stir the pot until you've been on for four or five years, and even not then. And so I said it would be helpful if Clair would call also and raise this because, bear in mind now, that back in November of '93, I had sent a pretty detailed memo to the board which said that the atmosphere of the board chokes debate. And so I was already, I was sort of outside of the mainstream. So I said to Clair, "You ought to write the president along with me asking. Let's both independently call the president and ask the president to put this on the agenda." So we both did.[30]

Although Regent Connerly believed his request to place a review of affirmative action on the Regents' agenda would not be as well received as one made jointly with Regent Chair Burgener, there were other constraints on Connerly's placing such an item on the Regents' agenda. Under Regents Bylaw 10.1, no item may be placed on the agenda of a standing committee except by direction of the university president or the chairman of the Board of Regents, with one exception. An item may be placed on the agenda for committee consideration with an affirmative vote to do so by two-thirds of the Regents present at a regular meeting of the board. In light of President Peltason's previous comments on Regent Connerly's confirmation hearing, Connerly may well have been anticipating resistance from the president when he requested Regent Burgener join him in his request for a place on the agenda.

There was also a broader issue of board dynamics and to what degree Connerly's relative lack of experience on the board would affect his relations with senior members of the board throughout a protracted policy struggle. Former Student Regent Jess Bravin described the larger board dynamic:

I think it is accurate to say that personality had much to do with the way things worked within the board on SP-1 and SP-2. I doubt, for instance, that Regents Bagley and Brophy gave a second's thought to affirmative action prior to Connerly raising the issue. I know, however, that some Regents were resentful of the attention that Connerly, then relatively new to a board where most menbers hold 12-year terms, was receiving long before he got onto affirmative action. Connerly had been raising serious questions about the day-to-day administrative practices of the university and challenging fee increases, which are things the Board of Regents just doesn't do. The Board of Regents—I mean when I was there—we spent (you couldn't quantify how much more time we spent) trying to think of ways to raise the salaries of bureaucrats than we did on issues central to the future of the university, or on other matters one might expect to be worth some review, such as the quality of the student experience or the impact of our campuses on surrounding communities. The University administration set the agenda and catered to Regents' egos, soothing them into feeling that they were on the team. So any challenge to the status quo would upset Regents who were cozy with the administration and believed they were the boys who really ran the show.[31]

At the end of August 1994, Regent Burgener sent a letter to each of the Regents describing his contacts with the Cooks. He included the original correspondence he received from the Cooks, the General Counsel's response to the Cooks' complaint, and the Cooks' comments on the General Counsel's report. The Office of the President agreed to a discussion on the issue at the October 1994 meeting of the board in San Francisco.

Just a few weeks before receiving his copy of the Cooks' materials, Regent Connerly went to testify in support of California State Assemblyman Bernie Richter's legislative bill to place the language of the CCRI directly on a statewide ballot. While Connerly would subsequently state in a number of open sessions of the Board of Regents that he was open-minded about UC's policies on admissions, his testimony before the Assembly left little doubt about his position on affirmative action. Connerly testified:

There was a time when affirmative action had a value. There was discrimination in all sectors of California and we needed some sort of shock treatment. The time has come to take off the training wheels.[32]

Throughout the summer of 1994, Regent Connerly and Governor Wilson had been meeting to discuss affirmative action, the Cook case, and the governor's interest in bringing a challenge to affirmative action before the UC Regents. Wilson agreed to support Connerly in his efforts to challenge the Regents' policies and urged Connerly to take the lead (Chavez, 1998). Although Connerly had relied on Regent Burgener to help place his request for a review of affirmative action on the Regents' agenda, there was no question of who the point man would be in the ensuing contest. As an activist willing to challenge the use of race in university policy, and who would invoke the Civil Rights Movement and Dr. Martin Luther King Jr. in the process, Regent Connerly had a unique platform on the board. Regent Carmona recalled it this way: "You can't underestimate Ward's impact. He's a Black man, he's articulate, and people became caught up in the polls and in what he was saying."[33]

Regent Russell, himself an African American, offered an assessment of the importance of Connerly's status as an African American Regent that echoed Carmona's, and Russell added his own perspective:

> One of the most poignant moments for me in those two years was when a student addressed the Board—an African American from Santa Cruz, I think. Again, his presentation was terrible, but he spoke in terms of "look at you, you stand up, you look at me, you hate what you see." Ward was so upset, he first yelled back, and you've seen the board, we don't respond, and then Ward got up and walked out. I think maybe it hit a little close to home. Had John Davies been the author of this, he would have been referred to as a racist.[34]

CALM BEFORE THE STORM

At the October 1994 Regents' meeting, the Office of the President presented a comprehensive report on the faculty of the university. In the report, UCOP touched on a number of issues that would become major areas of conflict in the contest over SP-1 and SP-2, including shared governance, efforts to diversify the university's faculty, and diversification of the student body. At the meeting, President Peltason announced his intention to address the concerns raised by the Cooks, Regent Connerly, and Regent Burgener, through a presentation at the November meeting that would address admissions policies at the university's medical schools.

In between the October and the November meetings, the Regents received an advance copy of the presentation. Its nearly one hundred pages included a variety of summary matrices and charts showing the admissions policies at various UC medical schools.

The November meeting commenced as always with a public comment period, during which any member of the public might speak on any subject on the meeting agenda. At the November public comment period, only two members of the public spoke on the medical admissions presentation. The Office of the President's presentation was made to the UC Special Committee on Affirmative Action Policies within the Committee on Educational Policy.

UC President Jack Peltason opened the presentation with a reaffirmation of the university's commitment to affirmative action:

> There is nothing new about the University's efforts to diversify its student body. These efforts go back almost three decades. Our first student affirmative action program, directed toward undergraduates, was established in the mid-1960s and grew out of the emerging national consensus that our democratic ideals required us to extend educational opportunity to the widest possible range of people. It was a time when the admissions policies and practices at most American medical schools, including ours, resulted in a student body consisting almost entirely of White males. The University of California, like universities around the nation, began affirmatively to seek out qualified minority students, so that our educational programs would more nearly reflect the diversity of California's population.
>
> We did not undertake these efforts because any legislative act or court decision obligated us to do so. We undertook them because it was clear then, as it is clear now, that University cannot fulfill its mission to California, one of the most diverse states in the nation, without a commitment to encompass within our student body and faculty the cultural, racial, socioeconomic, and geographic diversity of this state. This commitment to diversity has been the policy of the state of California and the Regents, restated and reaffirmed over the years, and supported by every University of California president for the past quarter century.
>
> For the University of California, diversity is no longer an option. It is a necessity. To achieve diversity and meet our educational and professional needs, we must give some weight—among a wide variety of criteria other than grades and test scores—to the race or ethnicity of highly qualified applicants. The faculty of our medical schools devote a great deal of time and energy to individualized evaluation of every qualified applicant to assure a diverse class of excellent students whose presence will enhance the educational experience we offer and whose future service to their patients and their profession promises to be outstanding.[35]

Although the president's remarks clearly expressed the UCOP commitment to diversity, it was also largely a commitment to the status quo. The president did not refer to the growing controversy over admissions policy, or to the reservations already expressed by a number of Regents.

UCOP REAFFIRMS *BAKKE*

The president was followed by General Counsel James Holst and Deputy General Counsel Gary Morrison, who presented the University's position on

Bakke in some detail, and discussed the ways in which *Bakke* had shaped admissions policies at UC's medical schools. Deputy Counsel Morrison noted:

> Programs necessary to achieve educational diversity which do not set aside places for minorities, but consider race as one factor, have clearly been lawful since 1978, and remain so. The University of California has not had a single lawsuit challenging our programs since the *Bakke* decision.[36]

While the Deputy General Counsel was correct that no lawsuits had been filed, the Regents were aware at the time of his remarks of the two investigations of UC admissions practices that had been conducted by the U.S. Department of Education Office for Civil Rights (OCR). One of the reviews, of a complaint that admissions practices at the UC Davis medical school discriminated against Asian students, had been issued only two months prior to General Counsel Holst's letter to Regent Burgener. The OCR, while exonerating UC Davis, raised issues that were troubling to some of the Regents. In evaluating why underrepresented students with lower GPAs and test scores were admitted while Asian American students with higher GPAs and test scores were not, the OCR report noted:

> UC Davis stated to OCR that it seeks to enroll students with a "patient service orientation." Thus, the reason an individual with strong quantitative qualifications may be denied admission is that UC Davis uses qualitative criteria that it has concluded are better indicators of whether a candidate has a patient service orientation. OCR found that due to the high demand for admission to the medical school, UC Davis is not able to offer admission to every qualified applicant. UC Davis has created criteria in order to be able to select applicants. The criteria is *[sic]* wide ranging and is not solely limited to determinations based on GPA or MCAT scores. Other more qualitative criteria are used to determine admissions decisions.[37]

A number of Regents, while accepting the use of qualitative criteria in admissions, were at a loss to understand why any one group should benefit over another using qualitative criteria.

Some Regents were also aware of the *Adarand* case making its way to the U.S. Supreme Court and the pending review of *Hopwood et al. v. State of Texas* by the fifth circuit court in Texas. The possibility of litigation over UC admissions would become a key issue in the contest over affirmative action.

In his prepared remarks for the November presentation, Deputy General Counsel Morrison went on to make a prediction about the prevailing landscape for affirmative action litigation:

There are those who believe that the result would be different if the *Bakke* issue were to be litigated today. I disagree. Trial and intermediate courts are bound by the *Bakke* decision and, at most, I would expect even an unsympathetic lower court to find only a procedural flaw in any particular program, which could be corrected without undermining the objectives of the program. It is true that the composition of the United States Supreme Court has entirely changed since *Bakke*. But the court has a strong institutional role in settling great questions and leaving them settled for a long time. I would not expect the court to take review of a new *Bakke* case and, if it did, I would not expect a fundamentally different result.[38]

Less than two years later, in *Hopwood*, a federal district court did what Deputy General Counsel Morrison predicted such a court would not do. That is, the fifth circuit court not only revisited *Bakke*; they essentially reversed it. The court majority wrote:

We agree with the plaintiffs that any consideration of race or ethnicity by the law school for the purpose of achieving a diverse student body is not a compelling interest under the Fourteenth amendment. Justice Powell's argument in *Bakke* garnered only his own vote and has never represented the view of a majority of the Court in *Bakke* or any other case. Moreover, subsequent Supreme Court decisions regarding education state that nonremedial state interests will never justify racial classifications. Finally, the classification of persons on the basis of race for the purpose of diversity frustrates, rather than facilitates, the goals of equal protection.[39]

Deputy Counsel Morrison concluded his remarks with an endorsement of the university's medical school admissions process:

As I indicated in my letter which was sent to you by Regent Burgener, each of our schools continues to find it necessary to use race if we are going to have more than token numbers of minorities. Each uses race as only one factor among many. And none uses a quota or set-aside of any kind. Therefore, the Office of the General Counsel is very comfortable with defending our current practices as consistent with law.[40]

A close examination of the Office of the General counsel's presentation to the board in November reveals a shift in tone and presentation from the counsel's initial response to Regent Burgener's concerns in the July 12 correspondence. In the November presentation, Deputy Counsel Morrison did not repeat the assertion in his earlier letter that, on average, minorities were being admitted with lower grades and test scores than nonminorities. He also made no mention of the Office of Civil Rights investigations of the UCLA and UC Davis admissions processes, nor any mention of the adjustments that had been suggested by the General Counsel's Office after the initial review prompted by Regent Burgener's letter.

MEDICAL SCHOOL ADMISSIONS AT UC

Following the Deputy General Counsel's presentation, the November meeting continued with UC Vice President Cornelius Hopper introducing a presentation on UC's medical school admissions policies. Dr. Hopper noted that in 1964, 93% of medical students in the United States were men and 97% were non-Hispanic Whites. Of the remaining 3%, most were enrolled in two predominantly Black medical schools, Howard University and Meharry Medical College. Dr. Hopper, an African American, used himself as an example:

> I can speak from personal experience in that I filled the University of Cincinnati School of Medicine's 1956 entering class quota of one. And when I joined the faculty of the University of Wisconsin School of Medicine eleven years later, in 1967, the school had graduated only one African American in its entire history. A scan of American Medical Schools at that time would show that this was not unusual.[41]

After Dr. Hopper's remarks, the Assistant Dean of Medicine at UC Irvine, Dr. Ralph Purdy, presented a detailed picture of the medical school admissions process at UC. Dr. Purdy focused his presentation on the methods used by the medical schools as they worked through their applicant pools. He noted that UC medical schools were extremely selective. Each of the five medical schools enrolled some 100 students per year from 5,000 to 6,000 applicants. Approximately 600 students were selected for interviews in order to accept about 200. Of those 200, roughly half enrolled. Dr. Purdy used his own campus, UC Irvine, as an example to explain to the Regents that the selection criteria used by Irvine were divided into distinct categories: (1) academic performance and Medical College Admissions Test (MCAT) scores; (2) clinical and/or research experience; and (3) personal characteristics and experiences, including factors contributing to educational diversity. These categories were given equal weight in selecting candidates for admission to the medical school.

Students' academic criteria were evaluated in light of family responsibilities, outside employment during undergraduate education, and educational and financial disadvantage. A number of personal characteristics and experiences were considered, including an applicant's character, leadership ability and commitment to public service.[42]

Dr. Purdy was followed by the Associate Dean of Medicine for the UC San Francisco medical school, Dr. Michael Drake. Dr. Drake focused on the differential allocation of health care in the country and UC's obligation to provide health care for California's underserved populations. He commented on research that showed quite different rates of blindness from glaucoma in African Americans and Whites, and differential rates of surgery for glaucoma in the two populations. He also referred to a study of graduates of UC San Francisco's medical school from the years 1973 to 1988 which found that over half of the underrepresented minority physicians in those cohorts had practices that served communities made up primarily of underrepresented populations. Dr. Drake concluded with slides that demonstrated that despite entering the medical schools with lower average GPAs and test scores than Whites and Asians in the admit cohorts, for the period 1989 to 1993, underrepresented minority students at UC San Francisco had a 98% first-time pass rate on national board licensing exams. He noted a number of benefits emerging from diverse student populations in UC's medical schools, including that an increasingly diverse nation needs a diverse pool of physicians. He also suggested that while a race-blind admissions policy might function well in a color-blind society, in his opinion the United States was not a color-blind society.[43]

THE REGENTS REACT

In the two years prior to the November 1994 meeting of the board, the pattern of UCOP presentation and Regents' responses was fairly predictable. Even after Regent Connerly's call for increased activism in December 1993, and on contested issues such as fees and the management of nuclear labs, the Regents had consistently acted, at least publicly, with deference to the Office of the President. Regent Carmona described the prevailing belief of various constituencies about board deference this way:

> The problem was that the faculty, like the board and the president, the board was completely used to conduct themselves in terms of business as usual. That meant that everything was okay. That meant that the Regents were deferential to the administration and that was okay. That meant that the administration could go on with a dissertation-like approach to testimony and addressing issues, and life would go on.[44]

The first comment from the board after the medical school admissions report had been concluded served notice that in the case of affirmative action, the nature and level of negotiation would be quite different. Regent Connerly suggested that the presentation was "one-sided, because it did not take into account the evolving political view of the people of the State of California," and that "the most compelling aspect of being an American is the right of an individual to equal opportunity and equal access."[45] He repeated the remark he had made before the Assembly Judiciary Committee that it was time to remove the training wheels. Perhaps most important, he suggested, "the presentation had failed to explore the question of whether or not, at the present time, all applicants are being treated equally regardless of their race or ethnicity." Regent Connerly concluded that the university administration had not answered the questions raised by the Cooks, and he announced that he would soon be calling on the president to conduct a thorough review of all existing UC affirmative action programs.[46]

Regent del Junco, a physician with a practice in East Los Angeles, stated that, in his opinion, the admissions process as presented by Purdy did not treat White and Asian applicants with low grades and MCAT scores in the same way that underrepresented minorities were treated. He agreed that there was a need to increase diversity in the medical schools, but stated flatly that he did not believe that a quota system was the answer.[47] Regent del Junco went on to express his belief that the Davis medical school had not truly reformed its admissions procedures in keeping with the *Bakke* decision. Twice during his remarks Regent del Junco expressed irritation with what he perceived to be the failure of the system in defining sub-populations of Latinos in the calculation of underrepresented minority status. He expressed dissatisfaction with the overall presentation by the Office of the President and echoed Regent Connerly's call for a review of all of the UC system's admissions and hiring practices with regard to the use of affirmative action.[48]

Regent Kolligian also addressed the board, noting that he felt the UC Office of the President had presented a "rationalization" rather than an explanation of the admissions process. He did, however, express support for continuing affirmative action programs in order to achieve diversity in the medical school.[49]

Regent Davies addressed the board to state his belief that the admissions process as presented seemed to him to be consistent with the *Bakke* decision. He also supported the use of a variety of measures in admissions evaluations. He cited the example of the likelihood of serving in an underserved community as an acceptable factor, and expressed reservations about using race as a factor.[50]

AUTHORITY OVER POLICYMAKING

Regent David Flinn turned the discussion from the criteria used for admissions to the medical schools to the question of who should appropriately decide the criteria. Regent Flinn made a distinction between setting broad policy for admissions, which he saw as the role of the board, and the actual selection of the students who were to be admitted, which he saw as the role of the faculty. He went on to say that he believed the Regents would "destroy the University if they took from the faculty the right to decide which students to admit."[51]

Although these were the first mentions of the question of authority over admissions policy, that question, and the corollary issue of shared governance in the policymaking process, would reemerge throughout the contest.

Karl Pister, the chancellor of UC Santa Cruz at the time of the affirmative action deliberations, later offered another perspective on shared governance in remarks on the approach adopted by Regent Dean Watkins:

> Dean is a very conservative Republican. He served on the board with great distinction for a long period of time. The reason why I'm mentioning it is that he frequently reminded the Regents that, look, your job is not to try to talk to the president and the chancellors about developing policy, your job is to hire the president and to see that he does his job properly. Get out of his way to run the university, that's not your job. I must say, I was really devastated by what I felt was the creeping micromanagement by the Regents this last five years, last seven years now. I have a very sharply different view. I don't think the Regents—first of all they don't have the time—secondly, many of them are not qualified to get into the detailed management of the University of California. Any more than I'm qualified to do their business.[52]

QUOTAS

Another key issue invoked at the meeting was the question of whether or not the University of California medical schools had established quotas for underrepresented minority admissions. In his letter to Regent Burgener, Deputy General Counsel Morrison stated, "No school has a set-aside or quota for minority students."[53]

The quota issue was first raised in open session by Regent Kolligian, who stated that in his opinion, "the University's practices, in fact, amounted to a quota system."[54] Regent del Junco commented that he also believed a quota system was being used at UC Davis, and stressed his belief that quotas were no solution.

Regent Flinn had argued that while one could make a case for a color-blind admissions policy, one could also make a case for a system of specific quotas for admission of various groups. His own opinion, based on the data received, was that the medical admissions policies were not quota systems.[55]

Student Regent Wooten argued against the notion that the medical admissions were based on quotas, suggesting instead that the applicants were evaluated as individuals, with race only one of several factors in the admissions decision. Regent Wooten, an African American, also pointed out to the board that race can also be thought of as a factor, "which may have closed certain doors in a student's face."[56]

Regent Connerly later reiterated his fundamental belief that UC was using quotas in admissions, and his belief that much of the public agreed with him:

> What many public institutions are doing is just outright unconstitutional. Race is seeping out of every pore. They have forgotten about "one of many factors," assuming, and I don't know how, that you could use it as one of many factors, personally. But assuming that you could do that, most institutions have gone so far beyond the pale that they're breaking the law. And they don't understand that this isn't some benign transaction. There are moderate-to-liberal families whose kids are being turned down, and these families are having to go out and take out loans and send the kids out of state. When they go to the dinner table, they're talking to their kids about it, they've got this dumb letter from the University of California that says, "You are a great student, but we had to, you know, we're rejecting you. Diversity is important." I've seen these letters where you read between the lines. We're telegraphing our message. The family reads that. They see the word "diversity." It's a code word to them for "quota." They talk about it with the kid's friends, they talk about it with their relatives, and now instead of the student who is wondering why he or she was turned down with a 4.0, you now have got have got fifteen or twenty other people who know about it who also are wondering. It's that dynamic that it's creating that the university just doesn't seem to be aware of.[57]

A number of comments from the Office of the President and ex officio Regents on the board pointed to an essential polarization in responding to the Cooks' concerns. While a number of appointed Regents, including Kolligian, del Junco, Connerly, and Davies, wondered aloud whether the medical school admissions process was currently fair to all applicants, President Peltason, Vice President Hopper, Chancellor Young, and ex officio Regents Carmona and Wooten all focused on the use of affirmative action as an effective tool for redressing historical and contemporary inequity.

Vice President Hopper noted that there were three African Americans present at the table (referring to Regent Connerly, student Regent Wooten, and himself), and he suggested that fifty years prior to that time, "no personal attributes or intelligence would have brought them there."[58]

A number of Regents subsequently suggested that the UC Office of the President's presentation in response to the concerns initially raised by the Cooks did little to assuage their concerns. Regent Connerly noted in an interview that the Office of the President might well have ended the policy contest at the November 1994 meeting if they had taken a different approach to addressing the concerns raised by the Cooks:

At the end of the meeting I thought that they were really trying to shine us on and from a governance standpoint they had really been unresponsive and so I spoke up and said basically that. But the point of all this is that Peltason could have talked us out of it, out of even scheduling it for the agenda, and he tried. Peltason certainly could've talked me out of going any further with it and he tried. I don't want to sound like I'm pompous or whatever, because you can look at this two ways, but I'm absolutely convinced that had it been anybody else on that board, this item would have been sandbagged right there at that point. It wouldn't have gone any further, because the tradition of the board from a governance standpoint is that you just don't rock the boat. You don't go ahead with something that the president tells you that they really don't want to do, and that it's going to harm the university, and that was all the stuff he said to me.

He said, "Look, we've got a legislature to deal with that really has yes or no over our budget," and the code for everything that he was saying is that it's a Democratically controlled legislature. Willie Brown was the Speaker, and John Vasconcellos was chairing Budget Committee, I believe it was, and John took a real interest in the university and so Jack's concerns, legitimate concerns, were that "God, we're going to run into a buzz saw here, and looking out for the best interests of the university, don't rock the boat."

And I said, "Look, if we're breaking the law I can't pretend that nothing is wrong here, and the mere fact that you're saying race is one of many factors doesn't convince me," because I wasn't persuaded by what had been said at that meeting.[59]

This was not a problem that improved over the course of the debate. Longtime California political analyst Peter Schrag described a presentation made by the Office of the President toward the end of the Regents' deliberations:

The "analysis" University of California officials submitted to the Regents last week regarding affirmative action in UC admissions piles confusion on misdirection. Rather than the impartial report it's represented to be, it's a clumsy defense of existing race preferences. It combines straw-man comparisons with statements so internally contradictory they make your head spin.[60]

Regents had concerns over other issues related to affirmative action policy at the conclusion of the November presentation, including the question of the fairness of differential admissions standards and a concern that was not expressed publicly at the November meeting, that the Office of the President was not entirely forthcoming in its dissemination of information. Regent del Junco expressed a number of Regents' feelings on that point in a subsequent interview:

We had, I'd say, at least four or five board meetings for them to present the issues. I think, forgive me what I'm going to say, but I think a lot of the information was managed information. And they were managing the thing. They were massaging the thing from day one. This guy, Galligani (UC Assistant V.P. Dennis Galligani), or whatever it is, he's a nice guy, but he was doing a sales job. For instance, I said, "Would you tell me if at UCLA if you are a Hispanic of Mexican ancestry, will you be treated differently than if you were of Cuban ancestry?" It took him three months to answer the question. Finally I had to threaten to expose him, because I asked the question and he didn't answer. I told him, "Tomorrow I'm going to pose the question and I'm going to tell you that I am going to expose you for what you're doing." This was the problem that was going on all the time.[61]

Regent Connerly's announcement during the November meeting that he would be bringing a request to the board for a review of affirmative action presented a particular challenge to those Regents who felt the request should be made by a committee vote. After some discussion over whether an individual Regent (in this case Connerly) could bring such a request, it was left unresolved.

Despite the option of forcing a committee vote, or endeavoring to maintain control of the agenda going forward, President Peltason chose not to prevent Regent Connerly's unorthodox approach to agenda setting. It was an early example of a problem that would recur throughout the conflict—the effect of institutional norms and culture interacting with interest group challenges to the policymaking process. While the governor and his allies on the Board would fight an aggressive parliamentary and political battle, the Office of the President would often restrain itself in the service of administrative propriety and deference. In the matter of the request for a review, the Office of the President chose to take the symbolic high ground. Throughout the contest, UC President Peltason stressed the importance of the administration maintaining its role as provider of expertise and information. It was a strategic choice that might have served UCOP and the university in the long run, but it would come to haunt the system's defenders of affirmative action.

THE GOVERNOR'S PRESIDENTIAL AMBITIONS

November 1994 was a turning point for Regent Connerly and his friend and political ally of over twenty years, Governor Pete Wilson. While Assemblyman Richter's bill to ban affirmative action had not gotten out of the Judiciary committee, on the first Tuesday of November, Proposition 187 had passed with 58% of the vote. More important, Governor Wilson was reelected with 55% of the vote. Wilson's successful campaign and his stance in the forefront of the anti-immigration movement placed him among the early contenders for the Republican presidential nomination for 1996. Wilson's campaign for reelection had benefited significantly from the fact that Proposition 187 drew White voters from both parties to the polls. In the wake of the election, exit polls and political commentators pointed to the success of the strategies behind the "Gingrich revolution," and suggested that the midterm election results would only intensify the courting of "angry White males" (Chavez, 1998).

Regent Connerly found himself in a position to bring to the establishment's attention, or at least initially the education establishment's attention, the concerns of those White voters. At the same time he could carry forward an issue that would ultimately provide unprecedented publicity and attention for the CCRI and Governor Wilson's presidential campaign. That the three issues, carrying forward an effort to repeal existing affirmative action policies at UC, bringing the national spotlight to efforts to place the CCRI on the ballot, and advancing the governor's presidential campaign, were initially linked was noted by many of those involved in the UC contest. Regent Bagley's remarks summed up this perspective:

> Had Pete not been involved, had the governor not been involved, we would have never passed the resolution. The governor got involved because he was running for president. The governor used my university as a forum to run for president.[62]

Regent Connerly and a few others did suggest that the connection was more serendipity than strategy. He presented a different rationale for the governor's role as advisor to Connerly and as activist Regent in his own right in the contest over UC affirmative action:

> You know, so, it helped his presidential campaign, but Pete Wilson is the kind who says, "The reason I'm running for office is to lay my values on the line and if you agree with them, fine. If you don't agree with them, well, that's okay, too, but the role of my running for president is to put my positions to the test." That's how you make public policy. So he never had any apology for getting involved and using this to further his own presidential ambitions and when people say, "Oh, you made it a political issue," he says, "What the hell is politics? It's the art of shaping public policy."[63]

REGENT CONNERLY GOES NATIONAL

The combination of the passage of Proposition 187, the early word on CCRI, and the coverage of the November meeting of the Regents resulted in a burst of national publicity. In December, an article appeared in the *Washington Post* that reviewed the results of Proposition 187 and mentioned for the first time nationally the effort to put CCRI on the ballot and the UC Regents' initial deliberations.[64] It was an article that has been described as "the turning point in CCRI's life,"[65] and it would also mark a turning point in the contest over affirmative action policy at UC.

In the weeks prior to the January meeting of the Regents, the proceedings of the November meeting and the upcoming discussion of affirmative action at the Regents' meeting by Regent Connerly were being covered by every major newspaper in California. The *San Jose Mercury News* headlined its story on the day of the January meeting, "Regent Seeks an End to Affirmative Action."[66]

PRESIDENT PELTASON RESIGNS

Just prior to the Regents' January meeting, President Peltason submitted his letter of resignation. In it he explained that during his three years as president he had essentially accomplished his main goal of stabilizing the university's financial situation, and that he hoped to be able to step down by the following fall.

Student Regent Ed Gomez saw Peltason's resignation, and the subsequent announcement by University Provost Walter Massey that he too would be leaving, as detrimental to UCOP's legitimacy in the ensuing deliberations:

> Peltason knows that he's going to be going out the door. He's gonna go along, whatever he has to do, and he's hoping to get the golden parachute, which you can't blame him. Massey has not said anything, but he knows, I think, in his head that he's going somewhere soon, too, and nobody else might have known that. So he's not going to rock the boat because if he starts shaking the boat here, then maybe his opportunity to be given a good recommendation to go where he's heading, up at Morehouse, right? So you have two guys who are actually in a position of power to do something who aren't going to do anything, they're even less inclined now because one's taking the golden handshake and one wants the approval to get out of there.[67]

President Peltason's resignation was not a great surprise, though the timing might have been. As he noted in his letter of resignation, Peltason had taken the job in the wake of the abrupt departure of President David Gardner, as something of an interim president. What is of more than passing interest is that in his resignation letter he said nothing about the issue which would consume that day's meeting of the Board of Regents and the entire university over the next six months: affirmative action.

STRUGGLE FOR CONTROL

At the Regents' meeting held on January 19, 1995, the Special Committee on Affirmative Action Policies convened at the request of Regent Connerly to conduct a discussion of policies on affirmative action. The item was on the agenda as a discussion item, meaning there was no motion or recommendation before the committee in advance.

In his presentation to the board at the January meeting, President Peltason deviated slightly from his prepared remarks, which were distributed to the press and in the Regents' premeeting briefing packets. One key difference is that in his prepared remarks he had written that "no changes were needed" in the university's affirmative action programs and policies, a phrase that was not used during his presentation in public session. Perhaps more significantly, a number of differences in the prepared and delivered texts point to a struggle for positioning around the question of who should take the leadership in directing the review of existing affirmative action that was under consideration. Having received a copy in advance of the January meeting of the remarks Regent Connerly intended to make, in his own prepared remarks President Peltason wrote:

> In response to Regent Connerly's remarks, let me say that we are preparing an inventory and report on our affirmative action programs.[68]

That is, the written remarks prepared in advance of the meeting give the impression that the subsequent preparation of a series of reports on affirmative action practices at the university was in response to Regent Connerly's remarks. However, by the time of the actual meeting, President Peltason was apparently less willing to concede that Regent Connerly was driving the process.

In his public remarks to the board and the audience, President Peltason deviated from the prepared text to say:

> In response to Regent Connerly's remarks, let me point out that *we are already* in the process of preparing an inventory and a report on our affirmative action programs.[69]

President Peltason, in his public comments, did not mention Regent Connerly in presenting his rationale for undertaking the review:

> I want to make clear that we are not doing so because, in my judgment, the time has come to make any fundamental changes, but because we're aware of the fact that the question is arising in the Legislature and before the public of California. We want to be able to answer questions about these programs as they arise.[70]

The president did note the efforts of Assemblyman Richter, and Custred and Wood's nascent CCRI, but not Regent Connerly. Neither the president nor anyone else from the Office of the President mentioned an inventory or review at the November 1994 meeting. There is no indication from any other remarks or documents that the Office of the President had been planning any sort of inventory or review prior to Regent Connerly's request. Yet the president went on to say,

> I'll be happy to accelerate the production of our report about these programs and be prepared to bring you that report this Spring.[71]

The Office of the President further made its point by titling the affirmative action discussion item on the January agenda "Discussion of Calendar for Review of Affirmative Action Policies and Coordination with State Government Action (Regent Connerly) {Oral Presentation—No Item}." The discussion of a review of UC affirmative action policies and a motion to request such a review were two quite different procedural matters, hence the emphasis in the agenda on the phrase "No Item."

The question of whether Regent Connerly was in a position to appropriately bring the request for a review of affirmative action policies to the Office of the President without a vote of the board was again raised by several Regents at the meeting. Under the bylaws of the Regents, a committee chair, in this case Regent Flinn, in consultation with the president of the university, would generally place such a request on the agenda, or a majority of the appropriate committee would vote to place the item. During the January discussion at the board, Regent Gonzales questioned the appropriateness of any single Regent asking for a comprehensive report from the Office of the President:

> One other point I want to make, and this is in general to address all of us here is that I feel uncomfortable when a request is made of the president and/or his staff by one Regent to prepare reports. There's twenty-one of us here, and we could all ask the president and his staff for a report on a different subject. So I think that the reports that are requested from the president and his office and the staff should be with the concurrence of the Board members. And that's the end of my speech, and I guess you know how I feel about it.[72]

Regent Davies supported the review of existing policies, and also questioned the route the issue was taking to get to the board:

> I don't think this is something that should be allocated to one Regent, but it should be handled in the normal way.[73]

Davies concluded his remarks with a caution:

> And there are legal issues as well, so I just urge, Ward, that I sympathize with you and I appreciate your sense of urgency, but I beg you to be patient and let this thing go through our normal procedures.[73]

Another dissent to the approach Regent Connerly was taking came from Regent Brophy:

> At the outset I want to second what Regent Gonzales has said. It is true that if a member wants the President's Office to do something, be he the Chairman or just a member of the Board of Regents, it takes a vote of the responsible committee, and theoretically, having brought this up at this committee, it would take a vote of this committee to request that. However, in as much as the president is preparing for information and is not going to be making any special effort, I would assume then it's a rule that we've had, and there's been transgressions on more than an average basis, I think, on it, but that isn't the principal issue here today.[74]

Brophy cited the appropriate method for bringing an item, but stopped short of bringing a procedural question. With Brophy following the president's lead, they had in effect foregone any parliamentary rules they might have invoked to deny Connerly's effort to bring the issue to the board. While it would turn out to be a key strategic choice, and one that greatly assisted Connerly's cause, there was no effort on the part of the Office of the President to force an early committee vote on the issue. This may have been because they didn't think Connerly could ultimately succeed in eliminating affirmative action. President Peltason, in a later interview, described his assessment of the board prior to the January meeting:

> My estimate of it was that one third of the Regents, before the debate started, were for affirmative action fervently. They were knowledgeable and for it and considered it an essential tool. One third were against it and would have voted to abolish it any time given a chance. And one third was neither focused on it, or if they were opposed to it, didn't think that the Regents should be the place for the debate.[75]

REGENT CONNERLY'S VISION

After Committee Chair Flinn introduced the discussion, Regent Connerly was the first to address the board at the January meeting.[76] Connerly introduced a number of the themes he had presented at his testimony before the Assembly Judiciary Committee in August, invoking the issues of fairness, equity, legality, and civil rights. The Regent also questioned the willingness of UCOP to move on the issue and raised a number of symbolic flags. Regent Connerly's remarks constituted his most complete declaration to date of the concepts that would ultimately shape SP-1 and SP-2.

Connerly spoke of the basic fairness of people, stating that sometimes you have to coax or drag them into doing the right thing, as in the case of abolishing slavery and ending segregation, but that in general people wish to create a fair and equitable society. He praised the State of California and particularly the University of California for leadership in what he called "one of the boldest and most exciting experiments in the history of the world,"[77] the pursuit of a society in which people of many backgrounds, languages, ethnicities, and perspectives "can live and work and play together in harmony, with mutual respect and with no limitations on our ability to succeed placed on us by our government." Connerly pointed to the importance of affirmative action in getting society on the right track toward integration, and the continuing need for inclusive behavior, but he lamented the turn that the university's affirmative action policies had taken toward unfairness. He argued that affirmative action was unfair to qualified White and Asian American students who were not appropriately considered for admission, as well as being unfair to talented Black students who would carry the stigma of preferential treatment. The essence of his dissatisfaction with affirmative action seems to be distilled in the following:

> My point is that many of our institutions contribute to the worst kind of racism. Until we begin to move in a different path, until we recognize that affirmative action was intended to be temporary to remedy past discrimination, not to be the device for permanently allocating this great resource that we call educational opportunity at this great institution, they will always look at Ward Connerly as a Black Regent, as a product of affirmative action.[78]

Connerly then proposed a course of action that called for the university to lead the country in finding a replacement for affirmative action, a course that, he suggested, would be more fair to all concerned, with better preparation of students before they reach college age, more criteria for evaluating applicants to the university, and fairer ways to award contracts to small businesses. He invited members of the administration and the student body to help him move the university ahead, and hinted that the CCRI might have a life of its own:

> There are some who say that we at the University should follow and not lead. Let the initiative come. We're here to be the legislative body of this University, and whether it's sports, whether it's science, or whether it's social thought, as cliche as it might sound, I think the University of California is the beacon that lights the way. And I think we should begin.[79]

A number of Regent Connerly's comments framed the symbolic terrain of contest for SP-1 and SP-2 over the next seven months. While he raised a number of technical issues with regard to admissions criteria, he dwelt more in the realm of the philosophical, the political, and the symbolic. In particular, he invoked the legacy of slavery, linked zealous supporters of affirmative action with the arch-segregationist Alabama Governor George Wallace, and linked his own efforts to end affirmative action with the national Civil Rights Movement of the 1960s. He drew the boundaries of the contest around a much larger domain than the University of California's policy arena. Connerly's comments positioned the contest over affirmative action at UC as part of a much broader struggle over access and equity nationwide. This approach was evidenced in Connerly's call for the Regents and the university to be in the forefront of the contest, rather than awaiting the outcome of the CCRI or other legislative efforts. It was to the latter point that President Peltason spoke as he addressed the board after Regent Connerly concluded. The president began with an effort to reclaim control of the agenda and process of reviewing affirmative action:

> Mr. Chairman and members of the Board. In response to Regent Connerly's remarks, let me point out that we are already in the process of preparing an inventory and a report on our affirmative action programs. I want to make it clear that we're not doing so because, in my judgment, the time has come to make any fundamental changes, but because we're aware of the fact that the question is arising in the Legislature and before the public of California. We want to be able to answer questions about these programs as they arise. I'll be happy to accelerate the production of our report about these programs and be prepared to bring you that report this spring. But I would like to take a moment to put into context my present understanding of these programs and our policies.[80]

The president then went on to state a case similar to the one he made at the November meeting, that affirmative action was necessary, and that it had served the university well in its efforts to diversify over the past three decades. He concluded:

> In my judgment, these programs have been, and continue to be essential. I am proud of what they have accomplished for the University of California. Like those of other American colleges and universities, they grow out of a broad national consensus that such programs are indispensable to achieving equal opportunity in this country. If that consensus changes, so will federal and State policy and law, and the University, as it is obliged to do, will respond at the appropriate time.[81]

In his concluding remarks, the president endeavored to redefine the appropriate terrain for the contest over affirmative action, to keep the conversation at the university level, and to practice traditional norms of UC governance. His speech was remarkable for the degree to which it ignored the political nature of the emerging contest and attempted to place the university above the impending struggle. His remarks also evidenced a unique perspective on the emerging political climate in California and across the nation with regard to affirmative action. His reference to a "broad national consensus that such programs are indispensable"[82] did not reflect the increasing lack of consensus on affirmative action. After President Peltason concluded his remarks, a number of Regents went on the record with perspectives that reflected the division on the board over the question of reviewing affirmative action and the possible effects of such a review.

Regent Burgener, a former congressman and no stranger to the political value and effects of symbolic contest, urged caution, while also seeming to question the existing affirmative action policies in his comments to the board. He concluded as follows:

> Sixteen years ago, largely forgotten at a number of universities and in the Justice Department's civil rights department at times, is what Justice Louis Powell said in the famous *Bakke* case. You will recall the Court was divided 5 to 4 and Justice Powell broke the tie. In his swing vote, he did indeed rule that in admissions programs race may be considered as one factor among many but that set asides or reservations could not be made. Powell added, "Preferring members of any one group for no reason other than race or ethnic origin is discrimination for its own sake. This the Constitution forbids." So all I'm suggesting is in this very complex matter I make the assumption that we're all of good will. Some aren't, but I think overwhelmingly we are, and as we enter this very slippery slope, or highway to heaven, take your pick, keep your cool, folks. Thank you.[83]

Regent John Davies had expressed support for affirmative action at the November meeting, and he appeared to reaffirm that support. As a Wilson ally, his reservations were an encouragement to those hoping to preserve existing affirmative action policies:

> I think we all agree that we are embarked on attempting to have a successful multicultural society and that it is by no means a given that we will succeed. One of the key pieces in order to succeed will be to have a multicultural university. Everybody has to feel like they play a part in it, and that's been the goal of affirmative action. I know that we have not achieved the goal. Affirmative action has certainly helped. The problem is not yet solved. Nevertheless, I agree with Ward in much of what he says.[84]

The first public expression of the position of the faculty representatives on the matter was provided by faculty representative Arnold Leiman, who reflected on the history of affirmative action:

> Our tone in this discussion is quite somber, and I think its somberness doesn't really do justice to the energy, the commitment, the enthusiasm of a wide array of faculty, students, and Regents, in solving the problems that are reflected in this policy. Our tone should turn celebratory. We have done an enormous number of things over a long period of time. The University of California has been a sensitive player in this arena, and because it's a sensitive player, it has opened opportunities for people who weren't part of the story but a short while ago. And the game is not over; the task is not over. And I think in our discussions, when they come, we should look at what we've done, not to say it's something that we shouldn't be doing, but to say we've done something that we could be proud of as human beings.[85]

At that point in the meeting Regent Connerly was recognized to speak on the issue of whether or not he had the right to request action on the affirmative action review:

> Thank you, Mr. Chairman. First of all, to respond to Regent Gonzales. I can really proceed without a report from the president. There's nothing here that says I have to await a report from the president. But candidly, President Peltason and I jointly talked about the idea of him providing some input so that whatever I would come forward with would have the involvement of the president. So I think that President Peltason will tell you that this isn't my idea, loading something on his shoulders in the form of an additional report. Secondly, with respect to Regent Davies' comment, I'd be delighted if the affirmative action special committee would take this task on. I don't want it. I'd be delighted if they would take it on. Is there a motion?[86]

After Regent Connerly's request for a motion, he was reminded that the item on the floor was not an action item, but a discussion item, and therefore no motion could be entertained.

Regent Nakashima, a Japanese American who had been interned during World War II, commended Regent Connerly for bringing the issue to the board and expressed general support for his position:

> The first thing I have to say is that Ward Connerly has an awful lot of courage to come out with his position. He indicated, I think, that he's not advocating the complete abolition or doing away with the affirmative action program, yet this morning's *San Jose Mercury News* says that a Black Regent is advocating the elimination of affirmative action. I think Ward has a tremendous amount of courage because of his background. He is an African American, and I'm sure he's going to get a lot of negative telephone calls and will be vilified. There's only a few of us on this Board who actually would be affected by the affirmative action policies, unless

you as a White had a son or a daughter with a 4.0 from Menlo High School who was not accepted at Cal because of the admission of 30 percent of the first-year class going to the disadvantaged minorities. If you have a son or a daughter with a 4.0 average who is turned away from the University, what are your feelings going to be? You're not going to be happy. You're not going to say, "Well, it's because of affirmative action, and it's fine with me." Whether or not an affirmative action policy is fair or unfair depends on where you stand. For example, we had a lot of confrontations with Asian Americans at UC because they said they were relegated to a quota system and they weren't accepted at Cal on the basis of grades or performance. I think that affirmative action has been used as a convenience. In other words, Asians are minorities and get the benefit of affirmative action in certain situations, but in the area of education Asians are not considered minorities who would be entitled to the benefits of affirmative action. I asked Chancellor Tien today at lunch how many Asians receive football or basketball scholarships at Cal. Well, under the affirmative action policy, we should be represented. That's really reaching.[87]

Regent Meredith Khachigian also expressed admiration for Regent Connerly's effort to address a topic that most would just as soon avoid. She invoked what would become another powerful symbol in the debate, the specter of affirmative action as racism in its own right:

I agree with Regent Johnson and many others here who have said that we've created factions. And I think we've created racism by affirmative action that maybe wasn't necessarily here before. And those are issues that I can see being discussed over the years, probably not years but months, and there's another issue that I'll throw out with some trepidation, but I think we've gone a long way from disadvantaged minorities to the affirmative action the way it's carried out now.[88]

The first ex officio Regent to comment on Regent Connerly's remarks was the state superintendent of public instruction, a Democrat, Delaine Eastin. She raised an issue she would return to throughout the deliberations, that the university belonged to all Californians:

Everyone here, I think, wants two things for the University: excellence, because it is the finest public university in the world, and access for all students. And we have felt over the years the need to provide something called affirmative action because in fact there was not access for all students. About the time Ralph and I went off to UC we were confronted with a world that was very different than it is today. Indeed, there were very few people of color at the University of California even then, in the '60s. And I might add there were almost no women in any of the professional schools, veterinary school, dentistry.

We did not, in fact, open all of our doors, although we asked everyone to support the system. And they did, because they looked and said, "someday my kid's going to go to the University of California." My family supported it for five generations before they got anybody in, so in fact there was that belief. This was the light that we held out for everyone, and I think we ought be very careful that we don't do damage to the notion that every child, irrespective of income or background or ethnicity or whatever, has a chance to come here. Because in the end this idea of the common good is the thing that is at risk in our country.[89]

The Regent Designate of the UC alumni association, Ralph Carmona, related his personal experiences with racism and cautioned the board against making UC policy an issue in a broader political context:

I share a lot of the ideals that Ward has regarding fairness and the whole ideal of colorblindness, and Ward and I talked about this extensively previously. We live in a world that's very unfair, a world that is very color conscious. An example I shared with Ward at the time was a situation just recently where I was at a garage changing mufflers, and there was a Black guy working on the mufflers. The guy happened to be White who was having the work done for me, and he turned to me and said, "You know, I'd pick six Mexicans over this. It would take six of this guy to do what one Mexican could do." I guess he was making me feel a little bit comfortable in making that statement to me, but it was very clear to me that the person was very conscious of who I was and who the gentleman working on the muffler was. It's a very color conscious world.[90]

Chair Flinn closed the discussion and the meeting with the hope that the issue could be resolved without becoming political, and a caution to the Office of the President to be forthright:

I think we could really find some consensus from what we've heard at the table today. We find consensus in the fact that this is not a simple problem, it is a complex problem. It is a problem that requires deep thought, study by everyone involved in the process, and that is not limited to those that are sitting at this table. It expands to our campuses, our chancellors, our administrators. I think there is also a consensus which I found very rewarding that this is not a political issue. We are not interested at this table at putting right against left, we are not interested at this table of calling people right or wrong. We're interested at this table in finding the best solution for the University of California, and for its future and for the people in this State. I'm optimistic that we can find that.[91]

REGENTS' MEETING, FEBRUARY 1995

The Regents' meeting in February 1995 focused on issues other than affirmative action. As a result, there were no speakers from the public on that subject and little press attention. One notable occurrence at the February meeting was the introduction to the board of a new Student Regent, Edward Gomez, to replace Terrence Wooten. Gomez, a graduate student at UC Riverside, would later become one of the most active Regents in opposition to the effort to pass SP-1 and SP-2.

At the conclusion of the February meeting, President Peltason announced that he intended to present to the board a series of reports on various affirmative action programs over the course of the year. He also noted that he would provide the Regents with a schedule of those presentations before the next regular meeting.

GOVERNOR WILSON JUMPS IN

One week after the February meeting, at the Republican state convention, Governor Wilson made up his mind to join the battle for the hearts and minds of White voters, angry and otherwise. His decision ended several months of hesitation, during which his staff had studied polls on CCRI and on preferences in general.[92] Because of the solid support on the part of voters, particularly women voters, for "affirmative action" (as opposed to quotas, or preferences, which voters strongly opposed)[93] some members of the Wilson staff were reluctant to identify too strongly with attacks on affirmative action. For this reason, Wilson did not mention affirmative action in his State of the State address in January 1995.[94] Convinced by the polling data, by his conversations with Regent Connerly, and by his belief that the language in the CCRI challenged preferences rather than affirmative action, Wilson came out as the point man for a national movement to end affirmative action. At the convention, he endorsed the effort to place CCRI on the state ballot and asked the people of California to support him in an effort to "undo the corrosive unfairness of reverse discrimination."[95] The first place the governor would attempt to implement his new agenda was the University of California.

MARCH 1995—THE REVIEW BEGINS

The March gathering of the Regents was a key opportunity for the public to speak on the issue of affirmative action. Although a number of forces on the state and national scene were moving against affirmative action, outside of the Regents' meeting at the UCLA campus, more than 200 students gathered to express their support for UC's policies. In a sign of the Regents' apprehension over student mobilization, more than seventy-five police officers kept watch over the crowd. During the public comment period, eighteen individuals spoke in favor of retaining affirmative action programs. Despite the increased student awareness and organization, it was clear early on in the meeting that the battle would be truly joined further down the road, as neither Regent Connerly, Governor Wilson, Lt. Governor Davis, or State Superintendent of Public Instruction Eastin chose to attend. Much of the meeting was taken up with discussions of proposals to establish differential fee increases for professional schools and annual reports on the university's energy laboratories and clinical medical enterprises. The first of the Office of the President's reports on affirmative action programs and policies was presented late in the day and lasted less than two hours. The meeting did, however, provide a clear indication that the Office of the President would use the review to make a case for preserving existing affirmative action policies and practices.

President Peltason opened the joint meeting of the Committee on Educational Policy and the Committee on Affirmative Action Policies with a public declaration of the stance of the Office of the President on the issue of affirmative action:

> As we agreed at our January meeting, I will be bringing you a series of reports on the University's programs and policies that support equal opportunity, non-discrimination, affirmative action, and diversity. The purpose of these presentations, as you know, is to explain why the University has these programs for students, faculty, and staff, what they are designed to do, and the constitutional and legal obligations and constraints under which we operate. As background for today's meeting, you received an overview paper on the University's efforts in this area. Today we will have the first of our presentations, a discussion of the University's academic development programs for undergraduate students. Before we begin, however, I'd like to make a few general comments.
>
> I am aware of differences of opinion among individual members of the Board about the continuing necessity of race-attentive programs. I am also aware of differences of opinion about the proper action for the University to take in light of ACA 2[96] and similar proposed legislation. Our programs, particularly in admissions, will inevitably be raised in the intense political debate, which will surround this issue. But, as this political struggle is underway, I strongly believe the University should continue to pursue its deliberative collegial process for arriving at decisions regarding fundamental educational issues.
>
> It has been the policy of the Board for the past thirty years to encourage a variety of efforts intended to increase the diversity of our students,

faculty, and staff. As I told you in January, I will continue to reflect that policy on your behalf unless and until there are changes in policy or law. As I also said in January, I believe these programs have been and are essential, for several reasons. [97]

After President Peltason's remarks, Regent Flinn, chair of the Special Committee on Affirmative Action Policies, commented on concerns raised during the public comment section at the outset of the meeting. Regent Flinn promised that the board would take a deliberative approach to its review of affirmative action and that no action would be taken until the Regents were in a position to make an informed decision. He also addressed the growing public awareness of the campaign to put the CCRI on the ballot. He expressed his opinion that under the CCRI, the sort of academic development programs that were the subject of the day's meeting would be imperiled. He also suggested that while much of the public might not support affirmative action, they would support outreach initiatives, even where they differentially benefited underrepresented groups.[98]

DIVERSITY: AN INTRODUCTION

As part of the Regents' information packets prepared for the March meeting, UCOP presented a comprehensive statement on the university's admissions programs. The report addressed California's unique demographics and the need to provide access to a changing population this way:

> The University of California has responded to these challenges with a variety of programs designed to promote access and educational opportunity for minorities and women. However, finding an effective and fair mechanism to do this work has been difficult and controversial. For nearly a quarter of a century, the University of California has supported programs designed to diversify the student body, has modified programs as required by law or as a result of internal program review, or the desired results have been achieved. Diversity is the goal; affirmative action is one of many strategies used to achieve that goal. To increase the diversity of the student body, the University has devised specific outreach and development programs, admissions policies and procedures, and programs to create a welcoming campus climate which fosters an appreciation of diversity.[99]

The report also invoked a number of historical publications demonstrating the commitment of various university constituencies to increasing access and diversity. It cited three documents in particular, beginning with the following statement of principles:

> Mindful of its mission as a public institution, the University of California has an historic commitment to provide places within the University for all eligible applicants who are residents of California. The University seeks to enroll, on each of its campuses, a student body that, beyond meeting the University's eligibility requirement, demonstrates high academic achievement or exceptional personal talent and that encompasses the broad diversity of cultural, racial, geographic, and socioeconomic backgrounds characteristic of California.[100]

The report also noted faculty commitment to the goals of access and diversity and presented a pair of statements, one from the Coordinating Committee on Graduate Affairs of the Academic Senate and the other from the Council of Graduate Deans, both prepared in 1990:

> The University is committed to increasing minority access to its graduate and professional programs as a vital part of its mission of enhancing individual opportunities and helping meet the needs of minority communities. It is also committed to maintaining admission processes that are fair and honest, not arbitrary or capricious. The faculty in each school and department is responsible for implementing these goals.[101]

> Because the professions need a diverse membership and because the educational experience is enhanced by a diverse student body, the University views as a high priority the enrollment of men and women from different backgrounds and demographic groups.[102]

The report concluded:

> The rapidly changing demographic profile of the State of California heightens the necessity for continued attention to the issues which spawned outreach and affirmative action efforts to promote diversity. By the beginning of the next century, there will be no single ethnic group constituting a majority of the California population. The White and Chicano/Latino populations are expected to be approximately equal by 2020 and, by 2040, it is estimated that the Chicano/Latino population will become the majority group. Educating the citizens and the workforce of the future means educating people from all population groups, and it includes educating all to live and work together. It has been the general consensus of our faculty and staff shared by peers around the country, that we must continue to acknowledge race, ethnicity, and sex among the many factors used in selecting students and recruiting faculty and staff. The University of California is a better place today not only because it has consistently sought to encourage diversity but because in addition it has valued the contribution and encouraged the equal participation in all its activities of all members of the community.[103]

ACADEMIC DEVELOPMENT

The March meeting continued with a comprehensive presentation of the university's academic development programs.[104] Assistant Vice President Dennis Galligani gave a brief overview of the university's efforts and intentions with regard to academic development programs. He explained that the university's academic development programs were intended to increase the number of African American, Chicano, Latino, and American Indian students enrolled on the UC campuses. He agreed with President Peltason's contention that diversity was key to a quality undergraduate education for all UC students and pointed out that research had demonstrated that there were positive outcomes for all students in ethnically diverse academic environments. He suggested that given California's increasingly diverse ethnic profile, it was a responsibility of the university to educate students to live in a multicultural society.

The vice president reviewed several essential problems facing underrepresented students hoping to enter the University of California. He noted that as underrepresented students moved through the K–12 system, they often did not acquire the required courses and grade point averages they would need to be eligible. Further, underrepresented students participated in math and science programs in quite low numbers, and there was often a disparity in the counseling and other academic resources at California's high schools. These factors contributed to low rates of eligibility for students from underrepresented groups. Galligani cited CPEC data which showed that 95% of California's African American public high school graduates and 96% of the state's Chicano and Latino public high school graduates were not fully eligible for admission to UC. He contrasted these numbers with those for White students, 13% of whom were fully eligible out of high school, and Asian American students, 30% of whom were fully eligible for admission to UC at high school graduation.[105] According to Galligani, low eligibility rates for underrepresented students was a persistent problem, and in response the university used race as a criterion in its admissions policies.

The allocation of funds for "targeted outreach" first became an issue during Regents' discussions near the conclusion of the March meeting. Two distinctly different perspectives emerged: one, that outreach money was being targeted as a preference for certain groups, and two, that the cost of targeted outreach was relatively low and the benefit to the system quite high. Regent Carmona pointed out that the university contributed less than $150,000 to Puente,[106] a small portion of the program's budget. Faculty representative Leiman suggested that the university should consider making a larger investment in academic development programs, particularly those that combined public and private investment and support, and Regent Johnson asked Vice President Galligani to prepare an accounting of the cost of the academic development programs.[107] That report, along with several other presentations on affirmative action, was put off until the next regularly scheduled board meeting in May.

5

The New Politics of Governance

THE LIMITS OF INTEREST ARTICULATION

Whatever hopes the administrative leadership at UC might have had for an institutional solution to the affirmative action contest were soon to be ended. Old patterns of mediation and interest articulation were being challenged by an increasingly zero sum admissions process, rising fees, and an emerging cohort of conservative politicians bent on using higher education as a site of contest. A new administrative strategy was called for, one that conceptualized the university as an instrument in a contentious national interest group struggle over control of the allocation of State resources. At a moment when the University of California was called upon to rethink its mission, the nature of its constituency, and the efficacy of its organization in a time of crisis, it turned for the most part to a time-tested strategy of relying on appeals to shared governance, faculty expertise, and a history of success. It was a strong hand, but the game was changing rapidly.

In the spring of 1995, the combination of Governor Wilson's attack on affirmative action at the California Republican convention, the increasing attention drawn to the nascent efforts to place CCRI on the ballot, and the growing state and national publicity generated by the Regents' review of affirmative action forced politicians and interest groups at every level of the state and national political system to rethink their current positions and their future courses. The newly installed Gingrich Congress was looking for legislation to force the issue and bring pressure on President Clinton as he geared up for his own run for reelection. Both Clinton and the front-runner to be his opponent in the 1996 presidential election, Senator Bob Dole, had been longtime supporters of affirmative action, as had Pete Wilson. But that spring the political tides were turning, with opponents of affirmative action mounting a charge against it, and traditional proponents of the policies looking for cover (Chavez, 2000; Schrag, 1998).

Clinton advisor George Stephanopoulos recalled that political moment this way: "In March of 1995 we thought that this (affirmative action) was going to be the issue that was going to race through America."[1]

In response, President Clinton issued a statement in March 1995 in which he suggested that it might be time to reconsider affirmative action programs, a foreshadowing of his emerging "mend it, don't end it" strategy.[2] Senate Majority Leader Dole also took the opportunity to challenge affirmative action in a speech on the Senate floor in mid-March. Dole tried to draw a sharp line between his position and Bill Clinton's:

> Race-preferential policies, no matter how well-intentioned, demean individual accomplishment. They ignore individual character. And they are absolutely poisonous to race relations in our great country.[3]

Not to be outdone on the issue that was taking off in his own state, less than two weeks later Governor Wilson announced his candidacy for the presidency, with the end of affirmative action a key plank in his platform. In the announcement, he stated:

> Some things are right and some plainly are wrong. It is wrong to engage in reverse discrimination, giving preferences not on the basis of merit but because of race and gender.[4]

In New Hampshire in late March, Wilson announced that he was disbanding a set of California state advisory panels on affirmative action, ordering a complete accounting of the cost of promoting diversity in state hiring and contracting, and he expressed his support for the ongoing review of UC's affirmative action policies.[5]

THE REGENTS MOVE TO RESCUE A MORIBUND BALLOT INITIATIVE

Despite the rising interest in revising affirmative action, the CCRI was a long way from becoming a part of the state constitution. Custred and Wood were finding it extremely difficult to raise the more than $1 million they would need to collect 700,000 signatures to place the initiative on the November 1996 ballot. They had sought help from sources as disparate as State Senate Democratic leader Bill Lockyer and Congressional Majority leader Newt Gingrich. Without Lockyer's support, a bill put forward by Senator Quentin Kopp that would have placed the CCRI on the March 1996 ballot was unable to move out of committee. Custred and Wood turned their attention to fund-raising, and relied on Governor Wilson and Regent Connerly to keep the initiative and the issue of affirmative action in the headlines (Chavez, 1998). One of the primary venues for doing that was the Board of Regents.

Prior to the May meeting of the Regents, despite maintaining that his mind was not made up on how the Regents should vote, Connerly published an opinion piece in the *San Francisco Chronicle*, which was also circulated throughout the country by the governor's press office. In the piece, "UC Must End Affirmative Action," Connerly asserted that the UC administration was using quotas to reach affirmative action goals, and in the process engendering racial hostility. He wrote:

> This brings me to another kind of affirmative action, the kind that I believe the overwhelming majority of Americans finds offensive. This is the concept of quotas, or "goals" as the term is more euphemistically used. Although the use of this term pushes the hot button of supporters, it is deceptive to try to honestly discuss the issue without acknowledging that the ultimate goal of most affirmative action practices is the attainment of numerical parity. In the University of California system, when our administrators and faculty talk about "underrepresented minorities" they are saying that certain groups do not have sufficient numbers of their group included in the mix. When the argument is then made that our goal is to achieve diversity and equal representation, it seems to me that the logical conclusion one can draw from this is that we want to achieve some measure of parity, and the only way I can see this being achieved is by the use of quotas.[6]

The University of California had been put in play in a broader political strategy, and as UCLA Chancellor Young described it in an interview conducted for this study, the university was a very key component of that strategy:

> Those engaged in politics today are much more willing to use the university for their own purposes than they ever were before and I think that is really the change. And that is true of the governor, that is true of the leaders of the Assembly and Senate, it is true of Republicans and Democrats. It is a very difficult situation. And it is not higher education generally; the situation with regard to the University of California and the state college university system is very different, just on the issue of affirmative action that we are talking about. This never became an issue in the state college university system because I guess in a way that does have something to do with the importance of the university. The university was a very strong and effective tool to use; the state college university system would not have been.[7]

UC REGENTS' MEETING—MAY 18, 1995

At the May meeting it was clear from the outset that organized student resistance to the Regents' efforts was increasing, and that despite increased security, business as usual would be difficult to sustain. Before the beginning of the meeting, over 250 students marched on the Regents' Laurel Heights headquarters, demanding the preservation of affirmative action. At the conclusion of the march, the students, who had traveled to the meeting from all nine UC campuses, attempted to enter the auditorium en masse. Security managed to limit access to only a few of the students, but the rest rallied outside the building.[8] Twenty members of the public, including three campus student body presidents and representatives of UC staff organizations, addressed the board to speak in favor of preserving existing programs.

At the March Regents' meeting, President Peltason had promised a series of reports on the university's existing affirmative action programs and policies on admissions, hiring, and contracting. It would be hard to fault UCOP on the quantitiy of material generated. Between the March and May meetings, alone, the Regents were sent several hundred pages of briefings on a variety of topics related to affirmative action.

UNDERGRADUATE ADMISSIONS OVERVIEW

One of the key documents provided in advance to the Regents was a statistical overview of the 1994 fall undergraduate admissions process at the university. The overview showed that over 90% of the applicants were from California and that the number of first-time freshman applicants had increased by 7.9% between fall 1991 and fall 1994, when just under 44,000 applications were received. The number of community college students applying to transfer to UC over the same period was relatively stable, some 18,000 applicants.

In the total pool of fall 1994 applicants, there was no majority ethnic group. Whites comprised 40% of applicants, Asian Americans 26%, Chicanos 11.6%, African Americans 5.0%, Filipino Americans 4.5%, Latinos 4.1%, and American Indians 0.8%.

In the California transfer applicant pool, Whites comprised 50.2% of applicants, Asian Americans 20.3%, Chicanos 9.5%, African Americans 3.9%, Latinos 3.9%, Filipino Americans 3.0%, and American Indians 1.2%.

The size of the entering freshman class had grown 11.1% in the previous three years. A number of groups showed significant increases: Chicanos 30.8%, Asian Americans 28.3%, Filipino Americans 17.9%, African Americans 16.5%, and Latinos 11.3%. The number of White students decreased by 5.5%.[9]

The overview also addressed the issue of underrepresentation. Underrepresented minority students were defined as "applicants belonging to ethnic groups whose UC eligibility rates are significantly below the statewide average of 12.3% reported in the 1990 California Post-secondary Education Commission's (CPEC) eligibility study." The underrepresented groups at the time were African American, American Indian, Chicano, and Latino. The 1990 CPEC study estimated eligibility rate for African American public high school graduates to be 5.1% and for Chicanos/Latinos, 3.9%.

For all California ethnic groups, the percentage of admitted freshmen that actually enrolled declined between 1991 and 1994, from 61.2% to 58.8%. The largest declines were for American Indian, Latino, and White students.

The report estimated that 54% of eligible public high school graduates enrolled at UC; the estimate for UC-eligible African Americans was 62.9% and for Chicanos/Latinos, 77.8%.

The overview also pointed to the fact that among newly enrolled California students, both freshmen and transfers had become more ethnically diverse over the previous three years.

In the new student cohort, Asian American enrollments increased from 1991 to 1994 by 36.8%. Chicano enrollments increased by 30.7%, African Americans by 19.5%, and Latinos by 13.3%. In total, the number of new students from underrepresented ethnic backgrounds increased by 22.1% between 1991 and 1994. White enrollments decreased by 5.0% and American Indian enrollments decreased by 5.4%.

The average high school GPA of new enrolling freshmen was 3.77, while 33.5% of enrolling students had GPAs of 4.00 or above.[10] The median parental income for new fall 1994 applicants was roughly $50,000. Chicanos had median parental income of approximately $30,000, African Americans $34,000, and Whites nearly $70,000. About 64% of fathers of freshmen and 46% of mothers of freshmen had a four-year college degree or higher. For Chicanos, 29% of fathers and 13% of mothers had four-year degrees or higher; for African Americans the numbers were 38% and 34% respectively. Among White applicants, the figures were 74% and 59%, respectively (Table 3.3).[11]

UNDERGRADUATE ADMISSIONS

At the May Regents' meeting, the joint meeting of the Committee on Educational Policy and the Special Committee on Affirmative Action Policies convened around a topic titled "Affirmative Action: Undergraduate Admissions and Graduate and Professional School Admissions."

The committee meeting began with a report from Assistant Vice President Galligani on undergraduate admissions and the use of ethnicity as a criterion in the admissions process. The report began with an overview of the process and statistics on the admissions class of 1994:

The University's admissions process is shaped by four elements. First, commitment to the tenets of the California Master Plan for Higher Education, assigning to the University responsibility for admitting students from the top 12.5% of California high school graduates; second, commitment to sound educational principles, especially academic excellence and diversity; third, commitment to admit all of the State's eligible applicants to one of the University's campuses; and finally, to ensure fairness in the admission process.

First, let me address the University's commitment to the guidelines of the Master Plan. Under these guidelines the University draws its freshman class from the top 12.5% of the public high school graduates in the State. By Regental policy, the faculty is charged with determining eligibility requirements to select this group. These requirements call for prospective freshmen to complete a minimum of fifteen units of high school coursework in specified academic subjects, to complete this coursework with a grade point average at, or above, a specified level, and to present a set of standardized test scores.

These eligibility requirements are exclusively academic in nature. They include no consideration for other criteria, such as ethnicity or disadvantage. It is important to highlight that almost all of our admitted students fulfill these requirements. Regental policy allows up to 6% of new enrolled students to be admitted by exception to the eligibility requirements. Two-thirds of these may be used to admit students from underrepresented minority, low income or educationally disadvantaged backgrounds.

In Fall 1994, out of 22,400 enrolled freshmen, 1,025 (or less than 5%) were admitted by exception. Of these, 31.9% were Chicano, 20.6% were White, 19.0% African American, 15.0% were Asian American, 8.8% were Latino, 2.5% were unknown, and 2.2% were American Indian. Included in this category are athletes, musicians, and other talented students, as well as students from underrepresented and low income backgrounds.[12]

Mr. Galligani then moved to a discussion of variations in rates of eligibility:

The University designates as underrepresented any ethnic group whose rate of eligibility falls significantly below 12.5%. And as you can see, the groups underrepresented using that definition are African Americans, and Chicanos/Latinos. American Indian students, although not identified in the CPEC eligibility studies because of small numbers, also are considered underrepresented because of their low participation in higher education overall, while California's Asian American and White high school graduates achieve eligibility at much higher rates.

What you see, then, is a very substantial eligibility gap separating Whites and Asian Americans on the one hand, and African American and Chicano/Latino students on the other. This is the problem. This is why we use ethnicity in the admissions process. The University has made a concerted effort to raise the number of eligible underrepresented students and actively encourages enrollment among the small number who are eligible.[13]

After some historical reflection, Mr. Galligani turned attention to specific admissions processes:

> To guide the University in the task of selecting students from among large number of eligible applicants, The Regents approved a University Policy on Undergraduate Admissions in May 1988. This statement reinforces both the tradition of the University as a public land-grant institution and the University's commitment to the Master Plan. It also underscores another of the University's goals, and I quote: "to enroll, on each of its campuses, a student body that, beyond meeting the University's eligibility requirements, demonstrates high academic achievement or exceptional personal talent, and that encompasses the broad diversity of cultural, racial, geographic, and socioeconomic backgrounds characteristic of California."
>
> To carry out the directives of the Policy, a set of University-wide guidelines were issued in July 1988. Following the Guidelines, campuses select approximately 60% of their prospective class solely on the basis of their outstanding academic criteria. The individuals who present the highest academic qualifications are admitted first. The remainder of the selected candidates, approximately 40%, are reviewed not only to determine their academic accomplishments, but also to assess their background, including ethnicity, and other non-academic accomplishments to determine how they can contribute to the academic, cultural and social life of the campus.[14]

The associate vice president then went on to review the "supplemental criteria" that were cited in the Cooks' original challenge as the key to the UC admissions policy. He defined and enumerated the following supplementary criteria:

> The use of academic criteria in combination with what we call the supplementary criteria, which we see detailed in this slide, are based upon sound educational principles; principles that most selective institutions in the nation follow in selecting their classes. It widely is recognized that success in college depends on both good academic preparation and also other personal attributes, such as leadership, creativity, motivation, tenacity and similar factors, special talents, interests, or experiences that demonstrate unusual promise for leadership, achievement, and service in a particular field, such as civic life or the arts; special circumstances adversely affecting applicant's life experiences, such as disabilities, personal difficulties, low family income, refugee status or veteran status; ethnic identity, gender and location of residence.[15]

While Mr. Galligani did not address the Cooks' assertion that supplemental criteria favored applicants from traditionally underrepresented groups, he did specifically cite ethnic identity and gender as supplemental criteria.

UCOP'S VISION OF FAIRNESS

Galligani also addressed the concern that had been raised by several Regents at the January meeting, the fairness of the process. He put it this way:

> The current process is fair. As noted above, the students with the highest academic qualifications are admitted, as are those who have the potential of contributing to the campus learning community. In the process, some students are not admitted to the campus or program of choice, but all receive a review of their academic record and their special achievements and background; and all who wish one are offered a place at one of the University's campuses. In sum, all have access to a University of California education. A brief comment regarding fairness of the admissions process. Because of changing circumstances, the admissions process periodically is scrutinized to determine its effectiveness. This is an evolutionary process and changes are made as appropriate. For example, we have discontinued the practice of admitting all eligible underrepresented students at their campus of choice. Also, we no longer set system-wide goals for the numbers of underrepresented students each campus should strive to enroll. There are no goals, and therefore no quota, in undergraduate admissions. The recent review initiated by the president led each campus to review its practices and make changes as appropriate.[16]

The assistant vice president also made some remarks on the small pool of eligible African American and Chicano/Latino students, and cautioned the board that changes in policy might further shrink the already small pool. He also reiterated that the efforts to select a diverse class had not lowered the university's high quality standards, noting that eligibility requirements had been strengthened five times over the past decade, and that both the overall graduation rate (75%) and the underrepresented student graduation rate (64%) had been increasing over the same time period. Assistant Vice President Galligani concluded with an equity argument:

> In sum, what we finally must ask about the University's admissions process is whether it serves its most fundamental purposes—these are to select the students best equipped to benefit by the undergraduate program UC offers and to provide opportunities for developing a new generation of leadership for California and for the nation. At the same time we must not forget that enrollment at UC is a very significant public benefit for

young people and that we bear a great responsibility for distributing that benefit in a fair way and in a way that contributes to the betterment of society overall.[17]

Despite the significant ground covered in Galligani's remarks, his statement that a UCOP review had shown that all eligible underrepresented students were admitted to the campus of their first choice (which was not the case for all groups) had significant impact with the board. This despite the fact that UC had already discontinued the practice.

In 1989 a committee chaired by UC Professor Jerome Karabel had reviewed admissions at UC Berkeley in response to criticism of the admissions practices at that time. The report led to the adoption of a number of specific new guidelines for admissions policies, including that admission to a specific campus would not be guaranteed to all UC-eligible applicants from particular categories. It seemed clear to some Regents that the two campuses in question, UCLA and UC Berkeley, had been violating Regents' guidelines by guaranteeing admission to all UC-eligible underrepresented applicants. It reinforced the beliefs of Regents Connerly and del Junco that the campuses were not abiding by their own policies.

A DEFINING MOMENT AT UCLA

The May meeting continued with presentations on the admissions process and a profile of the entering class at UCLA. Perhaps no other presentation in the entire conflict had more impact than UCLA's depiction of its admissions process. In attempting to explicate the fairness of their approach, the presenters from UCLA appeared to have motivated opposition in ways they never anticipated.

The presentation was introduced by UCLA Vice Chancellor Winston Doby and presented by UCLA Professor Philip Curtis, chair of UCLA's Academic Senate committee on undergraduate admissions. In his introduction, Vice Chancellor Doby stressed the difficulties posed by the intense competition for admission to UCLA, noting that for fall 1995 over 25,000 applications were received for some 3,700 slots. With that competition had come an increase in the academic qualifications of the admitted freshman class. Doby pointed out that in a comparison of the admitted class for 1984 with the admitted class of 1994, based on high school GPA, SAT verbal and math scores, and numbers of advanced placement and honors courses, the class of 1994 had a better record. The average GPA had increased from 3.66 in 1984 to 3.90 in 1994. Despite the increased competition, the University had managed to increase the overall ethnic diversity of the campus and to improve the retention and graduation rates of underrepresented students. In tracking the entering cohort of 1988, Doby pointed out that while underrepresented student graduation rates lagged behind those of Whites and Asian Americans, underrepresented students in 1994 graduated at rates comparable to those of the entire campus cohort of 1984. According to the vice chancellor, "We could not have achieved the current level of diversity without our current use of ethnicity as one of the supplemental factors in the selection process."[18]

At the conclusion of the vice chancellor's remarks, Professor Curtis gave a detailed presentation of the UCLA admissions process. To begin, Professor Curtis noted that the UCLA process was designed to implement the "1988 Regents Policy Statement on Undergraduate Admissions," and he emphasized a portion of that statement that Assistant Vice president Galligani had also cited, addressing the need for a student body that reflected the broad diversity of California.

Professor Curtis then listed six primary objectives of the UCLA admissions process:

1. UCLA should draw its students from all segments of the top 12.5 percent of high school graduates.

2. Every applicant should compete for every available admission position. There should be no set asides or separate tracks.

3. UCLA should use a wide range of academic and supplemental criteria, as specified under Regental and Office of the President policy.

4. No single criterion, academic or supplemental, in isolation would assure selection, or rejection, although academic factors remain the prime determinant of selection; all elements should be balanced by human review.

5. No applicant should automatically be admitted solely on the basis of satisfying the minimum eligibility requirements.

6. Each applicant should be reviewed together with applicants from the same secondary school, thus ensuring that applicants are compared with others who have had similar educational opportunities.[19]

THE RACE FACTOR IN ADMISSIONS

Professor Curtis then explained the UCLA admissions matrix. In the UCLA process, each applicant was ranked on two dimensions: academic and supplemental. The academic ranking was compiled through an analysis of such factors as the applicant's high school GPA, college entrance test scores, honors and advanced placement courses, and proposed curricula for the student's senior year. Each applicant was then assigned a rank from 1 to 6 (with 1 the highest ranking) on the academic criteria. The supplemental ranking was derived by taking into account the applicant's socioeconomic status, educational background, personal disabilities, ethnicity, and place of residence. Each applicant was also assigned a rank from 1 to 6 on the supplemental criteria, with 1 representing a high level of socioeconomic need or educational disadvantage and 5 representing little if any disadvantage. Level 6 on the supplemental criteria was reserved for out-of-state applicants.

A key attribute of the admissions matrix was that while an applicant from any ethnic group could be ranked from 1 to 6 on the academic criteria, this was not the case with ranking on the basis of supplemental criteria. A White or Asian American individual could be given a rank of 1 to 6 on the supplemental criteria, depending on that individual's socioeconomic need or educational disadvantage. However, African American, Mexican American, and American Indian applicants were given supplemental rankings ranging from 1 to 3, since, according to Professor Curtis's presentation, "These students have the lowest UC eligibility rates and have a historically low participation rate in higher education."[20]

Those applicants in the African American, Mexican American, or American Indian cohorts with a "moderate to high level of socioeconomic or educational disadvantage" were assigned a supplemental ranking of 1; those with "low or no such disadvantage" were assigned a supplemental ranking of 2. Out-of-state students from these cohorts were assigned a supplemental ranking of 3. According to Professor Curtis, "with these assignments, affirmative action enters the ranking process."[21] This separate scale for determining supplemental ranking would later be cited as a revelation by a number of Regents. Those Regents, in their comments prior to the votes in July and in personal interviews, pointed to the UCLA matrix and a similar matrix from UC Berkeley as prime examples of what they found inappropriate about UC's affirmative action policies with regard to admissions.

The Curtis presentation indicated that a California resident White or Asian American individual with low or no socioeconomic or educational disadvantage would be given a ranking of 5 on supplemental criteria, while any California resident member in the applicant pool of Mexican American, African American, or American Indian students with low or no socioeconomic or educational disadvantage was given a 2 on supplemental criteria. Several Regents later cited this as an example of allocating "group rights" and institutional action on the basis of race, which they felt was contrary to the spirit of meritocracy and the Fourteenth Amendment. Regent Montoya would sound that theme in the opening of her remarks to the board just before casting her vote at the July meeting:

Governor Wilson, Chairman Burgener, President Peltason, I do not favor admitting students based solely on their membership in a group.[22]

And as Regent Kolligian would testify prior to casting his vote at the July meeting:

> Our constitution is based on equality. We offer equal opportunities to all K–12 students; it's fair, free and equal. Those who assert themselves and achieve should not be discriminated against a lesser qualified student solely because of his sex or race or religion.[23]

Professor Curtis's presentation also provided evidence for what would become a powerful symbol for those opposed to affirmative action. Over the course of the debate over SP-1 and SP-2, there was the repeated invocation of a hypothetical applicant from a wealthy family who was also a member of an underrepresented group. This hypothetical applicant was held up as an example of "privileged" individuals who gained advantage on the basis of their membership in a "protected" group over "unprotected" students with similar economic and educational circumstances.

Professor Curtis's presentation also appeared to some Regents to call into question his assertion that there were "no set-asides or separate tracks." After explaining the ranking of academic and supplemental criteria, he described how they were combined to make actual selections.

The chart that he placed before the Regents demonstrated that a UCLA applicant in 1994 with an academic rank of 3 and a supplemental rank of between 1 and 3 would be directly admitted. A student with an academic rank of 3 and a supplemental rank of 4 would not be directly admitted, and even after a secondary reading was unlikely to be admitted.[24] What that meant was that a California resident African American, Mexican American, or American Indian applicant to UCLA with an academic ranking of 3 and "low or no socioeconomic or educational disadvantage" (supplemental ranking of 2) would be directly admitted, while a White or Asian American student with an academic ranking of 3 and "low or no socioeconomic or educational disadvantage" (supplemental ranking of 5) would not be directly admitted, and likely not admitted at all.[25] For a number of Regents, this meant not only separate tracks for consideration, but it also meant that applicants with equivalent academic rankings, and equivalent socioeconomic and educational advantage, were being treated quite differently. The underrepresented applicants were being accepted in circumstances where White and Asian American applicants would likely be rejected. This also seemed to call into question, in the minds of some Regents, UCLA's fourth objective, that "no criterion, academic or supplemental, in isolation, would assure selection, or rejection." It was this situation that was one of the key factors in the argument by Regent Connerly,

Governor Wilson, and others that race was not just one factor, it was potentially the defining factor in the admissions process.

Other dimensions of the matrix also raised the issue of differential treatment of applicants. The Curtis presentation showed that White or Asian American applicants with an academic index of 4.5 and very low or no socioeconomic and educational disadvantage would be denied admission without having an intensive reading of their files. That intensive reading was designed to allow for consideration of "special talents, leadership ability, motivation, academic interests and other evidence that the individual student has the potential for academic success at UCLA."[26] Under the matrix, a California resident applicant from an underrepresented group with an academic ranking of 4.5 and low or no socioeconomic or educational disadvantage would have his or her file given an intensive reading. This meant, from some Regents' perspective, that applications were treated differently on the basis of the applicant's race, and that some applicants were consequently given less opportunity to exhibit their potential, solely because of their racial identity. The central tenet that all applicants should have an equal opportunity to compete for admission would be cited by many Regents over the course of their deliberations. At the same time, the representatives of the campus administrations and the Office of the President believed the process was fair and that equal opportunities to compete were available to all.

ACADEMIC CRITERIA

The issue of admission on the basis of academic criteria alone also came to the fore in the May meeting. Under the Regents' 1988 Policy on Undergraduate Admissions, at least 40% but no more than 60% of the freshman applicants admitted by each campus were to be selected solely on the basis of academic criteria. In the case of UCLA in 1994, this meant that an applicant with an academic rank in the range of 1–2.5 was automatically admitted. This also meant that some of the students who just missed the automatic academic admission but who had lower supplemental rankings (4 and above) might not be admitted, despite possessing in some cases GPAs of 4.0 and above. These students were predominantly Asian American and White, and they would figure prominently in press accounts of the contest over affirmative action. If a White student did not get into UCLA through admission on academic criteria alone, that student had a slim chance of getting in. Of the 2,870 White students admitted, 96% were admitted on academic criteria alone. In contrast, 82% of Asian American applicants, 17% of Mexican American applicants, and 12% of African American applicants were admitted on academic criteria alone. Professor Curtis also pointed out to the Regents that for all students admitted to UCLA in 1990, the two-year retention rate was 88%, while for students admitted with academic ranks of 5 and 6 it was 78%. This latter rate was higher than the overall rate in 1980.

WHEN CULTURES CLASH

An important schism was revealed at the May meeting, when the Office of the President and the UCLA campus representatives delivered a presentation in defense of existing policies that seemed to a number of Regents to make the case against affirmative action. The interaction between UCOP and the Regents at the May meeting revealed two separate belief systems, one that many university leaders subscribed to, and a separate one that a number of Regents adopted. Regent Connerly described his perception of the administrative culture this way:

> I mean it's almost one of our traditions that the Academy is out of step with reality. They're the last ones to really understand what's going on. And they're especially not going to change what they've done, because they think they're doing the Lord's work. They're the ones who have bought into the notion race matters, that you have to use race to get beyond race, and they don't have to live with the consequences of some student who gets turned down with a 4.0 and 1500 SAT who happens to be White or Asian. Their parents have to take out a second mortgage to send them out to the University of Chicago. They don't have to deal with those harsh realities that we as Regents do see regularly on Thursdays. You know, we hear about these things. So they are, number one, just totally out of step because of the nature of that cloistered environment in which they live.[27]

Regent del Junco described his perception of the schism in these terms:

> I think that primarily it was that the chancellors had a program for affirmative action—they were the fathers of those programs, most of those guys, it was their program, so they were going to defend it. The reality of what went on was the following: a) there were existing programs which some of us felt had not resolved the problem, that here we were twenty-five to thirty years after these programs were put into place and we still were having 4% of Hispanics enrolled and actually eligible for the UC system, that was the number of Hispanics with exception. First of all, this program was only affecting UCLA and Berkeley, but we felt that these guys, chancellors, were the fathers of the program. If they were going to change it, they would have changed it a long time ago or brought about some modifications.[28]

GRADUATE AND PROFESSIONAL SCHOOL ADMISSIONS

The Office of the President offered two other presentations on affirmative action policies and programs at the May meeting, one on graduate admissions and one on admissions to professional schools. The presentations were accompanied by a comprehensive report titled "Affirmative Action and Graduate and Professional School Admissions."[29] The introduction of that report summarized the university's approach to affirmative action in graduate and professional school admissions this way:

> In examining applicants' backgrounds and experience, admissions committees consider the contributions of ethnic and racial diversity. Students, and the faculty themselves, benefit from a diverse student body. In the world of ideas, the greatest source of intellectual growth comes from the challenge to one's assumptions, perspectives, and ways of thinking. Exposure to peers with varying backgrounds is an important source of this kind of challenge. Exposure of members of the dominant American culture to other U.S. subcultures is of particular benefit in the academic setting because, while members of minority groups are expected to understand and adapt to the majority culture, the majority may well remain relatively ignorant of U.S. subcultures and the perspectives therein. It has been a long-standing practice for colleges and universities to admit students from different states and countries as a means to create a stimulating learning environment. More recently, the University's faculty, who work closely with graduate students, has actively sought broader kinds of diversity in the graduate and professional school programs. Accordingly, by admitting a student body with a variety of backgrounds and experiences, including race and gender, graduate schools draw from the perspectives of all demographic groups to enhance the quality of the environment of learning in graduate school itself.[30]

To emphasize the importance of race and ethnicity in building a diverse student body, the report also contained the following statement with reference to distinctions between race and socioeconomic status:

> Sometimes, upon mutual consultation, sometimes independently of each other, and without external compulsion, the deans and faculty admissions committees of the Medical, Law and Business schools and the graduate academic departments have also found race/ethnicity to be an important factor, apart from considerations of economic or social deprivation, to consider in the admissions process. In the areas of student outreach and retention, the University has devised programs which consider race and, to a lesser extent, gender, to achieve the racial and ethnic diversity the University deems necessary.[31]

UCLA Vice Chancellor Claudia Mitchell-Kernan presented a report that described an admissions process quite different than the one for undergraduate applicants. She noted that UC produced nearly 10% of all Ph.D. degrees in the nation each year, drawing from an international pool of applicants. While undergraduate admissions were handled centrally and applicants selected by admissions personnel, graduate students were selected at the departmental level by the faculty, with admissions criteria set by the academic units. The basic admissions requirement for entrance into a UC graduate program was a B.A. from an accredited institution with a GPA of 3.0. Standardized test scores, letters of recommendation, and the applicant's statement of purpose were the primary supplemental factors cited by the vice chancellor.

Mitchell-Kernan also noted UC's commitment to diversity in the graduate admissions process:

> At the doctoral level in academic fields, UC has long been concerned with the training of scholars and teachers from underrepresented backgrounds, particularly in the face of dramatic demographic change in the ethnic composition of California's student-age population. Ph.D. candidates are the faculty of the future, and they are the future experts in business and industry. The presence of all races and ethnicities, and both genders, among our faculty and within the leadership echelons in the private sector is growing steadily, but that growth has been, and continues to be, slow. The University has—over the last 20 plus years—made a concerted effort to increase the numbers of underrepresented minorities and women in its graduate student body, with mixed results.[32]

Despite the university's success—according to Mitchell-Kernan, UCLA ranked first nationally at the time in the number of doctoral degrees awarded to minorities with Berkeley second, while UCLA ranked second and Berkeley sixth nationally in the awarding of master's degrees to minorities—the absolute numbers at UC remained small.

The vice chancellor presented data for 1993 showing that African Americans received a total of 47 doctoral degrees from the entire UC system, just 2.3% of the total awarded; Chicano/Latinos received 89 doctorates, 4.4% of the total; and American Indians received 11 doctoral degrees, .5% of the total. She also pointed out that African Americans, Chicanos/Latinos, and American Indians were barely represented in doctoral programs in the physical sciences. From 1989 through 1993, UC conferred nearly 500 doctorates in mathematics, of which 5 were awarded to African Americans and 30 to Chicano/Latinos. In the same period, of over 650 doctorates awarded from UC in physics and astronomy, only 6 recipients were African American and 21 were Chicano/Latino. The vice chancellor noted that while UCLA awards graduate degrees in 107 academic areas, in 1993 over half of those areas had either zero or one

African American candidate, over half had zero or one Chicano candidate, and over three-quarters had zero or one American Indian candidate.[33]

PROFESSIONAL SCHOOL ADMISSIONS

The admission process at the UC law schools generated significant response from the Regents, and ultimately would become one of the more widely publicized areas of university admissions in the wake of the Regents' votes.[34] Dean Herma Hill Kay of UC Berkeley's Boalt Hall School of Law presented the admissions process, making frequent reference to a 1993 report on law school admissions provided to the Regents in advance. Less than a year before the meeting, the Boalt faculty had completed a major review of the admissions process. At the conclusion of the review, the Boalt faculty adopted the following policy governing admissions to the school:

> The Law School is proud of its past success in training academically excellent, diverse student bodies and seeks to build on this experience in achieving its present pedagogical objectives. Therefore, it is the policy of the School to admit a class with diverse characteristics, in a manner that takes into account past admissions experience, pedagogical considerations pertaining to the dynamics of critical mass, and annual fluctuations in qualified applicant pools. Given the dynamics of critical mass, the Law School sets as a goal the admission of an entering class that includes roughly 8-10% African Americans, 8-10% Chicanos/Latinos, 8-10% Asian Americans/Pacific Islander Americans, has a significant presence of Native Americans, and continues, as in recent years, to have meaningful numbers of disabled and older students and a rough parity of men and women, as annual fluctuations in qualified applicant pools allow. The class as a whole should be diverse with respect to regional background, life experience, and academic training; and internally within racial and ethnic groups, the class should be diverse with respect to ethnic and cultural background.
>
> To achieve these goals, diversity factors are to be given weight in admissions decisions if it appears that without such weight the desired diversity would not be achieved. Yet, no student can be isolated from competition for any place in the class and this policy does not prescribe fixed maximum or minimum numbers of applicants to be admitted from any particular group. Rather, the Admissions Director and the Admissions Committee should weigh numerical and non-numerical evidence of qualification for each applicant against the combined qualifications of competing applicants. No applicant will be admitted unless he or she appears capable of completing the Law School's course of instruction without falling into serious academic difficulty.[35]

A key factor in the UC approach to law school admissions, a factor that would prove troubling to some Regents, was the concept of "critical mass." The concept was further explained this way in the 1993 Boalt report distributed to the Regents:

> For intellectual diversity to emerge, the law school must include persons with a wide range of backgrounds and experiences. Diversity does not happen simply because some students with different perspectives are admitted to the law school. Rather, diversity can flourish only when the admissions process contributes to and is a part of an institutional climate that welcomes and supports difference.
>
> Tokenism is the enemy of diversity. For groups previously excluded from access to legal education, feelings of alienation and isolation not only retard academic achievement but also silence the very voices that are the building blocks of a diverse law school. A critical mass of these students is necessary to achieve a truly diverse student body that contributes to the robust exchange of ideas.[36]

In its details, the admissions process for the law school was much closer to the undergraduate process than to the graduate admissions described to the Regents earlier in the meeting. However, the use of supplementary criteria was more discretionary than in the undergraduate process. For the admissions class of 1994, Boalt received over 5,000 applications and ultimately enrolled fewer than 300 students. Women constituted 48% of the class; 52% were men. African Americans comprised 12% of the class; Chicano/Latinos, 13%; Native Americans, 1%; Asian, 14%; and Whites, 60%.[37]

While many criteria were used in the Boalt admissions process, undergraduate grade point averages and Law School Admission Test (LSAT) scores were the most significant. Boalt admissions committees also evaluated letters of recommendation, earned degrees, leadership qualities, and work experience.

Dean Kay reported to the Regents that race and ethnicity were never the sole basis for admission. Each application was given an index number derived from a formula that considered the applicant's LSAT score and undergraduate grade point average, adjusted for quality of undergraduate school. Each file was then examined by the office of the Director of Admissions in order to factor in difficulty of course work, employment while in school, residency, extra-curricular achievements, personal accomplishments, underrepresented status, and other factors. Approximately half of the entering class was chosen by the director on this basis, while the remainder of the competitive applications was then forwarded to an admissions committee of faculty members and student readers. The remaining students were admitted "with a view to meeting the target for overall class size, assuring proper representation of residents, and achieving appropriate diversity and critical mass, including internal diversity among ethnic subgroups as provided by the Faculty Policy on Admissions, in enrollment, and any other matters determined appropriate by the Chair."[38]

Dean Kay further defended the selection criteria in noting that UC's law students overwhelmingly completed their courses of study and passed the California bar exam with an average pass rate of nearly 94%. She went on to explain that if Boalt were to admit students only on the basis of their index numbers, the number of non-Asian American minority students in the 1994 entering class at Boalt would have dropped from sixty-six to nine.

Dean Kay's closing comments addressed the collective social benefits of the school's admissions program:

> The need to diversify the legal profession is not a vague liberal ideal: it is an essential component of the administration of justice. The legal profession must not be the preserve of only one segment of our society. Instead, we must confront the reality that if we are to remain a government under law in a multicultural society, the concept of justice must be one that is shared by all our citizens. This is especially true in California, where lawyers need to learn how to work effectively across racial and cultural lines, to help resolve social conflict, and to facilitate effective solutions to difficult problems. The University's law schools can best contribute to this goal by continuing, and continuing to refine, our existing admissions policies. Only by doing so can we hope to educate all our students in the context of such a multicultural society.[39]

Dean Kay's remarks pointed to an essential tension between Boalt's operational policy of seeking to create broad social benefits through admitting a diverse class and some Regents' perception of equal opportunity in access to Boalt.

At the conclusion of the presentations on graduate and professional schools, the Regents weighed in with a number of concerns. Regent del Junco made two points of significance to those attempting to count votes on the board. First, he said it was incorrect for members of the public who addressed the board in public session that morning to have suggested that he was not in favor of affirmative action. He stated that he was in favor of affirmative action and that he thought the board was as well. This point was echoed by Regent Khachigian, who stated that she did not believe there was a need to get rid of affirmative action but that it was necessary to determine whether abuses of the process had occurred and to support outreach. Regent del Junco also noted that he felt outreach was essential to improving minority enrollments and that the key to achieving greater numbers of underrepresented students was to improve K–12 student preparation. He made a similar comment in a subsequent interview:

I was personally extremely frustrated because the issue was not addressed as to what I think is a solution. Because in the final analysis, the solution is not to throw a bone to a half a dozen kids, ten, twelve, fifty, a hundred, when you're dealing with a population which is so large. I talked with [UCLA] Chancellor Young and I said, "Chuck, 50% of the graduates of this city are Hispanics, so you have a couple of hundred. What are you doing to the rest of them?"[40]

Regent Watkins suggested that while each of the reports pointed to the increasingly high GPAs of applicants and higher retention rate of students in the more ethnically diverse admissions classes of recent years, there was an alternate explanation: it might be the case that these rates were due to "grade inflation, as well as self-selection of less rigorous courses of study by less scholastically able students." Vice Chancellor Doby responded that given the competition for admission, even the least qualified applicants exceeded all minimum eligibility requirements, and the improvements could be attributed to the quality of the students.[41]

Regent Connerly questioned whether the university used any percentage goals for determining admissions classes. Berkeley Director of Admissions Robert Laird responded:

> No percentage goals for ethnic categories are set by the faculty. The Senate Committee on Admissions and Enrollment, in crafting the Karabel Report, used enrollment levels of the mid-1980s to define a critical mass of students of each ethnicity in the undergraduate student body at Berkeley. They set a flexible target range based on those levels for underrepresented students.[42]

This exchange was another example of the administrative officers of the University and some Regents speaking in parallel languages, where "flexible target range" and "critical mass of students" based on enrollment levels did not translate into "percentage goals." This sort of dialogue was at best confusing to many Regents. Some Regents believed the administration would not, or could not, clearly state the situation, despite UCOP's contention throughout the conflict that its intent was to provide prompt and accurate information.

Just before the adjournment of the meeting, Regent Preuss asked for a clarification of how the concept of critical mass differed from quotas in the admissions process. Dean Kay responded, as Director Laird had earlier, with an answer that did little to clarify the situation. She explained that Boalt does not look at the specific number of people from each group, but rather "at the number of people who will not be silenced in the classroom by their minority status."[43]

The report on graduate and professional school admissions distributed to the Regents prior to the May meeting had described the distinction this way:

The faculty policy governing admission to Boalt Hall sets goals for the admissions process based on sound pedagogical considerations. The objectives here are in no way intended to create quotas. There are no fixed maximum or minimum numbers of applicants to be admitted from any particular group. Rather, this plan sets flexible goals that permit each candidate to compete for every space in an entering class without wholly losing sight of general institutional objectives. Moreover, the Policy ensures that only applicants capable of pursuing law studies without falling into serious academic difficulty are admitted. The Policy in no way supports admission of unqualified applicants in a blind pursuit of critical mass.[44]

The concept of quotas had been broached at many of the Regents' meetings since the issue of affirmative action had been raised by the Cooks in July 1994. However, nearly a year later, the Office of the President and the various campus representatives had not yet dispelled the belief on the part of some Regents that the admissions process entailed quotas. Interviews with Office of the President personnel and chancellors indicated that they felt the Regents never came to understand the university's position. The Officers of UCOP and the Chancellors were fundamentally academic administrators, while the majority of the appointed Regents were wealthy businessmen, active in state politics. It should come as no surprise that each side sensed that the other did not understand the situation. However, it is worth noting that much of the research on higher education organizations and governance suggests that institutional leaders are able to bridge these divides (Pusser, 2003).

SOCIOECONOMIC STATUS IN PLACE OF RACE

Another document presented to the Regents for the May meeting was a report from the Office of the Assistant Vice President for Student Academic Services titled "The Use of Socioeconomic Status in Place of Ethnicity in Undergraduate Admissions." The report was prepared in response to suggestions by Regent Connerly and others that the university might ultimately preserve diversity and increase fairness in the admissions process by substituting socioeconomic status (SES) for race in the admissions process. Based on a computer simulation of the 1994 admissions process in which race/ethnicity was removed, the report concluded that the use of SES in place of ethnicity would result in lower levels of ethnic diversity at UC campuses. Specifically, it suggested that African American enrollments might be reduced across the system by as much as 50%, American Indian enrollments reduced by 50%, and Chicano/Latino enrollments reduced by 15%. Further, Asian American admitted applicants could increase by 25% across the system and White enrollments might remain at a fairly constant level. Perhaps the most controversial finding in the study was that replacing ethnicity/race consideration with SES might result in decreased average SAT scores and high school grade point averages of incoming students.[45] While the report was not discussed by the Office of the President, or mentioned by Regents at the May meeting, it would later figure prominently in the public debate over affirmative action.

RISING STUDENT PROTEST

The May meeting was also the first in several years in which the auditorium's nearly 300 seats were filled to capacity. In part this was due to increased requests for seats from the press covering the meeting. However, a large and organized group of students also came to the meeting from the nine campuses to implore the Regents to preserve affirmative action. Members of the student contingent were more raucous and demonstrative than many Regents had ever seen, particularly those Regents who had joined the board after the demonstrations in the mid-eighties over South African divestment. There was also a large contingent of students outside of the auditorium who were not allowed inside due to the capacity crowd. That group demonstrated its discontent by chanting and singing. The students were greeted by greatly enhanced security. As early as the May meeting, the grounds of the Regents' Laurel Heights headquarters, bordered on four sides by the streets of San Francisco, were dotted with armed police and security personnel. Members of the public who did get into the auditorium were patted down by security at the door and frisked with metal-detecting batons. All briefcases, bags, and packs were searched at the entrance to the auditorium.

Mystery Guests

The majority of students inside the auditorium fell into two primary camps: officers of systemwide student associations and their affiliates from various campuses, and those students who were attending as representatives or members of individual campus associations and clubs such as MECHA[46] and the Berkeley Young Republicans. One small group was consistently and particularly disruptive, a cadre known as the Coalition to Defend Affirmative Action by Any Means Necessary. The coalition appeared at the March meeting and was ejected from the meeting room for chanting in unison so loudly that the meeting had to be recessed. It was not the last occasion on which the coalition would contribute to a recess and the clearing of the auditorium. The actions of the coalition contributed to the development of a tense relationship between the board and audience throughout the contest over SP-1 and SP-2.

The representatives of the UC Student Associations and their affiliates were well known on the campuses, and to many of the Regents, on the basis of their frequent appearances before the board. Few knew the origin or the campus affiliations of the members of the Coalition to Defend Affirmative Action by Any Means Necessary. UC Student Regent Ed Gomez was a primary student organizer in support of affirmative action. Gomez had visited each campus on numerous occasions prior to the votes and was convinced that the members of the coalition were not UC students. He believed they were agent provocateurs working against the effort to preserve affirmative action. In an interview, he explained his view of the role of the coalition this way:

> There was a group that was constantly disrupting events; they were all from Detroit. They would always take the left side and then they would act ridiculous, and they would get the left arrested or evicted, or the meeting stopped, and the left gets thrown out. So it's used as a tactic, as if they were sympathetic to our means. Then what happens is actually they go "cuckoo" and then that makes everybody in the audience who is a liberal person or progressive person get kicked out with them, so it's used against us, and I believe that those students were infiltrators.[47]

At the May Regents' meeting, despite the general policy on public comment, a number of students who had requested permission to address the board were not able to speak.[48] During the subsequent outburst of chanting and complaints, the Regents ordered the meeting room evacuated. When several students would not go, they were forcibly removed. This caused UC Provost Walter Massey to try to personally intervene with security officers, as the crowd of students chanted, "Shame on you!" and "Let her go!"[49]

Student Regent Gomez described his own experience with UC security at that meeting:

> The security didn't know who I am, because they're not from there. They get imported from different campuses, and they just come in and do their jobs. And so here I am standing there and one says, "You need to get out of here." And I said, "I need to leave when I'm sitting on the board?" And he says, "Yeah," and I said, "What are you going to do otherwise?" He said, "I'm going to arrest you." I said, "You're going to arrest me right here at the board?" He said, "Yes, I'm going to arrest you, boy. You've got two choices, either I carry you out, or you walk out." I said, "Well then you're going to arrest me," and he did.[50]

Between the May meeting and the June meeting, the Office of the President received letters from students opposing the treatment received by those who attended the May meeting.[51]

GOVERNOR WILSON TURNS UP THE HEAT

In the month between the May and June Regents' meetings, a period in which he was in consultation with Regent Connerly nearly every day (Chavez, 1998), Governor Wilson pursued a comprehensive attack on affirmative action in the State of California. On the first of June he issued an executive order, which established "individual merit as the new standard for employment and contract decisions in state government,"[52] and repealed prior executive orders on affirmative action. The executive order was largely symbolic, as its prohibition on preferential treatment based on race or gender not required by law applied to very few state policies. The executive order did dismantle some state advisory boards on affirmative action, abolished recognition awards based on race and gender, and revised some definitions of state hiring pools. As a measure of how far the politics of affirmative action had shifted, Wilson's executive order removed as a portion of the official policy of the executive branch of the state the following language placed in the state code by then Governor Ronald Reagan:

> Time and experience have shown that laws and edicts of non-discrimination are not enough; justice demands that every citizen consciously adopt and accentuate a personal commitment to affirmative action which will make equal opportunity a reality. This is not only necessary in the internal affairs of state government, but also in its relations with the general public, including correction of any past inequities which may tend to deny equal opportunity to all.[53]

Wilson's executive order was accompanied by a call for all state employees and public institutions to comply with his proposed merit-based standards for public employment and contracting. On the same day, Wilson wrote to then Chair of the Board of Regents Howard Leach, announcing the executive order and suggesting,

> In our efforts to promote equal opportunity we should not perpetuate a system that confers special preferences upon individuals based on their membership in a particular group. It is simply unfair to the children and serves no purpose except to foster resentment and divide us as a people.[54]

He concluded the letter with this comment:

> Mr. Chairman, I call upon the Board of Regents to accept its responsibility to restore fairness and merit to the UC campuses and begin the process of uniting the people of this great state. I look forward to working with the Board on this important public policy issue.[55]

CAPTURING THE DISCOURSE OF CIVIL RIGHTS

The language of the governor's executive order previewed some of the key concepts that Governor Wilson would bring to the debate at the Board of Regents. Two in particular stood out. First, Wilson stressed the need to make a move away from state policies that guaranteed "equal outcomes" to policies guaranteeing "equal opportunity." The second concept was the invocation of the national Civil Rights Movement of the 1960s. This shift was designed in part to mirror the title and the spirit of the California Civil Rights Initiative. Wilson took a step further, as he pitted quotas against civil rights. His press release on the executive order stated:

> Throughout his career, Pete Wilson has opposed granting preferences according to rigid quotas based on race or gender. He believes quotas stand in the way of achieving the nation's long-standing goal of equal opportunity for all in a color-blind society. As governor he is working to ensure that people in California are judged according to their merit and qualifications, not their race or gender. And as governor, Pete Wilson has continued his career-long battle against quotas. We must replace the discredited policies of preferential treatment with a new vision built on merit and the original Civil Rights principle of equality under the law.[56]

In an open letter to the people of California released with the executive order, Wilson invoked both Thomas Jefferson and the Reverend Dr. Martin Luther King Jr:

> In fact, the success of the civil rights movement—against enormous odds—was very much based on its appeal to our heritage that this nation was founded on the principle, as Thomas Jefferson said, of "equal rights for all, special privileges for none." Martin Luther King invoked that principle in his most famous speech, when he described his dream that his children would one day live in a nation, "where they will not be judged by the color of their skin, but by the content of their character." That principle, however, is slipping away from us when we allow affirmative action programs that grant preferential treatment based on race or gender.[57]

The governor also used the open letter to discuss what he saw as the privileging of race and gender over merit and achievement in higher education, citing a case of a White, widowed mother who was allegedly denied admission to a community college English class because it was reserved for African Americans. He criticized funding set aside for several faculty positions at a state university that were allocated specifically for "diversity hires." He concluded with the following:

> Tomorrow, I will also ask the leaders of our public colleges and universities to end the unfairness of granting seats in our finest schools on the basis of skin color and ethnicity.[58]

Wilson's actions brought swift state and national attention. Major media covered the issuance of the orders and noted that the fight against affirmative action would further Wilson's campaign for president. The *Los Angeles Times* began its coverage this way:

> Seeking to establish himself as the political leader of the movement to abolish racial preferences, Governor Pete Wilson is preparing this week to begin dismantling a wide range of affirmative action policies affecting everything from higher education to state hiring practices.[59]

The *New York Times* covered the governor's actions on its front page and declared:

> With the letter the governor moves on his own toward curtailment of affirmative action, acting affirmatively on the issue, as it were, in the nation's most politically important state, while other candidates have only been talking about acting. That kind of move fits nicely into his vision of himself as a candidate who has actual experience in running a government, as opposed to candidates like Mr. Dole and Mr. Gramm, who Mr. Wilson casts as only players in a legislative system. With his letter, Mr. Wilson, generally regarded as a moderate in a party run by conservatives, also edges distinctly to the right on a matter of great importance to many prospective delegates to the Republican nominating convention.[60]

The *Times* piece went on to explain the limited effect of the executive order, but pointed out that Wilson's personal authority might extend further than the power of the order, all the way to the Board of Regents:

> Mr. Wilson has no direct authority over the state's public colleges and universities, and so he will have to rely on his appointees to those systems' boards to put his philosophy into practice.[61]

ADARAND CONSTRUCTORS V. PEÑA

For the June meeting of the board, the Office of the President was scheduled to present reports on existing affirmative action policies covering staff and faculty hiring and business contracting. Just prior to the meeting, the U.S. Supreme Court issued a landmark ruling on affirmative action in federal contracting, which attracted major media attention. On the *NBC Nightly News*, Tom Brokaw began the show with these words:

> The fuse that has been burning toward an explosive political confrontation on affirmative action in this country is burning even faster tonight. The United States Supreme Court, in a ruling on federal programs designed to help minorities, set new, tougher standards. Those standards will make it much more difficult for affirmative action.[62]

In *Adarand Constructors v. Peña,* the Court considered the case of a White subcontractor who sued the federal government when his low bid for installing guard rails on a federal road project was rejected in favor of a higher bid by a minority-owned business. The Court ruled that any preference based on racial or ethnic criteria could only be justified as a remedy for historical patterns of discrimination, which they did not find in *Adarand.* The Court further held that any official action that treats a person differently on account of race or ethnic origin was inherently suspect. Justice O'Connor, in the majority opinion, wrote, "Distinctions between citizens solely because of their ancestry are by their very nature odious to a free people."[63] Justice Thomas wrote an argument that resembled the one that Regent Connerly would soon bring to the Board of Regents: "These programs stamp minorities with a badge of inferiority and may cause them to develop dependencies, or to adopt an attitude that they are entitled to preferences."[64]

Republican presidential candidates Bob Dole, Phil Gramm, and Pat Buchanan all lauded the Court decision and stressed that the Court was, as Senator Gramm put it, "obviously moving in the direction that America's moving in."[65] For Democrats the Court had sent a less favorable political message, one that they feared would both energize Republican moves against affirmative action in California and elsewhere, and give an advantage to Republican candidates. Democratic campaign strategist Brian Lunde summed up President Clinton's position: "It is to get affirmative action off his political plate. For Democrats to have a public national debate over affirmative action can only hurt us."[66]

In the week prior to the Regents' June meeting, UC made headlines again, as a result of a report issued by a conservative think tank, the Pacific Research Institute for Public Policy. The report, a study of 519 UC Irvine graduates who sought admission to UC's medical schools, suggested that underrepresented students were receiving preferential treatment. The report claimed that some minority applicants, Chicano/Latinos, American Indians, Puerto Ricans, and African Americans, were given preference over other minorities such as applicants of Vietnamese ancestry. It also claimed that if race and ethnicity were not a factor in admissions, the odds of some of the admitted applicants being accepted would have been less than one in a million. Although the findings were quite similar to those reported by the Cooks nearly a year earlier, the response from the Office of the President was less diplomatic than the one the Cooks had received. UCOP spokesperson Terry Colvin responded to the report in part by telling the media:

> What I find offensive in this kind of study is it implies that our students of color are somehow less qualified to sit in a school than their counterparts. Everyone enrolled at a University of California Medical school has earned the right to be there.[67]

Regent Connerly also responded to the report in the press:

> Many administrators have been in denial about race being dominant in the decision-making process, and this study shows beyond any doubt that race is a dominant factor.[68]

JUNE 1995—THE CONTEST INTENSIFIES

The June meeting began with a public comment period in which twenty-five members of the public spoke in favor of retaining University of California affirmative action programs. No one spoke from the public against the existing policies.

As the meeting began, the issue of what would come in the aftermath of the day's presentations—the last ones scheduled by the Office of the President—was still in doubt. Press accounts indicated that either Regent Connerly or Governor Wilson would soon be bringing motions to the board on the subject of affirmative action. The chair of the Special Committee on Affirmative Action Policies, Regent Flinn, spoke to this point at the opening of the committee session. He noted that initially the special committee had convened in January to begin a dialogue, which in turn led to the series of UCOP reports on affirmative action policies at the university. He went on to say that generally reports are either accompanied by, or followed by, the presentation of an action item. Those items, which require Regents' votes, should be preceded by sufficient public notice in advance of their presentation to allow for extended public discussion. He reminded the board that no proposal for action with regard to affirmative action was pending, though he expected something in the future.[69] This cautious introduction represented the feelings of a number of Regents that the governor's political campaign needs and the flagging CCRI campaign, rather than any norms of deliberative policy process, were driving the pace of the consideration of affirmative action. Regent Brophy later described the timing:

If you take a look at how the proposal was put into place, it's probably the best and the worst example of policymaking. Now there was a policy that was put into place by the majority of the board, but which was under pressure to make those moves. I was too, but I decided it wasn't good. Not because there aren't bad parts to affirmative action, but I wanted—my plan was to propose a codicil to it that would give us the eighteen months or the sixteen months to search out and determine what was good and what was bad. To take learned people who understand what is good and what is bad and have discussions with the faculty and the administration and so forth and see if we couldn't come up with something that is not tantamount to throwing the baby out with the bath water. There was political pressure to get it passed then for obvious reasons and so consequently my codicil wasn't passed. But there was no consultation. The first time that we saw that [Connerly's proposal] was ten days before the meeting where it was passed. And few if any people really understood it, with the exception of the governor and Ward.[70]

Early in the June meeting, President Peltason stated that as a result of the Office of the President's ongoing review he would bring a recommendation to the July meeting of the board for modification of some UC policies on affirmative action. He also mentioned that Regent Connerly intended to bring his own proposal to the July meeting. President Peltason expressed his desire that the Regents would debate the merits of affirmative action at the July meeting after they had sufficient time to hear a presentation of the overall findings of the review conducted by the Office of the President. He then addressed the governor's executive order on affirmative action and suggested that the review being conducted by the Office of the President was in keeping with the governor's order.[71]

AFFIRMATIVE ACTION IN FACULTY AND STAFF HIRING

President Peltason was followed by Vice Chancellor Claudia Mitchell-Kernan, who presented a review of faculty hiring at UC. She stressed the importance and success of UC's efforts to broaden the applicant pool for faculty positions, particularly through recruiting at the junior level. She noted that each campus had a faculty affirmative action officer with the power to extend or reopen searches that failed to attract sufficient diversity. She explained that a variety of programs were in place at the campuses, including President's Postdoctoral Fellowships, and the Target of Opportunity (TOP) program, and stressed that diversity and success were compatible with the overall faculty rate for advancement to tenure at 91%. For women the rate was 92%, for African Americans 95%, and for Chicanos/Latinos 96%. She also noted:

> There is no "value-added" percentage for being a woman or minority group member in the tenure decision. Women and minority faculty

achieve these high tenure rates despite the greater expectations and demands they face.[72]

Following Vice Chancellor Mitchell-Kernan, Assistant Vice President Lubbe Levin presented a review of UC Staff Diversity and Employment Affirmative Action. She identified three key areas related to staff employment. One was equal employment opportunity (EEO), an individual's protection from discrimination in the hiring process. The second was affirmative action, which she described as follows:

> It goes beyond EEO and involves a set of specific programs and efforts by the employer to assure that those who are members of "protected groups" (that is, groups which have experienced historical discrimination) have full access to job opportunities and do not face barriers to employment or promotion. Such efforts are designed to reach out to minorities, women, individuals with disabilities, Vietnam-era veterans, and special disabled veterans.[73]

Her third category was diversity, which she described as the university's process of creating an environment of inclusion, where individual and group differences are valued.

She pointed out that UC's hiring policies for staff were shaped by federal law and regulations governing all federal contractors. Under federal guidelines, employers must ensure that applicants and employees face no discrimination, and federal contractors must engage in affirmative action. At the University of California, efforts to meet federal requirements for equal opportunity and affirmative action in hiring had been met primarily through outreach, continuing training and development of existing staff, and internal promotion programs aimed at alleviating underrepresentation of minorities or women in the workforce. Levin noted that under equal opportunity there was no preferential selection of minorities or women and no hiring quotas. The assistant vice president concluded that the university's staff affirmative action policies not only complied with federal mandates, they were essential for providing services to the university's increasingly diverse student body.[74]

AFFIRMATIVE ACTION IN CONTRACTING AND BUSINESS ENTERPRISES

The final presentation at the June meeting was an overview of the university's business affirmative action programs covering purchasing, construction, and contracting of design and professional services. It was presented by Director, Office of Risk Management, Rod Umscheid. In his opening remarks, the director referred to the *Adarand* case and suggested that it might have significant effects on the university's business affirmative action program. As with the staff affirmative action program, most of the regulations and policies concerning purchasing and contracting at the university-managed Department of Energy Laboratories were dictated by programs, goals, and objectives established by Congress. Campus contracting and purchasing programs were also shaped by federal law, particularly in the case of federal contracts to the university valued at greater than half a million dollars. The director reported that there were nearly 200 subcontracts of that value on the nine campuses.[75]

In response to state legislation passed in 1984, the university had adopted policies to support small businesses, including those owned by disadvantaged individuals and women. The university optimized the opportunity for small businesses and those that are owned by women or the disabled in a number of ways, such as not requiring competitive bidding for contracts below $50,000, and by giving preference to targeted businesses in cases where bid prices and other conditions were substantially equal.

As with its other affirmative action programs, the university had established outreach programs designed to increase the pool of businesses in targeted groups able to bid for contracts. The university had also established a certification program to assist targeted companies in obtaining bidding authority. To qualify, a firm had to be at least 51% owned by a disadvantaged individual, or 51% owned by one or more women, or 51% owned and operated by a disabled veteran. Socially and economically disadvantaged individuals were defined by federal regulations as:

> Those who have been subjected to social, racial, or ethnic prejudice or cultural bias in the United States because of their identity with a particular group and whose ability to compete in the free enterprise system has been impaired due to diminished capital and credit opportunities as compared with others in the same line of business.[76]

In 1994 the university's total expenditures for contracted purchases of goods and services, construction, and design professional services was just under $2 billion. Of that amount, 7% was awarded to women-owned businesses, 10% to disadvantaged businesses and less than 1% to disabled veteran businesses. Director Umscheid noted that while the university had reached its goal for contracting with women-owned businesses, it hoped to increase contracting and purchasing with disabled veteran and disadvantaged concerns.[77]

AN OPPORTUNITY FOR COMPROMISE

The June meeting of the Regents seems in retrospect to have been an opportune time for the Office of the President to forge a compromise. Regent Connerly had not yet revealed the nature of the proposals he intended to bring to the board. He later said that throughout the contest the Office of the President could have talked him out of seeking an end to the use of race in policy. The June meeting was also the last scheduled opportunity for the Office of the President to explain its stance on affirmative action. Although a number of Regents were adamantly opposed to affirmative action in any form, a number of undecided Regents were still looking for a way out of an increasingly contentious debate. The Office of the President did not offer a significant alternative to existing policies. Rather, Vice Chancellor Mitchell-Kernan suggested that affirmative action and diversity might be closely linked, and questioned whether the university could reach its diversity targets without considering race in some of its programs.

The Regents raised a number of concerns throughout the day's presentations. Regent Connerly, in response to the barrage of comments from the public in favor of preserving affirmative action, attempted to clarify his view of the process the Regents had undertaken. He declared that his understanding was that no one wanted to remove outreach or supplemental criteria from UC affirmative action programs. Rather, he questioned whether race or gender should be a defining factor in any aspect of the university's admissions, hiring, or contracting policies. According to Connerly, the issue was not whether to dismantle all forms of affirmative action, but whether or not the Regents wanted to continue to allow race-based decision making at the university.[78] At the same time as he made these remarks, he was ardently supporting the CCRI, which was clearly designed to remove race and gender entirely as criteria in all state functions, including admission to UC.

The board conversation had also turned to faculty and staff hiring. UC faculty were largely absent from the debate except through their representatives to the board and their votes in the various faculty senates. The comments of those representatives essentially defined the faculty position. Faculty Representative Simmons pointed out that while outreach and affirmative action were key to initial faculty hiring, the tenure review process turned on well-understood standards of teaching, research and public service.[79] Provost Massey noted that "promotion to tenure is a formal and elaborate process which never takes race into account."[80]

A certain amount of jockeying for position also took place at the June meeting. Regent Designate Carmona asked Regent Connerly what his position was on university outreach programs as part of the broader process of affirmative action. Regent Connerly replied that it was his position that "outreach programs should be expanded, but that they should be made available without regard to race, or national origin."[81]

Regent Davies raised a question regarding the information presented on faculty and staff hiring. He referred to cases in which two applicants were substantially equally qualified. He asked for clarification of the earlier statement that in such a case, efforts would be made to correct disparities that might exist for minorities and women. Vice Chancellor Mitchell-Kernan responded that in such cases, race or gender would be used in the decision. Faculty Representative Simmons added that he did not believe that race was a tie-breaker in that type of faculty hiring case.[82]

Regent Leach weighed in with concerns about the continuing utility of the university's approach to affirmative action. He pointed out that affirmative action was a thirty-year-old effort to increase opportunity, and he suggested that legitimate questions had arisen as to whether it should be modified or perhaps eliminated. He also encouraged the board to consider alternatives to the existing policies.[83]

THE AFFIRMATIVE GOAL: HISPANIC

At one point in the meeting, Regent Connerly read from a UC job listing he had received in the mail. It was a document that Regent Bagley would later credit for helping to solidify opposition on the board to affirmative action. The listing stated that the affirmative action goal for the position was Hispanic. Regent Connerly asked why this should not be considered a quota. Senior Vice President Wayne Kennedy answered that this position advertisement was for a post in the Management Fellowship Program and he noted that in his opinion the listing was not appropriate and would be changed.[84]

At the May meeting, the matrix for undergraduate admissions and the percentage goals for underrepresented law school students had troubled several of the Regents. At the June meeting, it was Regent Connerly's presentation of the "targeted" advertisement. Taken together, they added to the Regents' uncertainty about the quality of information they were receiving from UCOP. This also pointed to a progressive shift away from the confidence expressed a year earlier by Regent Connerly in a letter to the board:

> It would be foolish for the Board of Regents not to place a great deal of confidence in the UC administration. In the particular case of Jack Peltason, I am convinced that our confidence is well placed.[85]

Former UC Santa Cruz Chancellor Karl Pister later assessed the information problem:

> I think you've put your finger on an unease among some of the Regents at least, that the university, the administration here in the president's office, was dragging its heels or not coming clean. Knowing Jack Peltason and Walter Massey, I can't believe there was a deliberate attempt to hoodwink the Regents. An institution as large and complex as the university

has lots of problems producing the facts in a timely way, particularly with nine campuses that exercise a tremendous amount of autonomy. We just have one hell of a time getting everybody on the same database and doing the same things the same way. I think it was a misfortune that perception was created, but it was a real perception. I know Connerly felt very much that way, and certainly Clark did as well.[86]

At the June meeting, many Regents commented on staff and faculty diversity. Student Regent Gomez expressed his dismay over data on faculty hiring which indicated that for academic years 1989–1993, there were 864 White assistant professors who received tenure and 6 Native Americans. He suggested it was inappropriate to consider reversing affirmative action in light of such statistics.[87] Regent Khachigian also noted that the number of Native American tenured faculty was disconcerting and wondered if the university was losing Native American candidates to other universities. She also suggested that the university received unwarranted criticism for failing to recruit larger numbers of underrepresented faculty from extremely small pools of eligible candidates.[88] Although the issue of eligibility had been mentioned in various forms since the January meeting, Regent Khachigian's shift of the responsibility for underrepresentation to small eligibility pools previewed one of the primary rationales a number of Regents would present in arguments for ending existing affirmative action policies. This "pipeline problem" would become a centerpiece of the Regents' debates at the July meeting.

Regent Sayles recalled his own undergraduate days as he pointed to the importance of minority faculty members as role models and mentors for underrepresented students on UC campuses. Vice Chancellor Mitchell-Kernan agreed that minority and women faculty did play significant mentoring roles, although she pointed out that minority students do receive support from other faculty as well.[89]

Regent Eastin followed up on Regent Sayles's remarks. She noted that when she was an undergraduate at UC Davis she had only one female professor, a woman who had also been the person that encouraged Regent Eastin to attend graduate school. She urged the board not to return the university to a time when women were underrepresented in professional schools. She concluded by urging the board not to make decisions on the basis of political trends.[90]

A number of questions from the Regents to Assistant Vice President Levin were in the spirit of Regent Leach's question on whether affirmative action had outlived its usefulness. After pointing out that nearly 80% of university staff positions were held by women and minorities, Regent Connerly suggested that "an infrastructure of inclusion" was already in place at the university.[91] Regent Preuss commented that the success in diversifying at the staff level indicated that the university's approach was now virtually color-blind. Assistant Vice President Levin expressed her opinion that without a concerted effort to practice inclusion in the interests of diversity, the university would probably not have achieved the staff profile that it had. Chancellor Pister remarked that the level of diversity achieved at the university was a tenuous achievement, and that if pressure on the campuses to diversify were removed, he doubted the rate of progress would continue.

Regent Connerly then asked Chancellor Pister whether affirmative action was a temporary remedy, and, if so, how much longer it might be required. The response further defined the polarization between the chancellors and the Regents. Chancellor Pister replied that despite the significant progress made on his campus over the years, Santa Cruz was so far away from what he considered to be a diverse campus that he did not imagine the need for affirmative action would end in his lifetime.[92]

Provost Massey then presented closing comments. He noted that as a result of the university's internal review of its affirmative action policies, the administration had identified a number of programs that needed to be modified. He reported that the Target of Opportunity program for faculty hiring would no longer allow campuses to set aside pools of faculty lines exclusively for women and minorities. He also stated that although affirmative action programs had benefited women and minorities, White males also benefited from a more inclusive hiring process and diminishing the effect of "the old boy's network."[93]

The latter point, the notion that all would benefit from the diminishing of the "old boys' network" may have been lost on a board that contained some of the most prominent "old boys" in the state.

ALL JOIN IN

In the closing moments of the meeting, Regent Brophy, in an effort to force Regent Connerly to show his hand, asked that the board and the members of the public be informed of any action items well in advance of the July meeting. Regent Bagley suggested that if Regent Connerly intended to make a proposal, he submit it in writing to the board within the next ten days. Regent Flinn stated that he was also working on a proposal for the board and he suggested that other Regents might want to bring forth their own proposals.

Regent Sayles suggested that despite the months of presentations, the Regents had not received a complete picture of the university's affirmative action programs, and he cautioned the board against rushing to a decision.

Regent Connerly announced that he would bring his proposals to the board at the July meeting. He reminded the board that he could have brought his proposals forward months earlier, but that in consultation with the president he had agreed to allow the president's presentations to be completed first.

President Peltason stated that he would expedite the preparation of his recommendations in order to have them ready for the July meeting, while Regent Carmona promised he also would present a statement on the university's affirmative action process.

Regent del Junco pointed out that the board did not have to wait for the next meeting to reaffirm that the intention of the board was not to abolish affirmative action. He suggested that the university should begin an information campaign to inform the public of that fact.[94]

President Peltason closed the meeting by noting that students and the public were aware that proposals would be made at the next meeting that would challenge the university's affirmative action programs. In the context of the day's debate, it was a rare moment of understatement.

6

National Contest and Conflict

On the eve of the July meeting of the Regents, it was becoming increasingly clear that absent some intervention, a steady march to a vote on affirmative action was inevitable. To many observers it appeared that the UC Office of the President was determined to continue on the path of mediation and articulation, hoping ultimately for something of a "mend it, don't end it" compromise. President Peltason later explained his position:

> My debate with the Regents was not about their jurisdiction but about the merits of the issue. I'm for affirmative action. I also tried unsuccessfully to persuade them that this was a very divisive issue. I asked them to let me modify the worst parts of it, the parts they objected to most, and to not involve the university in the debate. Because no matter how it comes out, you're going to make half the people mad.[1]

Other principals in the contest saw the Office of the President deferring to Governor Wilson in the interests of preserving the administration's ability to make other kinds of policy for the good of the university. Then UCLA Chancellor Young reflected on that period this way:

> I think it was very clear that the Office of the President, the institution, generally, felt that they would be bringing harm to the university by taking a position that was blatantly anti-SP-1 and -SP-2, that its job was to try to convince rather than to argue, try to convince through information, and not say, "this is a political attack." Indeed, I said that, and I was chastised for having done so. Improperly chastised.[2]

Student organizers had been having a hard time finding allies within the formal ranks of the policy process. Student Regent Gomez felt that only the students were willing to risk all to avoid a vote by the board that would end affirmative action at UC:

> I think that despite whatever will be written in the future, I really believe that in many cases the only people who put up a good fight for us were the students. The faculty had their interests and they had to protect them. They didn't want to cross the line.[3]

REVEREND JESSE JACKSON AND THE REDRESS OF INEQUALITY

Many student leaders eventually decided they had no recourse but to turn outside the university system for support, to find someone who symbolized the fight for racial and political justice in America. Student Regent Gomez and the University of California Student Association invited Jesse Jackson to address the board as a guest of the students at the July meeting, to speak for their cause. The invitation to Jackson was a bold move that would ultimately have great influence on the contest and its aftermath. Jackson's entrance further galvanized student interest and student support for affirmative action at UC, as it increased student organization, resistance, and protest. Given Jackson's association with the Reverend Dr. Martin Luther King and the Civil Rights Movement, the invitation further shifted media and public perceptions of the contest from an institutional policy debate to a deeper conflict, one that encompassed America's long and continuing struggle over race and equality. The invitation turned attention to the role of education in a national effort to redress racial inequality and to the ongoing linkages between education and income inequality.

Reverend Jackson Mobilizes

The day after the June meeting of the Regents, Reverend Jackson announced he would lead a rally at the July meeting designed to prevent any retreat from affirmative action. Governor Wilson promptly announced that he would attend the Regents' meeting in his capacity as president of the board, his first appearance at a board meeting in over three years. The entrance of Jackson into the deliberations had a powerful impact on the governor's role in the contest. For Wilson, it ratcheted up the level of national attention, and when Jackson threatened from Chicago to disrupt the meeting, the governor was able to cast himself as the defender of order. His response to Jackson's threat was to go on the CBS News program *Face the Nation* to proclaim, "If he seeks to disrupt the meeting as he has announced, he will, I suppose, succeed in being detained."[4] With the national attention came higher stakes for the governor's efforts. As the press account described the situation:

> Politically, as a GOP presidential contender struggling to break into double digits in national polls, Wilson needs the win to demonstrate that he can deliver on one of the key elements of his nascent campaign—repealing affirmative action.[5]

The *Wall Street Journal*, in an article titled, "Affirmative Action's California Battle Lines," noted:

> If Pete Wilson adopts a cause as his own, you can usually go to the bank with it. The California governor is running hard against official prefer-

ences based on race and sex, and acting against them too. He thereby anticipates the three branches of the federal government, now themselves enmeshed in the controversy. It may be classic opportunism, as this is one more "wedge" issue Mr. Wilson has seized only lately. However, as an article in the *New Republic* dated June 26 makes clear, this time he is way out ahead of the political and corporate establishment that is his set. The popular ground has shifted away from what goes by the label "affirmative action," but charting new policy is a brave exercise.[6]

Faculty representative Simmons had this to say about the effect of the arrival of Reverend Jackson on the contest at the board level:

> I felt during the year, all during the year, that we had enough votes on the board to put it off. And we did, I think, until the day Jesse Jackson announced he was coming to California. It was Jesse Jackson who lost the issue, because his announcement put the thing at a much higher level in terms of national politics. Now you had the opportunity for debate over the issue between two people ostensibly running for president of the United States. And then of course, Pete Wilson had to turn the screws on his people, and get them to go. The day I saw that headline—you know I had no advance warning—I just picked up the newspaper one morning and read Jesse Jackson is coming to California. I said to myself, "Oh s—t, it's all over!" And I believe that to this day.[7]

The sentiments expressed by Simmons were shared by some actors on both sides of the contest, while others saw the political dynamic developing well in advance of Jackson's entrance. It can also be argued that the university had brought his involvement upon itself through its inability to build a meaningful coalition with student organizers. Over the previous two years, the Office of the President and the faculty representatives had opposed the student representatives on the issue of fee increases, and students were further alienated from the Office of the President by the students' perception of a lack of access to the Regents' deliberations. The pluralist process at the board level, where the students cast only one vote, had left many of them disenchanted and ready for an alternate approach to making policy.

THE LACK OF A FACULTY PRESENCE

It wasn't only students who expected a greater faculty presence. A number of Regents felt that the UC faculty, with the exception of their two representatives on the board, were remarkably quiet. While faculty members appeared at rallies or in newspaper commentaries, there was virtually no talk of an organized protest, such as a faculty strike. Regent Designate Carmona described the faculty attitude this way in a subsequent interview:

> It speaks a lot to how faculty are sort of out of the realm of reality when it comes down to the hard issues. I think even when it [Connerly's proposal] was out there, there were probably the same presumptions as were made by the administration—I'm not talking about the policymakers, I'm talking about the administrators who are of the faculty; those who say, "Hey, this isn't going to happen, we can live on even if they do pass this, we'll get around it." That was sort of an elitist assumption. That was the sense they had. I remember being horrified by one guy who said, "Hey, even if they pass this, we'll work around it." I said, "What are you talking about? You guys don't understand what has happened."[8]

The faculty representatives on the board, while strongly supportive of the existing policies, were quite cautious in their advocacy beyond the board. Faculty Representative Simmons described the constraints on his position this way:

> Well, the faculty representatives are in a difficult spot there, because they are representatives. I think I and everybody I know who has held the position has been very careful not to speak beyond what's been authorized by the Academic Council. So yes that makes it hard to go out and build public coalitions on public issues, but that's not what I consider to be the job, I think not what others who've held the position have considered to be the job.[9]

A MARSHALING OF INTEREST GROUPS

While UCOP and the faculty representative might have felt constrained from taking an activist stand, others did not. Between the June and July meetings, over 100 individual letters and hundreds of signatures on petitions were received by the Secretary of the Regents from organizations and members of the public in favor of preserving affirmative action policies, while some 60 letters were received in support of Regent Connerly's position.

A list of interest groups favoring the preservation of affirmative action included all nine campus chapters of the University of California Student Associations; the California State Employees Association; the California African American School Superintendents; the Northern California Ecumenical Council; the Inland Empire Women's Summit; the California Federation of Business and Professional Women; the Association of Asian and Pacific Americans in Higher Education; the University of California Black Alumni

Club; the Filipino Civil Rights Advocates; the Human Rights Commission of the City of San Francisco; the Vietnamese Community Health Promotion Project; the Mexican American Bar Association of Los Angeles County; the Mexican American Legal Defense and Educational Fund; and the Alumni Associations of the University of California. Regent Bagley forwarded to his fellow Regents a letter of support for affirmative action from an alumnus who had just made a major gift to the university.

A number of appeals were also received in support of preserving existing affirmative action policies from groups and individuals connected with the California legislature and other elected officials including the Coalition of California's Central Valley Latino Mayors; the California State Senate Democratic Caucus; and the California Legislature's Latino Legislative Caucus. Several legislators and political leaders either sent letters or requested time to address the Regents at their July meeting. These included San Francisco Mayor Willie Brown, Senate Majority Leader Bill Lockyer, Senate Higher Education Committee Chair Theresa Hughes, Assembly Higher Education Committee Chair Marguerite Archie-Hudson, Assembly Judiciary Chair Phil Isenberg, and Assembly members John Vasconcellos and Barbara Lee.

Most of the letters received in support of Regent Connerly's proposals were from individuals. There were also a number of requests to speak before the board from political leaders in support of Connerly's proposals, including Assembly Republican leader James Brulte, who sent a request to speak and a letter signed by thirty-five Republican Assembly members denouncing affirmative action. Assembly members Richter, Takasugi, Brewer, and Poochigian requested an opportunity to address the board at the July meeting. A letter was received from yet another presidential candidate, Alan Keyes, who also wrote in support of Regent Connerly's efforts.

Many letters were generated by faculty members at the University of California and elsewhere. Although more faculty members wrote in support of affirmative action than wrote to oppose it, faculty letter writers were clearly divided on the issue.

As if to bring the correspondence regarding affirmative action to the board full circle, the Regents also received a detailed letter in support of eliminating affirmative action from Ellen Cook. She concluded with these words:

> I ask each one of you. Are you willing to sacrifice the education of your own child, so that a less qualified individual, who happens to be a member of an underrepresented group, could attend in your child's place? Please do not ask the parents of this state to sacrifice their children's education, unless you are willing to do the same. I ask you to stand for the hard right—change the system to remove racial preferences—against the easy wrong of maintaining the status quo.[10]

The correspondence received by the board was notable for its passion, with strong emotions expressed on both sides of the issue. Many letters in favor of the existing policies complained about the politicization of the process and the linkages between Connerly's proposals, the CCRI, and the governor's presidential bid. Others noted the lingering effects of racism in their own lives and suggested to the board that the nation had come nowhere near establishing a level playing field for admissions, contracting, or hiring. Those who supported Connerly's motions also complained of political intervention, but rather than citing Governor Wilson, they cited Jesse Jackson as the instigator of the politicization of the process. Some expressed their desire that Jackson be arrested in the event that he or his supporters should disrupt the July meeting. The issue of slavery was invoked on both sides of the issue. Supporters of the existing policies cited the historical legacy of slavery and oppression as it shaped and constrained the contemporary landscape for racial interaction. Those opposed to affirmative action also invoked slavery, in a different context, likening affirmative action to chains, and in one instance, describing Regent Connerly as an emancipator.

The Regents began preparing for the July meeting at the closing gavel of the June meeting, with various factions on the board generating proposals and lining up public and political support for their positions. If the majority of the Regents could be aptly described as cautious prior to the June meeting, as the July summit approached, both those who favored and those who opposed preserving affirmative action could best be described as frantic. Between the June and July meetings, Regents Flinn, Brophy, Bagley, Carmona, Gomez, and Connerly would present proposals or significant amendments to proposals for consideration at the July meeting.

REGENT FLINN'S COMPROMISE PROPOSAL

The first of these proposals, from Regent Flinn, was presented to the board only four days after the June meeting as "a compromise to the all or nothing debate which is in process."[11] Regent Flinn, an ex officio Regent as president of the UC alumni association, was an attorney who would later be appointed a superior court judge. His proposal, titled "A Compromise Concept on Affirmative Action Policy," offered nine substantive modifications to existing affirmative action policies at the university. Taken together, they had the effect of eliminating race as a consideration in admissions, contracting, or hiring, except where an individual could show that the fact of that individual's race had put that individual, personally rather than as a member of a group, at some substantive disadvantage in the admissions, hiring, or contracting process. The proposal clearly prohibited quotas and group entitlements, or any violations of existing state or federal law. It offered additional funding for outreach in an effort to help the university more clearly mirror the ethnic diversity of the state of California, and suggested that outreach should be made available to all prospective students.

Regent Flinn's proposal also raised a new issue, the question of what effect a retreat from affirmative action would have on UC's federal contracts for research and energy laboratory management. Federal funding to the university at that time exceeded $1 billion a year, and each of those contracts required compliance with federal nondiscrimination and affirmative action policies.

The day after Regent Flinn sent out his concept paper, President Peltason received a resolution on affirmative action from Faculty Representative Simmons of the Academic Council of the Assembly of the Academic Senate.[12] It read, in part, as follows:

> At its meeting on June 14, 1995 the Academic Council endorsed the following resolution: The affirmative action programs undertaken by the University of California have made the University a better institution by making it a more diverse institution in terms of the gender, racial, and ethnic makeup of its faculty, students, and staff. This work is not yet finished. The University should continue to act affirmatively to increase the participation of individuals from underrepresented groups, evaluating and modifying these programs in order to strengthen them.[13]

Faculty Representative Simmons' letter went on to explain that the resolution had been drafted by the Academic Council's Committee on Affirmative Action and endorsed by the executive committees of the Divisional Senate on each of the nine campuses of the university. He concluded by asking the president to share the resolution with all of the Regents prior to the July meeting.

THE LAW

On June 30, shortly after Regent Flinn's proposal reached the board, Regent Connerly wrote a long letter to Regent Burgener, with copies to members of the board. The letter constitutes a very direct and biting critique, one that addressed a number of Connerly's central concerns and foreshadowed his formal proposals to the board. In it he summarized the events in the year since he first met with the Cooks. He emphasized how hard it was to get clear information from the university administration, and he criticized the student leadership on the issue. He noted that the explanations of admissions practices appeared, from his perspective, to be rationalizations of heavy reliance on race and ethnicity, and that his research had led him to believe that the institution was, in fact, using quotas in defiance of the *Bakke* decision. He made two fundamental points that would form the centerpiece of his subsequent arguments for SP-1 and SP-2. The first point addressed the legality of UC's admissions policies, and was put succinctly:

> I came to the conclusion that we are breaking the law. There is no other way to put it. WE ARE BREAKING THE LAW!![14]

The second point addressed what might be termed a Fourteenth Amendment concern over "equal treatment."

> It is indisputable that we are applying far different standards to "underrepresented" applicants being considered under the "Supplemental Criteria" than we are applying to those who are not underrepresented (White and Asian, largely) applicants. Look at the Karabel Matrix (attached) and you can see what I mean. The category "California Resident" is shorthand for Asian and White students who come from middle-class families. They stand MUCH less chance of being admitted in relation to nonresidents who are wealthy and who are underrepresented. This makes absolutely no sense. Yet, a form of this admissions process is being applied at each of our more selective campuses.
>
> The Office of the President and the General Counsel have confirmed that two of our campuses (Davis and Irvine) are still automatically admitting all underrepresented minorities and that two other campuses (Berkeley and UCLA) conduct individual assessments of underrepresented minorities (thereby providing them with a much greater chance of being admitted) but do not do the same for other students.
>
> The practices of these four campuses are in clear violation of *Bakke*, because Asian and White students have a much higher standard to meet than African Americans, Hispanics and American Indians. Thus, innocent people <u>are</u> harmed, students <u>are</u> admitted solely on the basis of their race, and underrepresented minorities (as well as others, but disproportionately underrepresented minorities) <u>are</u> admitted who are not eligible.[15]

Regent Connerly's letter was notable for its timing and its distinctly personal style. He noted that he had struggled to bring Regents over to his side during the course of the previous six months. He also confessed his regret for alienating some Regents with his style, and seemed to intend to soothe relations with undecided Regents, foremost among these the diplomatic Regent Burgener.

Connerly's letter is also noteworthy for the degree that it criticized "administrators" while praising Peltason. Connerly accused unnamed administrators of having rallied students to preserve the status quo and suggested that without intervention by the Regents, the campuses would never change their affirmative action policies.

Connerly also endeavored mightily to give any undecided Regents a fear of inaction, pointing to the imperiling of society that would result if the Regents failed to curb the efforts of students attempting to obtain power. He also referred to the "major class action suit" that he suggested would result if the university continued its existing admissions policies. Connerly claimed UC was either breaking the law or out of compliance with *Bakke* twelve times in the letter.

Regent Connerly's letter served as another salvo in the ongoing war of wedge politics that Governor Wilson, the backers of CCRI, and the state Republican Party had been assiduously waging since the commencement of the campaign to pass Proposition 187. Connerly hit a number of the wedge chords, invoking quotas, several kinds of lawlessness, protected classes of undeserving beneficiaries, the harm done to innocent White and Asian American students, and the decline of California's image and standards. He made reference to a cohort of angry students whom he accused of seeking power and attempting to redress the impact of slavery. He suggested that other students were attempting to hold the system hostage, and made reference to Angela Davis, an African American and tenured professor at UC Santa Cruz who was acquitted of felony charges in a highly publicized California trial in the early seventies. Professor Davis did not seem to be cited in the letter for any public comment or stance on the university's affirmative action policies. However, the invocation of her name has long served as a rallying cry for some California conservatives.[16]

REGENT CARMONA'S RECOMMENDATION

On the same day that Connerly's letter was written, Regent Designate Carmona, who was working closely with Regents Gonzales and Levin, released a statement to the Regents and to the press. Carmona stressed the importance of a cautious approach, and urged the board to avoid political influence in their deliberations. The text began:

> As you know, I firmly believe it would be a mistake for the University to go on record as the first state constitutional governing board in the United States to take a policy position that eliminates consideration of racial, ethnic and gender factors involving affirmative action. The retention of these critical factors is central to a viable affirmative action program. Public comments of support for affirmative action notwithstanding, any proposal that suggests the removal of these factors will have the effect of ending affirmative action. Such a decision is contrary

to our public purpose and could well threaten our independence from the political process.[17]

Regent Carmona went on to question the impact that the elimination of affirmative action would have on early outreach programs and the eligibility rate of Blacks and Hispanics. He also asked for a special meeting of the board to give consideration to the affirmative action issue. He raised a concern that troubled Regents on both sides of the issue, the growing public perception of the Regents as a political instrument:

> Because we are an appointed, non-elected, body, we owe it to the Legislature, Governor Wilson and all Californians to engage, where possible, in a truly factual and thoughtful discussion consistent with democratic principles and the University's public mission. Our decision should not be driven by voter sentiment or emotions. If we fail to properly address this most divisive and volatile issue, the public will perceive our decision as something more akin to a political than deliberative body. This false reading of our role could jeopardize the University's autonomy and generate renewed pressures for a Board responsive to California's electoral—not higher education—interests.[18]

REGENT CONNERLY PRESENTS HIS PROPOSAL

Just two weeks before the July meeting, and almost a year to the day after Regent Burgener first shared the Cooks' complaint with him, Regent Connerly formally presented his proposals for revisions to the university's affirmative action policies in admissions, contracting, and hiring. Regent Connerly's proposals were prefaced by a letter to the Regents that, while reminiscent of his June 30 letter, was considerably less confrontational. He reiterated his belief that while the emphasis on racial preferences was illegal, as well as grossly unfair to many who were not among the underrepresented groups, a college education at the University of California was still not an option for most Hispanic and Black high school graduates. He stated that, "this reality is acute for Black high school graduates and is essentially of the same magnitude in 1995 as it was in 1980, two years after the *Bakke* decision."[19] Calling for a complete and orderly revision of affirmative action policies, Regent Connerly proposed to include the following points in the resolution he would offer at the July 20 meeting:

1. Reaffirmation of the university's commitment to affirmative action (advertising, outreach, and other similar efforts to ensure that minority group members and women are included in the pool of eligible applicants for jobs and contracts).

2. An end to race-based hiring and contracting programs effective January 1, 1996.

3. A greatly expanded and restructured academic outreach program to ensure that the university continues to proactively participate with the K–12 system in preparing young people for the educational opportunities that are available at one of America's finest public institutions, the University of California.

4. An end to race-based admissions practices, effective January 1, 1997. This will allow the university ample time to moderate the effect of this action.

5. An end to race-based "admissions in exception" to UC standards of eligibility, effective January 1, 1997.

6. Directing the president and the Academic Senate to develop and propose new supplemental admission criteria, consistent with the policy of non–race-based decision making, aimed at promoting individual assessment of applicants' probability of success.

7. Raising the percentage of students who must be admitted solely on the basis of academic achievement from 40%–60% to 50%–75%, effective January 1, 1997.

Connerly noted that he had endeavored to find common ground with President Peltason, but the stakes were too high for compromise:

> Although the ground has shifted considerably for each of us, it is fair to say that we have probably moved as close to a common position as is possible. It is doubtful that further compromises can be made, considering the fact that an issue of principle is at stake.

He again invoked the memory of the Civil Rights Movement:

> In America, we are all entitled to the presumption that the standards which will be applied to any of us will not be higher than they are for others, whether one happened to be an African American seeking admission to "Ole Miss" in the 1960's or whether one is a Chinese American seeking admission to Cal in the 1990s. That presumption should never be subordinated to a government agency's desire for racial diversity.

He concluded with the following:

> It is my fervent hope that my colleagues on the Board of Regents will join me in beginning the process of redesigning and adequately funding our

academic outreach programs, removing the stigma which currently affects our Black and Hispanic students, ensuring that fairness governs the University's admissions, contracting and hiring decisions, and reaffirming the University's commitment to academic achievement and the reasonable application of affirmative action policies. [20]

THE FUTURE APPEARS

Regent Connerly's letter was accompanied by the first public release of his proposed action items for board consideration at the July meeting. These action items would become, in a slightly revised version, Regents' items SP-1 and SP-2.[21] Connerly's long delay in releasing his proposals was cited by Regents Eastin and Carmona as a tactic that prevented a measured and consensus-driven approach to the votes. Connerly suggested the Regents had more than enough information and had spent more than enough time deliberating. He pointed out that he had already delayed bringing the proposals to the board for a month, and declared: "It is clear to me that for those who support race-based decision-making, any change between now and the end of time will be premature."[22]

Connerly's proposals were in keeping with what he had outlined in his letter of June 30. While the first proposal, addressing admissions, contained eight sections, the essence of the proposal was contained in section 2:

> Section 2. Effective January 1, 1997, the University of California shall not use race, religion, sex, color, ethnicity or national origin as a criterion for admission to the University or to any programs of study.[23]

A virtually identical passage was at the core of the second proposal, covering employment and contracting:

> Section 1. Effective January 1, 1996, the University of California shall not use race, religion, sex, color, ethnicity, or national origin as a criterion in its employment and contracting practices.[24]

Although aspects of the items had been previewed in the press, their appearance had a powerful public and political impact. National, state and local news organizations reported the release of the letter. At that point the pace of press releases, proposals, and efforts to organize for the July meeting increased significantly.

PRESIDENT PELTASON RESPONDS TO CONNERLY

Also on July 10, President Peltason sent a letter and a number of key documents to the Regents, including the text of remarks he planned to make at the July meeting. The letter noted the release of the Connerly and Carmona proposals, as it reaffirmed the president's commitment to affirmative action, and warned against politically motivated actions by members of the board. There was also a strong reminder that admissions policies had been traditionally determined by the faculty senates in collaboration with campus chancellors, and that faculty authority over admissions policy came from the Regents' Standing Orders:

> Second, if The Regents decide to modify the admissions process, it is essential to involve the faculty at every step and the Chancellors as the chief executive officers of the nine campuses. Under our system of shared governance, The Regents have delegated to the faculty responsibility for setting the conditions of admission. The faculty are closer than anyone else in the University of California to the process of teaching and learning. The Regents must look to them, through the Academic Senate, for advice on how we can meet our responsibilities under the law and our equally important obligations as an educational institution.[25]

President Peltason also previewed his own action item for the upcoming meeting. Given the thousands of pages of reports and the hours of testimony, the president's action item was remarkably concise. It constituted one long paragraph:

> The president recommends that The Regents adopt the following:

> That the president be instructed to develop, in consultation with the Academic Senate, appropriate changes in undergraduate, graduate, and professional school policies governing admissions; these policies to take effect on or before January 1, 1997 should state or federal law be changed to prohibit consideration of race, ethnicity, and/or gender. Further, that the president be instructed to increase, over a three-year period, the funds made available for student academic development activities. Funds for expansion of these activities would combine additional moneys obtained through the state budget and private moneys from employers and others with an interest in a well-trained, well-educated workforce.[26]

The president's proposed action item was essentially a request from the Office of the President for the Regents to leave the authority for setting affirmative action policy in the hands of the president and the faculty. It further suggested that the university take no action until such time as there was a change in existing state or federal laws covering affirmative action. This was in reference to the still fairly remote possibility that the CCRI could be revived and passed by statewide vote. The president's proposal was also accompanied by a comprehensive rationale for recommendation of the president's proposal. The rationale offered a number of justifications for leaving existing university affirmative action policies in place. These included that UC policies were consistent with other major universities, diversity was vital to the institution, and decisions on educational policy were traditionally the province of faculty. It also noted that eligibility rates needed to be increased through comprehensive academic development programs conducted in conjunction with the state's K–12 system and cautioned,

> An abrupt and precipitate decision of this sort upsets settled expectations about how decisions are made within the University and will appear to many to involve the University in a divisive political issue.[27]

STATEMENT OF THE CHANCELLORS

Also accompanying the president's letter to the Regents was the first formal statement from the nine campus chancellors, which arrived in the form of a document titled, "Statement of the President, Chancellors, and Vice Presidents of the University of California." It was notable for its mild tone, as it restated many of President Peltason's positions. It closed with an endorsement of existing UC policies on affirmative action:

> It is for these reasons that the President, Chancellors, and Vice Presidents of the University of California unanimously urge, in the strongest possible terms, the continuation of the May 1988 Board of Regents admissions policy, together with increased efforts in early academic outreach. For if we do not fulfill the promise of Daniel Coit Gilman, we cannot expect either the state or the University to grow into the 21st century.[28]

UC Santa Cruz Chancellor Karl Pister, one of the authors of the chancellors' statement, later expressed some dismay over the timing and the nature of the statement:

> The academic council spoke out, as did the chancellors and the president. It could have been handled better; there is no question about that. In a way we have nobody to blame but ourselves, not to say it wouldn't have happened anyway, but we didn't necessarily mount the strongest possible case. It would be interesting to know to what extent a different president might have handled this. I can't see David Gardner allowing that kind of thing to have gone the way it did. Or Dick Atkinson. I think they are very different people from Jack Peltason. Jack was more of a compromiser. The art of compromise was on his mind all the way along. For example, Jack was very reluctant at the beginning to have the chancellors make a public statement as we finally did. He urged us not to make the statement by ourselves but to include him and the vice presidents, excluding the legal affairs vice president, who was also General Counsel for the Regents. That's ultimately what we did.[29]

Chancellor Pister attributed some of President Peltason's caution to a legal constraint, state restrictions on employees and representatives of nonprofits involving those institutions in state political activities. He recalled an earlier case that may have shaped UCOP's responses in the deliberations over affirmative action:

> It was Proposition 9, during the presidency of David Saxon. Proposition 9 was called the son of Proposition 13. David Saxon, to his credit, wrote a letter to parents of all UC students, saying that if this proposition passed, he was going to have to ask for fee increases for students because of what happened to the University. [State Senator] Bill Leonard sued him because Saxon spoke out on that, and I think Leonard won. On Proposition 209 we were very careful about what we said about that. Even on such things as bond issues, we had to be careful about the way we directed any public statements we made. We are in a tough position politically.[30]

Despite his reputation, President Peltason's proposal offered little room for compromise. In essence, it asked the Regents to move aside completely, to accept that the Office of the President, the chancellors, and the faculty would make all the necessary modifications to accommodate law and fairness within the existing policies on affirmative action in admissions, hiring, and contracting.

REGENT CONNERLY RESPONDS TO THE PRESIDENT'S PROPOSAL

Two days after President Peltason released his proposal, Regent Connerly released another letter that spoke to the president's proposal, as well as to Regent Carmona's. In his response, Connerly answered Carmona's charge that the university was being used in a broader political project. Connerly reaffirmed his stance:

> Certainly, we all must know that there will never be a time when an issue affecting the use of race in the operation of the University of California can be discussed and resolved free from the influence of politics.[31]

He also reminded the board:

> Although it has publicly been noted that Governor Pete Wilson and Jesse Jackson have political stakes in the outcome of this issue, can we candidly say that other colleagues of ours, such as Superintendent Eastin or Lieutenant Governor Davis, can be unaffected by this issue? Obviously, they are affected, and that is a legitimate part of the process of shaping

public policy for a public agency such as the University. We cannot hide from that fact nor can we insulate the University from those who care to participate in our deliberations.[32]

Connerly also argued that to postpone the vote because the issue had achieved public and press attention would be to set a precedent whereby anytime a group raised a critical level of response to an issue, the Regents would be forced to hide and postpone action on the issue. Given the efforts of Regent Connerly and Governor Wilson to bring attention to affirmative action at UC, it seemed unlikely there would be any hiding or a postponement.

STUDENT PROPOSAL

On July 17, a proposal developed by Student Regent Gomez and the UC Student Association was distributed to the Regents. It was accompanied by an announcement that Regent Gomez would offer the proposal as an action item at the Regents' meeting in July. The proposal and the alliance between the Student Regent and the UCSA[33] followed a series of meetings and rallies across the UC system attended by thousands of students. Many of the rallies were monitored by campus police and security. Regent Gomez recalled that period of organization, and the toll it had taken on student organizers, this way:

> I put 40,000 miles on my car. And I went and talked to the Academic Senate, unions, staff people, at one o'clock in the morning sometimes. I spoke with students. I spoke with every single faculty until I had an understanding of what I believed the people wanted. I was on the Santa Barbara campus when they shut down the entire student center and turned off the electricity, sent the police, and I had to be protected by the Native American students. I was telling students last night, that from October until the votes, when we had the massive rallies, each month I slept ninety hours. On one day I went to five different campuses. It's important work, but we were so stressed out, it is the reason why the students weren't stronger.[34]

Regent Gomez had agreed to submit the student proposal for consideration at the July meeting. That proposal was quite explicit about the continuing inequality in California higher education, noting at one point:

> WHEREAS, it is an embarrassing injustice that, although the population of the United States, particularly California, has been the most racially diverse in the world, higher education has historically been accessible almost exclusively to men of European descent.[35]

The students' proposal was quite similar to the proposal offered by President Peltason; the fundamental resolution in the students' proposal was a call for the preservation of affirmative action and institutional autonomy to administer the program.

THE BATTLE IN THE PRESS

With the various proposals on the table, and the meeting still two weeks away, a torrent of press releases and statements by various actors dominated the state and national headlines. Regent Connerly and Governor Wilson took to the airwaves and the networks to ensure that the elimination of existing affirmative action policies was seen as a salient political issue that would be unconscionable to avoid. This approach was designed in part to convince undecided Regents, many of whom were Republican political activists, that they must take a stance. In the press conference that accompanied the release of SP-1 and SP-2, Regent Connerly made plain the pillars of his argument to the public against UC's existing policies:

> Personally I am convinced that we are lowering the standards with our race-based admissions practices and that the quality of the University is harmed.[36]

Second, Connerly reiterated his opinion that UC's present policies were against the law, and third, that the university would be better served by focusing on economic disadvantage than on race. He also expressed regret that he had not been able to reach a compromise with the Office of the President, and that he had not been able to work that compromise in private consultation.

> Right or wrong, I felt that I had no way of getting the University to take me seriously other than focusing the public spotlight on the problem.[37]

The same afternoon, the UC Office of the President issued a statement that included an opinion by General Counsel Holst that UC's existing policies were well within state and federal law, and that "No student has been selected for the remaining places in the class solely on the basis of race or ethnic minority status."[38]

FOUR REGENTS CHALLENGE THE PRESIDENT

A little over a week later, four more Regents responded to President Peltason's proposal with a letter to the president that was released to the press. The letter was described this way:

In a development reminiscent of the turmoil that engulfed the University of California in the 1960s, a group of Regents yesterday publicly criticized UC's president.[39]

In the letter, which was reported on the front page of the *San Francisco Chronicle* and the *Los Angeles Times*, Regents Campbell, del Junco, Kolligian, and Lee stated that delaying the vote would be a "dereliction of duty." In a neat bit of public relations spin, they accused the president of linking a policy issue to a political issue, precisely the linkage the defenders of existing policies had invoked in criticizing Regent Connerly and Governor Wilson. The four Regents further endeavored to refute the charge that SP-1 and SP-2 were linked to the CCRI:

> It is somewhat unsettling that you have juxtaposed our deliberations on this policy issue with ballot initiatives that may or may not appear on the November 1996 ballot. The Board of Regents is the governing body of the University, as you know. It is our duty to govern, not await speculative ballot propositions which have yet to qualify for the ballot. Regardless of whether we support the continuation of existing policies or their repeal, we believe the University is not well served by either acting on the basis of polls or failing to act pending the outcome of an election that may or may not occur.[40]

The Regents also turned attention to President Peltason's statement in his letter of July 10, 1995, that Davis and Irvine would no longer automatically admit all eligible students from underrepresented groups, and that UCLA and Berkeley would alter their process of reading applications separately. The four Regents insinuated that this was an admission that the university had been breaking the law prior to making those changes. In an indirect challenge to the veracity of the campus administrators, the four wrote:

> The candid admission that race has been a <u>major</u> factor in the admissions processes of Berkeley, Davis, Irvine and Los Angeles, to such an extent as to result, in accordance with your letter, in "automatic admission to all undergraduate underrepresented students who applied" at Davis and Irvine is very troublesome. Clearly such a practice violates the *Bakke* decision. The above revelation that this has been the practice at these two campuses, despite the fact that the Regents have been consistently informed that "no one was being admitted because of race" and race was "only one of many factors" is disturbing. Why has this not come to our attention sooner? Why has it taken the persistence of one Regent to bring the matter into the open? If all of the campuses concluded that this practice should have been discontinued in the late 1980s, why has it taken so long for Davis and Irvine to follow suit?[41]

In an interview accompanying a news article on the letter from the four Regents, Regent Bagley likened the allegations to an earlier era of UC conflict:

> It's reminiscent of a scene from the Reagan era, when the Regents fired Clark Kerr. They're taking on the president of the University in public. It's tragic.[42]

ETHNICITY AND SOCIOECONOMIC STATUS

Once Regent Connerly had stated in his proposals that consideration should be given to individuals who had suffered disadvantage economically or in terms of their social environment, the question of replacing race/ethnicity with socioeconomic status again came to the fore. California State Senator Tom Campbell issued a press release on July 17, 1995, attacking the May report from the Office of the President modeling the use of socioeconomic status in place of ethnicity in undergraduate admissions. The press release challenged three key points in the Office of the President's report. First, it questioned the methodology, suggesting that rather than replacing race with socioeconomic factors, the UCOP simulation used race in the model for determining admissions. Second, in the release, Campbell stated that UCOP was incorrect in stating that dropping racial criteria would diminish the academic qualifications of students. Third, he suggested that the existing UC policies favored higher-income African Americans and Hispanics over lower-income Asian Americans. In yet another example of the opposition's efforts to turn around the Office of the President's arguments, Campbell quoted a passage written by UCOP analyst Dario Caloss:

> Keep in mind that by using socioeconomic status (SES) in place of ethnicity, we would reduce the number of underrepresented students from middle and high SES backgrounds and replace them with additional Asian American students from low SES families.[43]

The press release then argued:

> Turn that statement around, and you have a frightening admission of favoring higher income African Americans and Chicano/Latinos over Asian Americans of lower income. At Berkeley and UCLA, that is the policy, as explained to Campbell by Assistant Vice President Galligani.[44]

Labeling the policy "reprehensible," Campbell went on to ask:

> What can we say to the child of a lower income Asian family, all of whom had to work extremely hard for the child to arrive at a chance to attend

Berkeley, when we pass that child up, and admit instead the child of a professional couple of upper-middle income, no more academically qualified, but possessing a different skin color?[45]

The next day, UC Provost Walter Massey wrote to the Regents in an effort to refute Senator Campbell's claims. Massey defended UCOP's methodology and reiterated the study's finding that the substitution of socioeconomic status for ethnicity would result in a significant decrease in the number of underrepresented students at UC.[46]

REVEREND JACKSON AND GOVERNOR WILSON IN THE NATIONAL PRESS

On the same day that Senator Campbell issued his press release, the Reverend Jesse Jackson announced that not only would he attend the July meeting, along with other civil rights leaders and ministers from churches around the state, he would address the Regents. Jackson vowed that if necessary he would lead others in nonviolent civil disobedience at the meeting and join students in an all-night vigil the evening prior to the July meeting. At the same time, additional national focus was brought to bear on the issue by a report that the White House would send a representative to the meeting to monitor the Regents' efforts.

On the weekend before the July meeting, Governor Wilson again moved to carry his efforts to end affirmative action in California to a broader national platform. First he appeared on CBS television's national broadcast of *Face the Nation*. During that broadcast, Governor Wilson held up a chart of the UC admissions process that would be replayed on countless television news programs and picked up by national newspaper wire services (Figure 6.1). It was a chart of the UC application process similar to the one demonstrated by Professor Curtis for the Regents at their May meeting. The graphic Wilson displayed referred to the admissions process for the UC Berkeley admissions class of 1992.[47] It was a chart that would figure prominently in the July Regents' meeting and lead to an intense confrontation between Governor Wilson and Berkeley Chancellor Chang-Lin Tien.

In his televised appearance, the governor pointed to the graphic and noted that it had been produced by UC itself. Wilson then proclaimed,

> What it says is that if you are of the right ethnic group, they won't even bother to read your essay. You are automatically admitted, even if you're a non-resident, even if you're high income, even if you have a lower test score than someone who is Asian or Caucasian who is a resident of the state, who is low-income, who has a higher test score. That's wrong.[48]

Academic

	1	2	3	4	5	6	7	8	9	10
A	Admit	Admit	Admit	Admit	Admit	Admit	Read	Read	Read	Deny
B	Admit	Admit	Admit	Admit	Admit	Admit	Read	Read	Read	Deny
C	Admit	Admit	Admit	Admit	Read	Read	Read	Read	Read	Deny
D	Admit	Admit	Read	Read	Read	Read	Read	Read	Read	Deny
E	Admit	Admit	Read	Options Letter	Options Letter	Options Letter	Options Letter	Options Letter	Deny	Deny
F	Admit	Read	Options Letter	Options Letter	Options Letter	Options Letter	Options Letter	Options Letter	Deny	Deny
G	Admit	Read	Options Letter	Options Letter	Options Letter	Options Letter	Options Letter	Options Letter	Deny	Deny
H	Admit	Options Letter	Options Letter	Options Letter	Options Letter	Options Letter	Options Letter	Options Letter	Deny	Deny

(Social Diversity — vertical axis)

Figure 6.1. Fall 1992 Freshman Admissions at Berkeley. (Source: *Berkeleyan,* Vol. 21, No. 3, Office of Public Affairs, UC Berkeley).

Wilson failed to mention that there were a number of conditions that entitled applicants to admission on other than academic merit. Students with outstanding athletic skills were often cited in the contest, as were students affiliated with wealthy donors, or who received assistance in the admissions process from Regents or state political leaders.

"IF PETE WILSON THINKS HE'S GOING TO BE PRESIDENT, HE'S TRIPPING"[49]

When asked about the Reverend Jackson's threat to engage in civil disobedience, Wilson told *Face the Nation*:

> If he seeks to disrupt the meeting, as he has announced, he will, I suppose, succeed in being detained. We are not going to put up with the kind of threats to disrupt a regularly scheduled meeting of the Board of Regents. He can't succeed. This is going to go off on the merits of the argument. And what merit can there possibly be in saying we should ignore individual merit and instead give preferences based on race and gender.[50]

Wilson positioned himself as something of the guardian of the Regents, despite not having attended a meeting in over three and a half years. He was going to end that streak on July 20, 1995, for a number of reasons. The *Los Angeles Times* reported:

> Strategists working for the governor's presidential campaign expect Wilson will receive his biggest national spotlight of the year when he is pitted against Jesse Jackson at the meeting of the Board of Regents.[51]

Although the meeting itself was only four days off when the governor appeared on *Face the Nation*, the contest was still in some doubt. At the press conference after the televised broadcast, one of Wilson's aides suggested that the key to the vote would be the number of Regents in each camp who attended the meeting. He went on to say that Wilson would attempt to persuade Regents who were on the fence not to attend the meeting in order to give himself a better chance to carry the day.[52]

Two days before the vote, Wilson addressed a meeting of the California Employers Group and laid out his plan for the meeting:

> On Thursday, I'm going to urge my colleagues on the University of California Board of Regents to make our University the leader it should be in moving our nation forward toward a new vision of equality, opportunity and fairness. Nearly two decades ago, the Supreme Court's *Bakke* decision chastised the University of California for making race a primary factor in admissions. The Court correctly noted that it violated the guarantee of equality at the heart of our Constitution. But in recent months, it's become clear that, despite official denials to the contrary, race is just as deeply imbedded in UC's admissions process as it has ever been. Most campuses really have two admissions processes: one for members of protected groups and one for everyone else.

Wilson again presented the ubiquitous UC Berkeley admissions chart:

> This chart diagrams the admissions policy at Berkeley. It shows that members of some preferred groups were <u>automatically</u> admitted at a given level, while White and Asian students <u>with the exact same academic qualifications</u> didn't even qualify to have their <u>essays read</u>, much less get admitted.[53]

Throughout the week prior to the votes, state and national newspapers, television, and radio covered the impending contest. Newspaper op-ed pieces were published that conveyed the positions of the governor, various Regents, and campus chancellors. The *New York Times*, in a feature article shortly before the vote, published the following:

With an agenda of hotly contested proposals to eliminate affirmative action policies at the University of California, the meeting of the University's Board of Regents Thursday will be a proving ground for a central social issue of the decade. Governor Pete Wilson, using the dismantling of affirmative action as a cornerstone of his Republican presidential bid, has announced he will exercise his right for the first time in years to preside over the meeting. Jesse Jackson is coming to town on Wednesday to lead protests. And the White House has announced that President Clinton will deliver an important address on the subject on Wednesday. The twenty-six Regents themselves appear to be sharply divided.[54]

In that same article, Regent Connerly gave some insight into the governor's role in turning Regents' votes in favor of his proposals. Addressing his conversations with Regents after Wilson had issued his executive order, Connerly remarked,

So I started talking to individual Regents, asking them, "Have you thought this through?" Only about three of the twenty-six were with me. The governor then began talking to them. Today, because of his efforts we have about fourteen or fifteen who agree with us. That should be enough to adopt the resolution, but you've got to get them there, you've got to get them to vote, and they have to find the courage to go through with it.[55]

PRESIDENT CLINTON SPEAKS TO THE NATION

The day before the July Regents' meeting, President Clinton delivered a national address on affirmative action. Although he made no specific mention of the UC deliberations, Clinton did make a strong call for the preservation of affirmative action. Clinton reported the results of a White House review of affirmative action and concluded,

In the fight for the future we need all hands on deck, and some of those hands still need a helping hand.[56]

President Clinton, speaking from the National Archives before the original copies of the Declaration of Independence, invoked Dr. Martin Luther King Jr.'s "I Have a Dream" speech, and declared that racial bigotry was still commonplace. He acknowledged that there had been abuses in the implementation of affirmative action, but suggested that was no reason to retrench from support for the policies:

Affirmative action has not always been perfect and affirmative action should not go on forever. It should be changed now to take care of those things that are wrong, and it should be retired when its job is done. I am resolved that that day will come, but the evidence suggests, indeed screams, that that day has not come.[57]

Both Jesse Jackson and Governor Wilson were quick to react to the president's remarks. While Jackson praised Clinton, noting that it was one of the finer moments of the Clinton presidency, Governor Wilson denounced the president's address:

> He is trying to keep in place a system that will contain the virus that threatens to tribalize America, and to divide us.[58]

Wilson's choice of the word "tribalize" was yet another piece of fuel for the fiery protest that would engulf the Regents at their meeting the next day.

7

Contest, Resistance, and Decision

On the morning of Thursday, July 20, the Regents' headquarters complex in San Francisco resembled an occupied territory. Police officers were posted on each of the four blocks surrounding the university complex, some in riot gear, others arrayed as part of an elite SWAT team. Hovering around the barricades, stringing cables and testing microphones was a small army of television and radio journalists covering the scene. Shortly after dawn a line of students, ministers, members of the Rainbow Coalition, and other interested members of the public gathered at the door of the auditorium in which the meeting would be held. The weather was gray, with wind and fog chilling the scene.

Many in the early morning crowd had attended a rally the evening before at a San Francisco church, with over 1,000 people on hand to hear Reverend Jackson (Chavez, 1998). Many planned to be arrested in an act of civil disobedience if the Regents voted to end existing UC policies on affirmative action. Organizers moved up and down the line with bullhorns, exhorting the crowd, explaining details of a rally scheduled for later that morning, where Reverend Jackson and Mario Savio, a leader of the Free Speech Movement at UC Berkeley in the sixties, would speak.

The first problem the protesters faced was how to get into the building. The auditorium held fewer than 300 people. Many seats were reserved for the press, invited guests, and individuals connected with the university and campus administrations. Nearly 200 requests had been received from members of the public hoping to address the board, and thirty guests had been invited to speak to the board. It was clear that most of those in line to enter would not be seated in the auditorium with the Regents. The Regents had arranged for a video broadcast in a room adjacent to the auditorium for the more than 500 spectators unable to obtain access to the main auditorium. Six protestors were arrested before the meeting began.

YOUNG REPUBLICANS

As the meeting was to be broadcast live over local radio and television, even the content of the crowd in the auditorium was contested by political actors.

The president of UC Berkeley's chapter of the College Republicans, Scott Kamena, described his role this way:

> My original assignment was to bring as many students as possible to picket against affirmative action outside. I was one of many organizers in this effort. We were supposed to concentrate on getting people there, while the Wilson campaign was to provide the picket signs. However, it soon became clear to Republican strategists that the picketing wasn't going to work. We just weren't getting the volunteers. Conservatives tend to have a real distaste for protests. They also tend to have jobs, which makes it difficult to dedicate an entire Thursday to a demonstration.[1]

Someone sympathetic to their cause seemed to have found the solution for the small numbers problem faced by the College Republicans: pack them into the few available seats inside the auditorium. Kamena explained it this way:

> While I can't prove it, I believe that somebody went to great lengths to make sure that we would get in. The auditorium was originally scheduled to open at 7:30 a.m., a half-hour before the meeting was scheduled to begin. On Monday night I was told (I won't say by whom) that the doors would actually open at 6:30 a.m. and that my group had better be there before then. I was concerned that we would be beaten to the punch by the liberal activists that had vowed to camp outside the doors the night before. But I was told that as long as we were there by 6:20 a.m. we would get in.[2]

Although the College Republicans did get into the meeting, most of the other students did not. The students were further frustrated by the rules for addressing the board. At prior board meetings, students had been asked to hold their comments for the July meeting. Yet at the commencement of the July meeting, it became clear there was no way to accommodate all of the members of the public who had signed up to speak, as well as the various politicians, activists, and interest group representatives who had been invited to address the board. Given their time constraints, the Regents opted to hold a lottery. They chose thirty-five members of the public at random, fewer than one in five of those who had requested time. Only four students were chosen to speak. After Student Regent Gomez protested, four more students were added to the list, meaning that nearly seventy speakers in total had been selected, each of whom was to be held to a three-minute limit.

THE DAYLONG PRESIDENTIAL CAMPAIGN AD BEGINS

First to speak, and to exceed the limit, was Governor Wilson, who defined the arena of conflict this way:

> This institution has a long and proud tradition of generating and tolerating diverse opinions and perspectives. We will carry on that tradition today. But as Regents of the University of California, we cannot tolerate university policies or practices that violate fundamental fairness, trampling individual rights to create and give preference to group rights.[3]

The governor then held up a copy of an admission application for the audience and the television cameras to see.

> This is the undergraduate application for the University. Inside the front cover, it says, "The University of California does not discriminate on the basis of race." That's a fundamental and cherished American principle that must not only be the policy, but also the practice of this institution. But it's become unmistakably clear that, despite official claims to the contrary, it is not the policy and not the practice. As President Peltason acknowledged last week, race has played a central role in the admissions practices at many UC campuses. Indeed, some students, who don't meet minimum academic requirements are admitted solely on the basis of race.[4]

The last comment, that students were admitted solely on the basis of race, was at best mistaken. Perhaps the governor was referring to students who were not eligible to be admitted solely on the basis of the academic index, those admitted on the basis of academic index and supplementary criteria. He may have been referring to special admits, those admitted on the basis of particular skills or talents in music, athletics, etc. In neither instance were students being admitted solely on the basis of race, a point the Office of the President had made over and again in the previous month. The governor surely knew this was the case, but he also was not going to let a careful interpretation of the issue get in the way of what one newspaper account the following day would call "Pete Wilson's daylong presidential campaign ad called a UC Regents meeting."[5]

Wilson then made an appeal to working-class taxpayers:

> It takes all the state taxes paid by three working Californians to provide the public subsidy for a single undergraduate at the University of California. The people who work hard to pay those taxes and who play by the rules deserve a guarantee that their children will get an equal opportunity to compete for admission to this university—regardless of their race or

gender. Simple fairness demands that we assure them that all eligible applicants go through the same process. I appreciate President Peltason's commitment to support change in the future. But it is the Regents' responsibility, not that of the administration or the faculty, to set policy and to ensure that university practices adhere to those policies. That responsibility cannot be delegated. This is a matter of fundamental fairness and justice on which the Regents, and only the Regents, can act. We cannot ignore or duck that responsibility nor temporize in making the required decision. The questions before us are simple and cannot be set aside. Are we going to treat all Californians equally and fairly, or continue to divide Californians by race? The answer we owe the people and the changes we must make are clear. By doing so we will keep faith with the principles on which the University and our nation were built, we must do no less.[6]

After the governor's opening statement, the Regents heard from the invited guests. The succession of speakers encompassed a number of key California legislators from both sides of the aisle, including Assemblyman Willie Brown, who spoke first. Brown, a longtime Speaker of the Assembly and the first African American Regent,[7] had been a key supporter of the university, and proponent of UC affirmative action programs. His address focused on his own experiences in attending the University of California and his belief in the continuing need for affirmative action for the current generation. He also urged the board not to succumb to the temptation to further any individual's political ambitions at the expense of the board's obligation to remain an independent governing body. Brown concluded his remarks by cautioning the board:

> To vote to change affirmative action, ahead of the people, ahead of a court order, ahead of a constitutional amendment, ahead of any statute, would be to move the Regents into the arena of politics, and once there, extrication will become an impossibility.[8]

Following Brown's remarks, a number of state legislators, both Democrats and Republicans, along with former Regents and leaders of a variety of interest groups, addressed the board. The speakers generally began by sharing their personal experiences with affirmative action and discrimination. The Democrats and others who favored preserving the existing policies testified that affirmative action was a useful tool for diversity, the product of a long struggle, and that to repeal affirmative action in order to advance the governor's political ambitions would be a terrible mistake. The Republicans and others in favor of eliminating UC's existing policies expressed the position that politics had nothing to do with the necessity to vote to do away with a group preference program that they felt did not even serve the groups it was intended to benefit.

REVEREND JACKSON SPEAKS TO RACE AND ECONOMIC PRIVILEGE

It was left to Reverend Jackson to bring closure to the first portion of the meeting. As he approached the podium, many in the auditorium and in the annex stood and cheered. He commenced by asking the Regents to stand in prayer. He repeated the request three times, until all but one of the Regents stood and joined hands; the lone exception was Governor Wilson (Chavez, 1998).

After the prayer, Jackson spoke for nearly forty-five minutes. He began his remarks with a direct challenge to the governor, for his mixed support for affirmative action and for his reference to "tribalism" in his remarks the day before. Jackson, like many others who addressed the board, spoke about affirmative action as an issue of both race and economic privilege:

> Today the eyes of the nation are upon California. Today and in the months ahead the issue of Affirmative Action will be debated. Today we're examining a microcosm of the great debate, a heated public discourse that could either inflame our worst tendencies toward racial animosity or elevate us to a more compassionate and fuller understanding of living in a more culturally diverse society. We often look at the same thing and see different things, not because of genetics, but because of culture and socialization. We observe that always we see forests in Europe, and always jungles in Africa. Both forests and jungles are thickets of wood and flowers and wild animals, but the connotation, like tribalism, takes on expressions that go deep to the heart of racism.[9]

The reverend also reminded the board of the danger of politicizing the debate over affirmative action:

> There's widespread support for Affirmative Action in the academic community. I stand in some comfort here identifying with the positions of University of California President Peltason, all nine chancellors, all nine Academic Senates, the student associations. They work on this all the time and this is their full-time duty, they are the best at this in the world. I take some comfort identifying with their positions. I hope we can keep the matter of academic freedom and their judgment from being polluted by political agendas.[10]

Reverend Jackson further admonished Regent Connerly and the governor for their repeated invocation of the Civil Rights Movement and the words of Dr. Martin Luther King Jr. Connerly had suggested earlier that Dr. King might not have been in favor of contemporary affirmative action.[11]

> I've heard too much today. This distortion of Dr. King's quote. Those who did not walk with him in life should not try to pervert his words in death. That's a sin.[12]

Reverend Jackson reminded the Regents of how far the university had come in its quest for inclusion, and of how far it had to go:

> Because of Affirmative Action this university is more diverse, and looks more like California. Thirty years ago the University of California was predominantly White. The response to the Civil Rights movement of the 60's and 70's was to raise a call for equality, enlightened leadership among the Regents and the University of California administration. The University began to devise methods to include people of color. At Berkeley, the Educational Opportunity Program was established in 1964. By the 60's and 70's minority enrollment increased, yet the University of California at Berkeley as late as 1984 was 61% White, 24% Asian, 6% Latino, and 5% African American, in a state where African Americans were 12%, and Latinos 30% of the population. Because of Affirmative Action programs a wide range of academic development and outreach programs to junior high and high school students, and the consideration of ethnic and racial group status as one factor, among many, for all qualified applicants, today African Americans are 6% at Berkeley and Latinos are 14%. These figures are still too low, but nonetheless significant in light of the tough economic straits of minority families and impoverished inner-city school districts from which a majority of people of color graduate.[13]

Reverend Jackson introduced a subject that would loom large in the Regents' deliberations and move to the fore of the state policy agenda after the Regents' votes, the construction of merit in admissions:

> I think what is the most disturbing, finally, is this: the most deceptive argument among the rationales for Regent Connerly's proposal is the idealization of bias-free meritocracy. Our being for color-blind and gender-blind admissions is a lot like appraising virtue. It is easy to say, but hard to do. In many ways judging merit is like defining virtue. It is subjective. Who decides what is meritorious? We cannot let merit be defined narrowly by grades and test scores, which are not intrinsically indicators of success, worth or service. The desire for the minority student to go back home and become a teacher in the ghetto, or for a woman to become a rape crisis counselor, are these not virtues that should be considered? Even if we accept grades and test scores as the basis for merit, and we should, how can we be sure that culturally biased tests could measure worth? Grades and test scores have never been the sole criteria for admission.[14]

Reverend Jackson also responded to two other significant points in Regent Connerly's argument, that affirmative action prevented the creation of a "color-blind" society, and that there was a stigma attached to students of color in institutions that used race as a consideration in admissions:

> I remember when the Blacks lived in a color-blind society. I was invisible. My thoughts, concerns and rights were of little or no importance to Whites who governed the political process and could control the economy of Greenville, South Carolina. Where I grew up, Mr. Governor, I never saw a Black policeman until I was an adult. I never saw a Black fireman until I was an adult. Blacks couldn't sell shoes downtown. We were qualified to sell them. Where I grew up, we couldn't use a single public toilet. We were qualified. We couldn't use a single hotel. We couldn't use the library. We were qualified. We couldn't buy a hamburger with money. We were qualified. We couldn't use the state roadside bathrooms. We were qualified. My father, God rest his soul, was a veteran of W.W.II, with shrapnel in his body. He couldn't use the public bathroom. His son couldn't go to Furman University though my mother washed the children's clothes there. I couldn't go to South Carolina. I couldn't go to Clemson University. That didn't make me bitter. It didn't make me better. But I am not at all bitter, because I've been blessed.
>
> But don't assume some self-righteous, arrogant stance, and assume for a kid like me. Because I don't feel any complex from opportunity, as we fight for racial justice and gender equality. Try saying to me that, "You might have had certain opportunities, don't you feel guilty?" That would be like saying the day after slavery had ended, "Well I'm a White guy and you're a Black guy, both of us are free now. But you had to have the Emancipation Proclamation. Ha ha ha, how do you feel?" "Wonderful! You did not need the Emancipation proclamation. I did."[15]

In his concluding remarks, Reverend Jackson again directly challenged the Regents, raising the issue of how they had obtained their seats on the board:

> Lastly, Regents, why do I make this appeal for you to open your minds? The appearance of corruption in appointments. Seats on this Board seem to be made not by merit but by stock purchase. It seems that way. I looked at this list before coming here to meet with you today. Howard Leach $82,000 contribution to the governor. Ward Connerly, $73,000 contribution, Stephen Nakashima, $33,000, Bill Bagley, $28,000, John Davies, $17,000, Frank Clark, $17,000. This may not be corruption, but it appears to be a conflict of interest. If it's true, this appears to be politics at its lowest and most irrational. I appeal to you today to rise above the politics of the moment, I appeal to you today to do justice, to love mercy and to use your power to save our children and make an investment in the healing of our nation. I urge all of you, through all of this pain, to keep hope alive.[16]

His allegation that many Regents were Republican fund-raisers and contributors was correct. The precise amounts of Regental contributions are difficult to determine because many Regents also made contributions through their businesses and associations. The actual amounts were likely much higher than those that Reverend Jackson cited (Schwartz, 1996).

RACE, ECONOMICS, AND THE STATE

One of the more notable aspects of Reverend Jackson's address was his linkage of racial and economic inequality to the broader topic of affirmative action in higher education. Jackson invoked the disparity in income and assets between African American, Latino, and White families, the effect of glass ceilings on women, and the major differences between expenditures on elementary-secondary schooling in California's predominantly White districts and districts serving African American and Latino students.

Reverend Jackson also pointed to the effect of broader American economic segregation on access to education, as he noted the pattern of awarding federal licenses and franchises to White investors, and the continuing efforts to limit inheritance taxes in order to reduce the redistribution of wealth. In these latter remarks, Jackson spoke directly to the role of the State in redressing economic inequality, and he suggested that one of the foremost tools at the State's disposal should be affirmative action in higher education. He contrasted the cost of an academic scholarship with expenditures on incarceration and suggested that any rollback in affirmative action in higher education be considered in light of the vast increase in the nation's prison population and the disproportionate percentage of African Americans in prison. He delineated a vital State interest in affirmative action, and as he related the stances of the Supreme Court and the president in supporting affirmative action, he pointed to the role of the State itself in the broader contest over affirmative action.

Reverend Jackson's final comment on what he saw as an inappropriate linkage between political contributions and appointments to the board challenged the elite control of access to public higher education and the tension between the perspectives of the wealthy individuals that dominated the board and the students struggling to preserve affirmative action. The tension between privileged, predominantly White economic interests and those seeking redress of historical inequalities generated both by racism and by the inequalities inherent in economic production served as a powerful underpinning for all of the reverend's remarks.

While Reverend Jackson's speech was one of the most eloquent and comprehensive presented to the board, whether he swayed many Regents was not clear. It is more clear that his powerful advocacy inspired students, who incorporated his remarks into speeches and rallies held on the UC campuses when the campuses reopened in the fall (Chavez, 1998).

At the conclusion of Reverend Jackson's remarks, the thirty-five members of the audience who had been selected by lottery each spoke for three minutes. The four students who had been added to the roll by Chair Burgener followed them.

Before the first of the four students spoke, there was some angry shouting from the audience referring to the limit on the number of student speakers. One of those shouting referred to the governor with language that offended Regent Brophy's sense of propriety. He threatened to change his vote, to join the governor, if the spectators did not improve their behavior. This was the exchange that took place, and it gives an indication of the sensitivity of the Regents, and the strained relations at the meeting:

> A voice from the audience: Why don't you change your dirty underwear, Governor Wilson.
>
> Chair Burgener: We're not going to tolerate that.
>
> Regent Brophy: Mr. Chairman, as a matter of public privilege...
>
> Chair Burgener: Regent Brophy?
>
> Regent Brophy: If I have to continue to hear this kind of vulgarity out of the back of the room, I'm going to leave this meeting and I'll take whatever Regents will go with me. That's completely unfair, those things they're saying about Governor Wilson. I won't listen to it. You might be surprised that I'm the only no vote sitting at this chair too, but you can sure switch me in one hell of a hurry.[17]

VOICES OF STUDENT RESISTANCE

The students addressed the board with remarks that differed quite substantially from those presented by many of the invited guests. The students commented more specifically on racial and economic equity, and to a far greater degree than the invited speakers or the board, they addressed the issue of gender, and the low numbers of women on the faculty and in leadership positions at UC. They invoked corporate capital flight and the effects of the continuing polarization of income and wealth in the country as key factors in the emergence of affirmative action on the national agenda. Like the Reverend Jackson, they conceptualized the contest as a struggle over more than race or gender in isolation, as a struggle that reached far beyond the institution itself. They also pointed to the role of the State in redressing inequalities central to economic production, and they noted the overtly political nature of the affirmative action contest. Their remarks were supported by shouts of encouragement and applause both in the auditorium and in the annex.

The initial student speaker was Colleen Sabatini, an undergraduate biology major at the University of California San Diego. She appealed to the crowd for calm and good manners, as she began her speech:

We are not Jesse Jackson, we are not Pete Wilson, business people or Assembly people. We are the people who work, live, learn and struggle in the University daily. We too deserve to be listened to. There are a large number of students outside this building that have been here since 6:00 this morning and we are representing an even greater number of students who could not be with us today. We are Black, Chicano Latino, Native American, Asian American, middle Eastern, White, we are male and we are female and we have come from all over the state to tell you how we feel. We are in strong support of affirmative action. My question to those of you who are trying to dismantle affirmative action is, why are you attacking a solution instead of the problem? Affirmative action attempts to address such racist and discriminatory actions as you have heard personal accounts of today. Affirmative action is an equalizing measure that must stay in place because we do not have an equal opportunity society.

I'm involved in this struggle and I'm here today because I benefit from affirmative action in many ways. First, I came to UC expecting a richly diverse student body representative of the diversity of the state of California. That is what the UC mission says. When I arrived at UCSD, I was deeply saddened and angry at what I found. My school has a 2.2% African American population, a 10% Chicano/Latino population and a .9% Native American population. I am being denied my education in learning how to work and live in a multicultural society by being exposed to a diversity of opinions and beliefs. I am not getting that. Additionally, a grave concern of mine is a representative faculty. Of the 24 classes I have taken in my two years at UCSD, one of my professors was a female. Where are my role models? Where are the role models for my Chicano/Latino and African American brothers and sisters when none of those 24 professors were either of those races? We will no longer need affirmative action when we achieve a color-equal society. This will only be achieved by combating the larger societal problems of racism and discrimination. Not by dismantling affirmative action. The students of UC are incredibly appalled and resent that this major issue has been thrown into the political arena, and demeans, solely for the advancement of certain persons' political careers. Take your politics out of our classrooms and the University. Regents, please stand up for affirmative action. We beg you not to bow to political pressure. Join with the Office of the President, the UC chancellors, the vast majority of faculty and staff, the vast majority of the students of this prestigious University who support affirmative action. Please keep the doors of accessibility open, expand and accelerate affirmative action by supporting Regent Gomez's and the UC students' proposal that you have before you today. Thank you.[18]

The second student to address the board was Ed Center:

> My name is Ed Center and I'm a student at UC Davis and I'm also a member of the University of California Student Association, which is the representative voice of the students of the UC. A lot of people have talked about their cultural backgrounds today. I come from a cross cultural background. My mother is Asian and my father is White. Asian and White, the two racial groups that supposedly suffer the most from the current affirmative action policies. But I'm here to argue and to beg and to plead in support of affirmative action. I support affirmative action because it is still a necessary mechanism to achieving educational equality. I work in outreach programs to low income and minority youth. Mr. Connerly's proposal also advocates the expansion of outreach programs and I support him on this and at least we can find some area of agreement.

Mr. Center shared his experiences with outreach programs and concluded:

> Students of color suffer because of race based problems and these race based problems demand race based solutions. Women suffer because of gender based problems and gender based problems demand gender based solutions. Until we create a culturally and gender sensitive UC system, we will need affirmative action. Until we create a culturally and gender sensitive community college and Cal State system, we will need affirmative action. Until we create a culturally and gender sensitive K–12 system, we will need affirmative action. We don't have any of these things. Before our children can pull themselves up by their bootstraps, we need to create an educational institution that can teach them how to tie their shoes. I would invite any of you to come down and meet with the students that I work with in order to understand their perspectives before you decide on policy that will affect their lives. Like I said, until we have achieved complete educational equity at all levels for all students from preschool through graduate and professional schools, we will need affirmative action. When that society is created, and I hope it will be, I will be the first to sit down and shake hands with Governor Wilson and shake hands with Mr. Connerly and say that affirmative action is no longer necessary because we have achieved equal status in our society. But until that point is reached, affirmative action is a viable, necessary moral institution within our system that we need to preserve so I would urge all of you Regents to please protect the students within the system and those that will be entering the UC system soon by rejecting Mr. Connerly's proposal and voting in favor of Regent Gomez's proposal that he will present before you soon. Thank you.[19]

The next student speaker was York Chang:

> My name is York Chang, I'm the newly elected Student Body President for UCLA. I am the second Chinese American to hold this position. And I'm also the outgoing Chair of the Affirmative Action Committee for the UC Student Association. I spoke to you earlier this year on this issue. Then and now the efforts of students are the culmination of months of trying to get the Regents engaged in a real discussion of how to improve affirmative action and access to the University. But there are some Regents that some people feel are interested in something wholly different than this. Their attacks on affirmative action are somewhat like little pop tunes that are catchy, easy to sing to and stick in your mind, but if you listen closely, really closely, you'll hear that it's being sung by a deadly pied piper that's leading us down a dead end path towards oversimplified short term solutions and desperate campaign gimmicks.
>
> The answer to the problem of fairness and equitability in the UC system is not to do away with affirmative action, it's not a preferential policy, it's an equalizing policy that attempts to recognize the blatant inequalities that are prevalent in our K–12 educational system which goes way beyond simple, socioeconomic status and cuts to the very culture of this anemic educational system that California has. And who is being encouraged to succeed? Who is being discouraged? Who has role models, who has peers? These things all cut to the heart of the matter, and that is, race matters in a society. Perceptions of inferiority of people of color and women are not caused by affirmative action. I would submit to you that we've suffered from these perceptions of people of color and women throughout our history and if you are successful in eliminating affirmative action, it will continue. Those things are there not because of affirmative action, but because of institutionalized racism and sexism. To do away with race consciousness is not the solution. The only real solution to this problem of educational equity is fundamental societal reprioritization of education that guarantees equal educational opportunities from the very beginning. To attempt to create a color-blind system at the University when the preparatory system leading up to it is fraught with discriminatorily imposed disparities of resources and opportunities and support is just plain blind.
>
> We must be conscious that racism still exists. Ward Connerly himself has admitted in discussions I've had with him that institutionalized racism and sexism does exist throughout our society today. That's a given, no question about that. And anybody in touch with the real world will not deny that. That we are free—nobody can say that we are free of that after only 30 years of some solutions that are laying out there. That's not the question. The tougher question is, what are people prepared to do about it? What are you prepared to do about it? When we begin talking about personal responsibility, we have a personal responsibility to combat these

> things. It goes beyond affirmative action. I think that the Regents at one point understood when it was less complicated and less convoluted with all this stuff going on out here. We saw them passing and allocating a million dollars to the UC Diversity Initiative. Now, let's ask what has changed since then? Pete Wilson has also supported affirmative action policies, just a few years ago. What has changed since then? The only answer to that I have is that there is a shift—a window of political opportunism and I urge you not to jump out of that window. It's a long, long fall to the pavement. And I urge you to reject...

At this point the Chair interrupted the speaker to warn him that his three minutes were up.

> Yeah, let me just—students are the ones in the trenches struggling for educational equity in our society. And Governor Wilson, unless the rest of us, all of us, can see that you are willing to join students in this fight for societal reprioritization of education, please, please don't tell us that you're talking about educational equity or that you're talking about leadership and a long term vision for our society. This is not for the sake of this program or that program; it's not for the sake of winning an argument, but what we're talking about is for the sake of diversity, access to education and a better society. I am personally responsible for that and that's why I'm submitting it to you that it is also your responsibility. Support the student proposal to be submitted by Ed Gomez asking for reaffirmation and expansion of affirmative actions programs. Thank you very much for your time.[20]

The final student chosen to address the board was Ralph Armbruster, a graduate student in sociology at University of California Riverside. After thanking those inside and outside of the meeting for the opportunity and inspiration to speak, he said,

> To put it concisely, as many other speakers have noted, racism and sexism continue to exist in this country. At UC Riverside, only 4% of our undergraduates are African American, while in sociology, political science, anthropology, and many other academic disciplines, we have zero African American faculty. In sociology we have only one African American graduate student, while we have three Latino graduate students, I'm one of the three. Even more troubling is that we currently have no graduate students who are women of color in our whole graduate department history, which is about 25 years, we've only had one African American female to graduate with a Ph.D. from our department. Do these numbers sound like reverse racism or reverse discrimination to you? These numbers solidly demonstrate that affirmative action needs to be strengthened and not weakened.

I was shocked recently to hear Regent Johnson state that affirmative action had gone too far. How could affirmative action have gone too far if we had numbers like this at UC Riverside? The numbers are appalling. Clearly then, race and gender matter in the educational admissions process at UCR and at other universities. I call on the Board and Governor Wilson to accept and to face this grim reality. The attacks on affirmative action come at a time when many people are experiencing downward mobility in our country. These folks, usually referred to as angry White males in today's society, are frustrated and alienated by changes in our economy and society. Instead of looking at those who are most wealthy for their own declining situations, they look to faces at the bottom of the well. And they blame them instead for what's happening in our society. This stratum of society is rightfully upset at their situation but they are wrong to blame people of color, women and undocumented workers for these problems. The problem is with blaming downward and not upward. This blocks serious progressive and radical social change which our country desperately needs.

The source of our nation's problems lies not with affirmative action, immigration, welfare, or with crime, it lies with corporate flight overseas, class polarization, increasing the concentration of wealth and income, the weakening of civil rights laws designed to strengthen anti racist legislation and so on. People's lives are becoming increasingly precarious in our society. People are becoming frightened. And in these trying times people lash out at convenient and powerless targets. Moreover, it is truly tragic that our nation's political leaders are exploiting these very real fears for their own advancement. Governor Wilson supported both affirmative action and immigration when it was politically expedient. But then strategically changed his mind on both issues when his governership was floundering. These waffles in political decisions are why people are fed up with politicians. People see politicians as nothing more than opportunist hacks who reinforce systems of exploitation and domination. I would suggest to the board that they reject simple analysis, which blames our nations problems on people of color and women. This is a grave misconception of reality. Race and gender still matter in education policy, hiring decisions, home loans, and in many other situations. I wish this was not the case. I wish we had a color-blind objective merit based system, whatever that means. Yet reality illustrates racism and sexism still exist. Just look around, Regents, you can see it wherever you go. Racism and sexism are there. I urge you to reject Regent Connerly's proposal and to accept continuing affirmative action in the UC system and accepting Regent Gomez's alternative proposal. Thanks very much, and this has been an enlightening experience.[21]

REGENT CONNERLY ADDRESSES THE BOARD

The first Regent to address the board after the students was Regent Connerly. Under Regents' bylaws, President Peltason could have brought his recommendations first, as an action item that Regent Connerly's forces would then have had to amend or vote down, before he could bring his own action item to a vote. Instead, as he had throughout the contest over SP-1 and SP-2, President Peltason graciously yielded the floor to Regent Connerly, promising to bring his own item to the board after Connerly had presented his item. This would later prove to be an important parliamentary point, as not only would Regent Connerly introduce his proposals as a motion to the board, he would put SP-2 forward first, so that the board would first vote on contracting and hiring, rather than admissions. This would have the effect of shaping the conversation around the board, and also allow Connerly and the governor, in the event that for some reason SP-2 did not pass, to seek a delay on the consideration of admissions (Connerly, 2000).

Just before he began his remarks, Regent Connerly interjected that despite some misunderstandings, he was not opposed to the Regents, in due course, considering the motion prepared by the UC Student Association and Student Regent Gomez. He noted that although he personally opposed the motion, he felt that on the basis of the energy the students had put into the motion and the distance many students had traveled, it would be only fair to consider their proposal. It was then agreed by acclamation that the student proposal would be voted on at some point after the end of debate on the Connerly motion.

Connerly began with an apology to the Reverend Jackson for some uncomplimentary comments Connerly had made earlier in the week. He then went on to explain how unpleasant it was for him to be the one to have brought so much discomfort to his colleagues, and to have been the focus of many uncharitable remarks, but that he felt it was his duty as a trustee of a public institution to challenge a system he thought was wrong. He said that he should not have to apologize for bringing an important issue to the table, and then proceeded with the following remarks that led up to the introduction of his proposals:

> Let me share a few observations with you, my friends. First of all I believe unequivocally that the goal of this nation and this state is to have its government institutions blind to the color of one's skin or the national origin of one's ancestors in the transactions of government. I recognize that we're not there. But that's still our goal. Two, for good purpose we have been granting what we call racial preferences. Let us not deny that.

We have been granting racial preferences. To remedy some of the historical unfairness and injustice, projected upon and practiced upon many Americans, particularly Black Americans. Three, the assumption has been made that these preferences would be temporary. And four, with each passing day, it should be clear to us that our system of preferences is becoming entrenched as it builds its own constituency to defend and sustain it as a permanent feature of public decision making. Five, it is equally clear to me as I suffer the characterizations of traitor, sell-out, Uncle Tom, that we're dividing ourselves and America along racial lines. Not as one nation indivisible, and we may have already passed the point where we can regroup and think of ourselves as individuals. Six, I am absolutely convinced that our excessive preoccupation with race contributes to this racial divide. And nowhere is the art of race consciousness practiced more fervently than on our University campuses. Seven, it is impossible for me to conclude that a preference to some, no matter how noble, no matter how noble, based on race is not a disadvantage, is not discrimination against others. The only question is the magnitude of the disadvantage. I believe it's considerable. Finally, the longer we wait before changing direction on this issue, the more difficult it will become to ever change.

After some further comments on his vision for the university, Connerly brought his motion with these remarks:

I just want to share a final comment because I think it tells, for me, why I'm doing this. And I often get the question of, "Why are you doing this?" Michael Jordan was once asked why he wasn't doing more to help Black kids. And he said, "Because I want every kid to think of himself as an individual, it does not mean that I'm not Black enough." That's what drives me. That's my belief. Now, this whole process for me has been a terribly revealing one because we cannot expect forever in the Black community not to prepare our kids to compete. We're doing that. But when I leave the office at the end of the day and when I spend my weekend I've asked, Ward Connerly are you doing as much to eliminate the need for preferences as you are proposing their elimination. And the answer is no. I'm not. I am not. And that is something that I, and all of you, and all of us need to do. But the fact is that there is still the burning question of whether race ought to enter into the equation. And grant me the right to believe that we should not. And on that basis, Mr. Chairman, I move the adoption of my resolution SP-2 relating to employment and contracting.[22]

Connerly's motion was seconded by Governor Wilson, and President Peltason took the floor to begin the discussion of the motion.

PRESIDENT PELTASON

The UC president began his remarks by noting the widespread support for affirmative action throughout the UC system and its leadership. He then turned to the changes that he had agreed to make as a result of UCOP's review of affirmative action:

> I have made some changes with the consent of the chancellors and the academic counsel and others. I just briefly call to your attention:
>
> That UCLA and Berkeley will institute a more comprehensive review of undergraduate applications background and qualifications. That UC Davis and UC Irvine have discontinued the practice of granting admission to all eligible underrepresented students who apply. I might also point out that the practice of that institution did not ever exclude any eligible students who might have applied. I have also initiated a review of whether race should continue to be used as one of the factors considered under admission by exception to the University's eligibility requirements. Specifically I've asked the Board of Admissions and Relations to schools to give its recommendation by next March 1 so that the proposed changes could be in place for the fall 1997 admission process.
>
> As I pointed out, we modified the target of opportunity program so that it will no longer be used to reserve faculty positions solely for the hiring of underrepresented minority and women faculty, as has been the case on some campuses. Second, a search under the regulation can be waived to hire any faculty member whose presence would significantly enhance the quality of the faculty.
>
> We've also taken action to insure that all of our management fellowships in similar development programs are not restricted to women or minority applicants but are open to all of the staff. I'll also ask General Counsel Holst to review all of our business activities at the request of the governor and the Regents, in light of recent Supreme Court decisions and to come back with specific recommendations if in his judgment any of them need to be modified as a result of these changes.
>
> We've tried to take an honest look at our programs and to change them where change is appropriate. It is equally important to emphasize that our review confirms my belief in the essential soundness and the value of these programs. In our admissions program there is no evidence that our efforts to increase diversity have compromised quality. On the contrary, our entering students have the highest academic qualifications in our history. We now have the highest graduation rates ever and the highest number ever of our students going on to graduate work. As the resolution approved by the Academic Council puts it, "We have made the University a better institution by making it a more diverse one."

The president concluded with a call for a commitment to diversity, and he promised to abide by the will of the board.

> As I said to you when I was inaugurated as your president, what happens to our university campuses will have much to do with our ability to forge an emerging new culture, a culture that is inclusive and respectful of difference which also unites us in the community that can live, work, prosper and flourish in our constitutional democracy. Our affirmative action and other diversity programs have been a powerful tool in helping us prepare California for its future. The chancellors, the provost, the vice presidents, the academic student leadership are united in urging the Regents to reaffirm our 30-year commitment to the twin goals of diversity and excellence. So let me reassure you that whatever the board decides, we will faithfully carry out your policies.[23]

As with his earlier letter, President Peltason's statement was remarkably mild. He did not invoke the shared governance issue, nor did he press on the issue of faculty or campus roles in setting admissions policy, other than to remind the Regents that the campus and systemwide faculty, administrative, and student leadership were united in support of preserving the existing policies, with the modifications that he had outlined.

In seeking support for UCOP's proposal, President Peltason was also arguing for preserving the norms of postsecondary governance. That is, after a thorough and consensual process, with information and expertise provided by the administrative leadership under the direction of the oversight board, the administration of the campuses and the system had recommended significant modifications in existing policy, in keeping with the concerns of the Regents and existing law. At the time of the president's proposals, the system was not under legal challenge, nor had the CCRI qualified for the ballot. Given the traditions of shared governance, the administration's willingness to make changes to established UC policies, and the traditional understandings of governance as the process of using expertise and oversight together to secure policy, existing governance models would predict that the board would have supported the president's proposal. That they did not was in part testimony to the influence of the next speaker, the governor of the state of California, who addressed the board and the state and nation with a hoarse and unsteady voice, still not entirely recovered from throat surgery. After an homage to Connerly's character, courage, and intellect, Governor Wilson began by displaying a chart (Figure 6.1) from an admissions handbook for UC Berkeley. He used that slide to articulate his case against existing UC policies, beginning with a challenge to supplemental criteria:

What this template shows is that there are some who are applicants, who by virtue of their membership in a particular racial group, are admitted to the University at the Berkeley campus without any reading of their essay on their application. What it also shows—those by the way are those in the green—and it also shows that even those who are non-resident as members of those particular favored ethnic groups are admitted even without any reading of their essay. What that shows very plainly and very graphically is that there is presently and has been a policy, not simply of explicit racial preference, but one that has been interpreted to permit what is clearly a discriminatory practice. It will not make right 200–300 years of discrimination against African Americans. But it is not going to make for the kind of California that we all want, one where there is genuine equality of access to opportunity to succeed to deprive a new group on racial grounds.[24]

Next the governor turned to his fundamental themes, linking the constitution and the redress of slavery as part of his own initiative to end affirmative action, and suggesting that there was a lesser standard for particular groups, with a stigma attached to the admission of underrepresented students:

After a bloody civil war, one consequence of which was to abolish slavery as a legal institution, we adopted an amendment to the Constitution which has come to be known as the equal protections clause. It protects the rights of individuals and yet this policy which is so graphically illuminated overhead is a policy that defeats the purpose, the expectation, indeed the protections afforded by the 14th Amendment and the Equal Protection Clause. This afternoon I've listened to a number of eloquent witnesses as I did this morning. A number who side with Regent Connerly and who support his proposal, did so for very personal reasons arising from their own experience. From their own resentment at the suspicion that their legitimate, genuine high achievement is not high achievement but that it is instead simply recognition of their race. There is a suspicion they find that somehow they have not earned their distinction when in fact they have. I can understand their resentment. Underlying all of affirmative action is an assumption somehow, a terrible false mistaken assumption that members of a particular racial group need special protection, need to have the bar lowered so that they can participate. Well, very clearly, that is not true. The abundant evidence is all around us that members of every race can excel and indeed do.[25]

In his conclusion, the governor stressed the need for his supporters on the board to act, and without further delay:

My friends, I would ask that as Regents we recognize our responsibility. It is ours. We cannot delegate it. We should not be sued into submission and surrender on a policy that however well intentioned is indefensible thirty years after the passage of the civil rights laws. Yes, discrimination continues to exist and yes we must oppose it with every fiber. We must enforce the protections afforded the prohibitions against discrimination and must do so conscientiously and vigorously and we must do more. We must in fact level that playing field in the way that we are seeking to do, but we cannot do it artificially in a way that produces simply a new class of victim. That's wrong. It is a matter of fundamental fairness. Don't duck this issue. Don't temporize. The time to act is now. The change must be made now.[26]

MOVING BEYOND *BAKKE*

In his remarks, Governor Wilson had articulated a number of themes that he had put forward in his press blitz over the previous month. Once again he had displayed the ubiquitous admissions chart from UC Berkeley, and reiterated that it enabled members of certain groups to receive preferential treatment. In this case the chart would do more than reinforce Wilson's contention; it would become an element in the departure from the UC system of the popular and successful Berkeley Chancellor Chang-Lin Tien.

Wilson hammered again on the notion that there was something particularly inappropriate in out-of-state applicants who were also members of underrepresented groups receiving preference over California's Whites and Asian Americans. His reference to "non-residents" brought back memories of Proposition 187. He invoked the national debate on race relations, through his reference to the Civil War and the Fourteenth Amendment. He insisted that despite the findings of UC's legal staff, there was evidence of clear discrimination and legal violations. He also raised the highly sensitive issue of "stigma" being visited upon members of underrepresented groups under affirmative action, a point that Reverend Jackson had attempted to refute in some detail. Finally, the governor offered an olive branch, holding out the possibility that the truly disadvantaged could be admitted through careful screening of applications without using race as a criterion.

Ultimately the arguments of both Connerly and Wilson could be stripped to an essential element: race as an admissions criterion was unacceptable. Neither mentioned the modifications promised by President Peltason, which would ostensibly have ensured fair readings for all applications. The president's compromise would have held all UC admissions policies up to a more strict legal standard, would have removed any guarantees of admission to particular classes of applicants, or set-asides designed to diversify the faculty. With those modifications assured, and a stated commitment around the table to diversity, the essence of the debate had shifted. At the beginning of the contest the question was whether UC was using race as one factor in admissions, contracting, and hiring, as *Bakke* allowed, or whether UC was using race as the defining factor in admissions, contracting, and hiring. But with the UCOP modifications in hand, the battle line was much more finely drawn: would the Regents allow the university to use race at all, in efforts to diversify the campuses? To vote for SP-1 and SP-2 was to vote to disallow any consideration of race, to go beyond *Bakke*. By the time of the July meeting the earlier invocations of "quotas" had given way to "preferences," the harsh accusations leveled against Reverend Jackson given over to apologies. Governor Wilson hoped not only to carry the day, but to look presidential in doing so. As the meeting continued, the audience would have a strong say in whether the governor would be able to do both.

After Governor Wilson's remarks, the Chair called for a clarification of the motions on the floor. General Counsel Holst advised the board that they could now continue discussion on Regent Connerly's motion to consider SP-2, governing contracting and employment.

REGENT RUSSELL

The next Regent to request the floor was Regent Designate[27] Russell, an African American attorney and a representative of the UC Alumni association, who as a designate could not cast a vote. He was twice interrupted in his remarks, and both interruptions would be significant for the course of the day's events and votes.

Regent Russell began by explaining that although he had no vote, he had a voice, and that although Governor Wilson had no voice, he had a vote. Russell offered to trade and the governor declined. Russell then started to talk about the political nature of the proceedings and how he wished that it were otherwise, because he felt that affirmative action could bear some honest scrutiny. At that point Regent Russell was interrupted by Regent del Junco, who asked the General Counsel for a ruling on whether Regent Russell was speaking to the motion that had been seconded. The General Counsel opined that Regent Russell probably had some latitude but that it would be well to keep in mind that the motion on the floor addressed employment and contracting, not admissions. It is worth noting that Governor Wilson had spoken at some length on admissions after Connerly's motion had been offered, but Regent del Junco said nothing during Governor Wilson's remarks. Russell then continued:

> It seems to me that Regent Connerly's proposals all have to do with really two guiding principles, that is fairness and opportunity. Is it fair to act on behalf, to use race as a factor for a given individual as compared to others who are not of that race? And there is also a question of opportunity. I

don't have examples and in terms of hiring because I'm not someone who has been hired or sought employment with the University. I do know as a graduate of this university that fairness and opportunity are important. I come from a family in which none of the members of my family prior to me had ever graduated from high school. I graduated from high school and went on to the University, specifically Berkeley. I was given an opportunity, and some might say it was unfair that I was given that opportunity, because my grades were not as good as a number of my classmates. I was someone who was subject to affirmative action. Now it's true that some of the factors that made that possible or caused me, for example, to not have the grades and perhaps the test scores of others, have to do with socioeconomic status. But some of them, and I don't think this point has been made adequately today, there is racial discrimination. And I know I face it today. I know my children face it today. My children face racial discrimination despite the fact that we are not of a low socioeconomic status.[28]

At that point Regent Russell was interrupted again, as the Chair announced that a bomb threat had been called into the auditorium, and the entire auditorium needed to be evacuated. After huddling with Regent Connerly during the bomb threat, while the auditorium was searched and the board and audience returned to their seats, Regent del Junco motioned for the question. If passed, the motion would have closed debate and caused an immediate vote on SP-2.

The ensuing vote to close off debate was 15–10, failing for lack of a two-thirds majority. This vote, coming some four hours before the end of the meeting, was an interesting harbinger of things to come. That is, of the fifteen Regents who voted to close off debate and vote immediately, ostensibly signaling that they did not need to hear any more debate in order to make their decision, only one, Regent Montoya, would not vote in the same bloc when the votes on SP-2 and SP-1 finally came to pass; the other fourteen would vote in favor of Regent Connerly's motions.

THE BAGLEY AMENDMENT

While awaiting clearance to return to the auditorium, Regent Bagley, who had written the legislation that became California's Open Meeting law[29] and who had a reputation as an astute parliamentarian, wrote out an amendment stressing the university's commitment to outreach and diversity, which he intended to have Regent Connerly append to SP-1 and SP-2. Bagley later told the story this way:

So I wrote it out, and I wish I had it, in fact I xeroxed it and sent it to Chancellor Yang in Santa Barbara. He says he carries it around with him and anytime a student complains he reads this to him. It's number nine paragraph of the resolution. But it changed. So everybody is for diversity, so I write this amendment. It was forceful. We are for diversity! I gave it to Ward, or I sent it around the table. I've used this expression before—he was counting his votes and feeling his oats. He refused to take the amendment. "I'm not going to take any amendments." At which point I said, "You either take this amendment or I shall give notice of reconsideration and hold this thing up for months." In order to give notice of reconsideration you have to be on the winning side or abstain. You can't vote no and then ask for reconsideration. You can only reconsider when you voted yes or abstained. So having said that, Ward and Pete motioned to me. Then we went out back to the coffee room and I had my draft written down and Ward and Pete [Wilson] had another thing written down. I remember saying to Pete, "Oh, my God, I don't want to negotiate with you; whatever you write is fine." So Pete wrote paragraph nine or ten on diversity.[30]

While Bagley's amendment would prove quite significant at the close of the day, it also gives an indication that Regent Bagley at least believed the ultimate vote would not be close enough for his "no" vote to make a difference. For his threat to the governor and Regent Connerly that he would call for reconsideration to have any force, he had to abstain, depriving the "no" camp of one key vote.

Bagley also related that during the bomb scare there was a great deal of vote counting. When Regent designate Russell resumed, he alluded to just how close both sides thought the vote might be:

First of all, with regard to the governor's reference to lowering the bar, I would suggest it's been my experience and I believe the experience of others that perhaps we stand in a hole and it makes it difficult. And that's just in terms of experience. Secondly, I would hope that the Regents should, as opposed to voting on something as divisive yet as important as this, that the Regents make an effort to—instead of coming down on a 13 to 12 vote or a 14 to 12, what have you, I believe it would be important and in the best interests of the University of California to seek to come to a consensus of the Board and efforts be made in that respect. Thank you.[31]

Regent Bagley then took the floor and raised the issue of the politicization of the process and the timing of the votes, holding out to the Regents the possibility of delaying action until after the CCRI made its way to the ballot. He noted his respect for all participants in the debate and emphasized his notion that the Regents' primary duty was to the university.

I want to make a point. Please. There is an urgency I think however, to come out of this meeting positively. Because as everybody here knows, and you've experienced it today, by having this matter before us, and Willie Brown said it so much better than I: we have already politicized the University. And that gets back to my thought. My deep thought on our fiduciary duty after 125 years of UC's existence not to do that. So instead of deferring, instead of tabling, I think we should come out with something positive.[32]

Regent Bagley next made an appeal for the Regents to avoid sending the message that UC had turned its back on race as a criterion for admission:

> If, however, we continue to say as a part of a resolution that Ward has adopted that maybe we're going to defer implementation, that's been proposed here in informal discussion, but we still adopt that basic sentence that says, "race is no longer a criterion," the message that we give to the world, and I mean the world, is that we are the first university, and now the greatest university, who have "abolished" and I know you're not abolishing, but the message will be that this university today had abolished affirmative action. If we don't adopt that aspect that says we got rid of race, and adopt those positive programs that are good, Ward, then we come out with progress and we take away the politicization that has occurred.[33]

Bagley's remarks reflect his years in the legislature and his experience as a negotiator. Through his proposal to defer implementation, he offered a compromise through which the governor and Regent Connerly would be able to announce the end of race as a criterion in UC admissions and changes in procedures on several campuses, while the UCOP would be able to delay implementation until it was clear whether CCRI would make it onto the California ballot.

LIEUTENANT GOVERNOR DAVIS

Regent Bagley was followed by Regent Davis, lieutenant governor at that time. The lieutenant governor, as one of the state's leading Democratic figures, had been an early opponent of Regent Connerly's effort to end existing affirmative action policies. He concentrated his remarks on the governor's presidential ambitions and urged the Regents to avoid partisan political action:

> Now, the governor has every right to run for president. He has every right to campaign for the Civil Rights Initiative. He has every right to propose the abolition of affirmative action. He has every right to come here and ask you to join him in that effort. But you have a right, actually you have a duty, to do what you think is in the best interest of this university and that is why you are given a 12-year term. So you are not buffeted by the exigencies of the moment and you can make a wise, judicious thoughtful decision, which is what I urge you to do.

> So you're not just being asked to participate in a political campaign, you're being asked to fire the first shot. And what we do here will be commented on David Brinkley, *Meet the Press*, criticized by some, praised by some. I mean we'll be kicked around literally like a political football between now and November of 1996. I think it's unwise, I think it's unbecoming to the greatness of this university. And I've said to some of you informally, there is a reason why institutions like the judiciary and great universities are respected. They do not get involved in politics. Now I'm not saying that you can't have a private position. I'm not saying you can't publicly articulate it. I'm not saying you as individuals can't decide what you think, how you should vote on the Civil Rights Initiative, I'm just saying don't put this university on the battlefield before anyone else gets out of the locker room if I can mix a metaphor here.

Davis also urged the Regents to think beyond their allegiance to the current governor and to again recall why they were granted long terms on the board by the California constitution.

> So I would like to close by urging that you search your soul as Regents, realize this will be one of the most important votes you'll cast in your lives. Realize that you have 12 years, even if someone might be upset with you for a moment or two if you cast a vote a certain way and to close by offering as a substitute motion President Peltason's remarks, to incorporate those remarks into a motion so we have that before us as a motion.[34]

At the close of his remarks, the lieutenant governor had offered President Peltason's action item as a motion in substitution for the motion offered by Regent Connerly, SP-2. This was the first instance where the parliamentary strategy of Regent Connerly came to fruition. What the lieutenant governor hoped to do was to force a vote on President Peltason's item. That item stated that the board should accept the modifications to existing policies recommended by UCOP. It also called for the board to authorize the president and the faculty to prepare a provisional plan for making the additional changes to existing affirmative action policies that would be needed if the CCRI were to be placed on the ballot and passed.

While President Peltason's compromise statement might have gained a majority of votes, Lt. Governor Davis's effort to substitute the president's action item for Regent Connerly's SP-2 never came to a vote. The General Counsel ruled that one motion can only be substituted for another if the subject matter under amendment is essentially the same. Given the specificity of SP-2, as it dealt with employment and contracting only, President Peltason's item strayed into too many other realms to be substituted. To try to get around the bind created by Regent Connerly's having offered SP-2 first, Regent

Carmona then offered a motion to table SP-2 until SP-1 had been resolved. This motion was defeated by a 15–10 vote, and debate resumed on SP-2. The next Regent to address the board was Howard Leach.

REGENT LEACH

Regent Leach began by offering up a number of quotations on the appropriateness of preferences. One in particular had a startling effect on the audience:

> The next quotation is from the 1995 membership card of the National Association for the Advancement of Colored People. From the NAACP purposes, and it has six purposes, I will only quote two. The first purpose is, "to eliminate racial discrimination and segregation from all aspects of public life in America." Purpose number five is, "to secure equal job opportunities based upon individual merit without regard to race, religion or national origin."[35]

Just as Reverend Jackson had warned about invoking Dr. Martin Luther King Jr.'s name in the service of ending affirmative action, there were many in the crowd who reacted vocally and angrily to Regent Leach's use of the NAACP's membership card as part of his argument for eliminating "preferences." It was interpreted by some as a hubristic performance from one of the more privileged actors on the board, a performance that puzzled his fellow Republican Regent Bagley. Bagley described Leach, who would later be appointed ambassador to France by President George W. Bush, this way:

> Howard is another player. Howard does not have to go along with the governor. The governor has to go along with Howard. Howard not only contributed $88,000 to the governor, but I think at that time, he was national finance chairman. Hard not to go along with Pete? Howard is a nice person, he's decent, he's civil, he's polite to me so I won't characterize, other than to say he could have done more. Why in the hell he had to follow Pete Wilson, I don't know. I didn't have to follow Pete Wilson. Pete never called me.[36]

Regent Russell also took exception to Leach's use of the NAACP membership card, noting in a subsequent interview that, in his opinion, when Regent Leach read from the membership card, "He'd never seen it before that moment."[37]

Throughout the conflict at UC, the proponents of SP-1 and SP-2 invoked metasymbols like fairness, equality, and color-blindness, and they often appropriated symbols that were previously equated with progressive struggles for equality, civil rights, and justice. Regent Leach's display of the

NAACP card, Governor Wilson's reference to the Civil War, Regent Connerly's invocation of Dr. King, and Regent Nakashima's allusion to internment camps were all elements in a battle over the symbolic high ground. It was a battle that—at least at the board level—the opponents of affirmative action would win.

SUPERINTENDENT EASTIN

Once the clamor over Regent Leach's presentation subsided, State Superintendent of Public Instruction and Regent Delaine Eastin addressed the board. She described her own experience with racism in California:

> I'm sad to say that when I was at UC Davis there were almost no minorities there. The fact is that many were not there because in fact there was terrible housing discrimination and employment discrimination in California. Although, Governor, I agree with you, the 14th Amendment is a wonderful part of our Constitution, it was not being enforced in California in the 50's and 60's. My hometown was a working class community, but we didn't sell homes in that hometown, the realtors had a deal and they didn't sell to minority families. Ward Connerly could not have bought a home there. And so, in fact a wonderful guy, R.C. Owens, Alley Oop from the 49er's, bought the first house owned by an African American in the city of San Carlos. And so over time we've improved on some of those things but there are these long-standing effects of discrimination that have affected us.[38]

As with the earlier comments from Assemblyman Brown and Lieutenant Governor Gray Davis, Superintendent Eastin concluded with a caution that the board not participate in the political gambit of the governor.

> When you open up this Regent body to the criticism that we do sway in the political wind, then we open up the finest public university in California and America to be tampered with by other political forces. Ladies and gentlemen, one last thing. This university was built by Earl Warren and Pat Brown. It was built by great people of both political parties. Nobody should ever let this subject of education become the bailiwick of one party or the other and nobody should ever let this university be subject to the winds of any, any political tide. Governor, you and I've had differences. I know you care about this university. I hope that in the end you will help us to rebuild K–12 and to add the 10th campus under Governor Wilson's term of office. Thank you very much.[39]

While Regent Eastin's comments added to the litany of historical references by proponents of affirmative action, she did not bring much of the data collected by her own office to bear on the argument. Eastin could have shared her knowledge of the declining UC eligibility rates of California high school graduates from underrepresented constituencies, or detailed information about the changing profile of California's K–12 system over the previous two decades. With those data she might have challenged one of Connerly's key contentions: that improved K–12 outreach by the university would ultimately compensate for the elimination of affirmative action. Eastin might have pointed out that given the cost and enormity of improving the K–12 system sufficiently to meaningfully improve UC eligibility rates, Connerly's contention was a form of wishful thinking. That she did not choose to challenge Connerly by pointing to the remarkably low percentage of UC eligible high school graduates from underrepresented populations may be less surprising, given that she was the elected head of California's K–12 system.

VOTING ON THE STUDENT PROPOSAL

At the conclusion of Regent Eastin's remarks, Regent Gomez attempted to substitute the motion prepared by the UC Student Association for the proposals put forward by Regent Connerly. The students' proposal was quite similar to President Peltason's, in that it would have authorized the University of California to continue to implement its existing affirmative action policies. After some discussion of the parliamentary propriety of Gomez's effort, it was agreed by unanimous approval that the board would vote on the students' proposal. A roll call vote was called, and after nine hours of meeting the first vote on a proposal was held. The students' proposal failed by a vote of 18–6. Although only Regents Davis, Carmona, Eastin, Gomez, Gonzales, and Levin voted for the student proposal, it was not a clear referendum on Regent Connerly's proposals, as a number of Regents were waiting for SP-1 and SP-2 to come to a vote before fully committing themselves.

CHANCELLOR TIEN AND GOVERNOR WILSON CLASH

Regent Carmona then asked UC Berkeley Chancellor Chang-Lin Tien to clarify a point. He asked for the admissions matrix Governor Wilson had referred to earlier in the meeting to be placed again on the overhead projector (Figure 6.1). Wilson had claimed, as he had at various press conferences prior to the meeting, that for students with particular combinations of academic and supplemental criteria, Whites and Asian Americans would be denied admission without having had their applications read, while underrepresented students in the same categories would have their applications read, and in some cases be admitted. President Peltason had announced at the June meeting that in the future all applications would be treated in the same fashion. One dispute between Wilson and Tien, and between Wilson and Connerly and UCOP, was based on whether the administration had voluntarily abandoned the differential treatment of applications, or whether they had done so only after Regent Connerly brought attention to the practice. In that light, the dispute revisited the issues of communication and trust that had been a point of contention throughout the deliberations. At that point in the meeting, those simmering issues came to a boil.

Regent Carmona asked Chancellor Tien to comment on the governor's interpretation of the matrix. Chancellor Tien promptly criticized the governor's understanding of the matrix, in measured tones, carefully choosing his words:

> Well, I'm on the spot. With due respect to Governor Wilson, a very strong supportive alumnus of Cal Berkeley, but I must say perhaps due to some miscommunication or misinformation, some of your statements are either outdated or not entirely accurate.[40]

The crowd, still angry from the vote against the students' proposal, vocally expressed their approval of the chancellor, until gaveled to order by the Chair. A number of Regents attempted to declare Chancellor Tien out of order. After some parliamentary wrangling, the chancellor began again:

> I will keep it very short, in fact I'm going to write to the governor, who I admire and I've loved for many years. [41]

The governor interjected, in a voice laden with sarcasm, "Still do, huh?" Chancellor Tien continued:

> But let me keep it very short. The chart here was outdated. That was 1992. Since then we have changed. Every year we review and we correct and refine. And also I want to say, the governor made a big point about our not reading all the files and in fact we have already changed the policy and that was before Regent Connerly's proposal, motion, and orders.
>
> We are going to read all of them and not only that, I want to point out, the reason we couldn't read all of them at Berkeley. We have 23,000 applicants. To read all the essays, not just once, you have to have two people read in order to be fair. To read all of them, due to lack of budgetary support, it's very hard for us to read all of them, that's why we have this process. But now, because we want to be fair and also due to the discussion in the media and so on, we have independently decided to change the practice to read all of them. This was before, I emphasize, before Regent Connerly's motion and before the governor's good suggestion. But we need more support. And I just want to say it's a tough

process. Just look at the chart. To make it fair and also fair to everyone, it's not an easy job. We are doing the best we can, and every year we review. I am the one who actually already took some of the automatic admissions criteria out of the picture. We have improved a lot. And I must say we can still improve and we will continue to improve and with due respect, I was caught on this, I was not prepared. I'm sorry if I feel, if some of you feel, I shouldn't speak that way. But I really love the University. I think we should get on with the right business.[42]

At the time of the meeting, Chancellor Tien was thought by some observers to be on two short lists: one to be the successor to President Peltason as president of the UC system, and the other to be the secretary of energy in the Clinton cabinet. One Regent later noted that he believed Chancellor Tien had already committed to the position of energy secretary, and that his expectation of a new position might explain why he would publicly challenge the governor.

After more parliamentary clarifications, Regent Carmona continued to focus on the effect of Regent Connerly's proposals on the admissions of African Americans and Chicanos to UC. The meeting was now in its tenth hour. Regent Carmona's attention to these issues, in the aftermath of the bomb threat and the crowd's reaction to Chancellor Tien's challenge to the governor, caused a constant stream of interruptions and asides by the tired, irritated members of the board.

Regent Carmona raised a question for Robert Laird, director of admissions at Berkeley, harking back to the debate over the UCOP simulation of admissions patterns:

> What would be the impact of these policies at UC Berkeley specifically in terms of the number of Blacks?[43]

Laird replied:

> The simulations that Berkeley conducted on our Fall 1994 process, everything held the same but minus consideration for race and ethnicity, indicated that the number of African American freshman at Berkeley would decline from 207 which was the actual number to some place between 44 and 74.[44]

Again the crowd had to be gaveled to order. Regent Carmona then concluded his remarks:

> Let us not forget why we took this treacherous path to this day of controversy. As you may recall, last November, Regent Connerly emphasized that the passage of Proposition 187 was a harbinger of things to come. In

Contest, Resistance, and Decision

that same breath, he made reference to that draconian, anti-affirmative action initiative that has yet to qualify for any ballot, or be passed by any state constitutional body. He of course suggested at the time, and now proposes, in my view, the essential elimination of the heart and soul of affirmative action.[45]

WILSON AND TIEN AGAIN

When Carmona finished, the governor reclaimed the floor. He asked for time to respond to the comments made by Chancellor Tien:

> This is a point of personal privilege. Regent Carmona asked the Chancellor to come forward and to make some comments about the template that I had earlier offered into evidence. And the response from the chancellor was that the changes had long ago been made. Let me just ask President Peltason. I will simply make the statement and if he thinks it's inaccurate, he can correct it. On July 10, President Peltason sent a letter to all the Regents. July 10. The attachment to it was his statement about his feelings on affirmative action and his concession that a number of modifications needed to be made. At page two and I quote, his letter reads, "UC Berkeley and UCLA will institute a more comprehensive review of undergraduate's background and qualifications. These campuses currently give a special reading to applications from underrepresented students." This is the key sentence. "In the future, written on July 10, all eligible applicants will go through the same process." That contradicts the chancellor, who, if I understood him, made the point that this has already been done.[46]

Chancellor Tien then responded:

> If I may make two points: This particular matrix is from 1992. I stand on that fact. Second, we had made the decision to read all files before President Peltason's memo. So President Peltason was not wrong.[47]

Governor Wilson demanded:

> You mean he just didn't know?

Tien replied:

> No, he did.

Wilson repeated his question, with some amazement:

> You're telling me the president didn't know this?

To which Tien responded,

> He communicated that this was decided already and from now on that will be instituted. There is no contradiction.

Wilson continued:

> Well, the rest of the Regents were not permitted to share in that knowledge until July 10th. The rest of the Regents did not learn of this until July 10th. And evidently the president felt it necessary to let us know that then because to my knowledge, they had not been informed before that. There is one more thing that I would like to ask and then I would be happy to hear from the President. The third page of this statement, I quote, "in the late 1980's most of our campuses discontinued the practice of granting automatic admission to all eligible undergraduate underrepresented students who applied. UC Davis and UC Irvine are the only remaining campuses, (on July 10th), that automatically admit all eligible underrepresented applicants. Now, they will discontinue the practice."[48]

President Peltason then responded to Governor Wilson:

> I believe that in the case of Berkeley and UCLA they are two separate things. One is what matrix are they using and they have changed that matrix. The prospective thing is that they will in addition to the matrix read all applications. The governor is correct in saying that that is a new thing, reading all applications. I think what the chancellor is referring to was the change in the matrix that they used.[49]

Chancellor Tien then added,

> We decided to read all files independently before Regent Connerly's motion. But that was communicated, but not communicated directly to the president's office, to the Board of Regents. So the governor was correct in that sense. But my statement was also correct. We decided, through our review, to read all files before, independently, before Regent Connerly's motion.[50]

While the governor and Regent Connerly could have left it there, they continued to press the point. Their insistence reflected their anger over their perception of continual information management and poor communication from the Office of the President.

Regent Connerly then requested the floor and began his own line of questioning:

Connerly: Chancellor, in 1994, were you using a form of that matrix for admissions?

Chancellor Tien: Maybe. That was already changed.

Connerly: Were you reading all essays in 1994?

Tien: No, we were not.

Connerly: Okay, did you have a letter from general counsel in March or April of this year after I'd asked for this evaluation advising you that you needed to make the change?

Tien: I don't recall.

Connerly: General Counsel, did you send them a letter?

General Counsel Holst: Yes.

Connerly: So the change you're talking about making is next year, prospective, right.

Tien: Yes, but the decision was made before Regent Connerly's motion.[51]

At that point Chancellor Tien sat down and the meeting continued. The intense exchange between the popular chancellor and the governor over this point represented a microcosm of the broader struggle that enveloped the UC governance and policymaking process. Regent Lee expressed his admiration for Tien in a later interview:

Chancellor Tien is a good friend. I have a lot of respect for him, especially because he is a Chinese American like I am and succeeded through education. I take off my hat to him. On the other hand, he also has his own agenda of what he wants to do. I think he wanted to be the secretary of energy, because he would be the first Chinese American to hold that position in the U.S. government. He really wanted that job. I think he was offered that job; therefore he resigned from UC.

For some reason the nomination was withdrawn on short notice.

He went to Washington for the announcement. Then in the evening things changed. I feel bad for him. I blame Clinton. I was an advisor to Clinton. I believed Clinton was changing on it and I think at the last minute he made the change. I feel bad that Tien became caught up in it.[52]

Next to address the board was Regent John Davies, one of Governor Wilson's most reliable allies on the board. A college friend of the governor's, Davies assisted Wilson in several aspects of his professional and personal life.

His comments reflected the contradictions inherent in the governor's position on SP-1 and SP-2. Davies admitted that eliminating the use of race would lead to a precipitous decline in admissions of underrepresented students. He also asserted that he, like many other Regents, was in favor of diversity. However, he could not, he concluded, give privileges to one group over another on the basis of race. Davies expressed the position this way:

> We then had presentations throughout the first six months of this year on various aspects of the subject of affirmative action. I feel like we've studied it thoroughly and it has been a very difficult process. And what I've learned from that process is that we use race in an impermissible way to govern admissions and contracting and hiring. The proof of it is a statement made here in response to Regent Carmona's question as to what would be the effect at Berkeley of eliminating race as a factor in admissions. It would take the admissions from 207 to 44. If that isn't a significant factor, I don't know what is. That's a dominant factor. And besides that, it's wrong.[53]

Like many of the proponents of SP-1 and SP-2 before him, Davies had announced support for diversity and discomfort with affirmative action. Despite pointing to the potential declines in underrepresented students that would result from the elimination of race as a criterion in admissions, Davies marched rhetorically forward:

> In my opinion, what we've learned is that this tool does more harm than good. I'm determined to find a different way. And I think Regent Connerly's proposal to direct the Academic Senate to develop supplemental factors that can be used, excluding race that will get us a diverse student body, that we should have. And if they can't come up with supplemental factors that will achieve that diversity, then we need new faculty. Because that should not be that difficult. It's not just economic factors. I'm not talking about just economic factors. The whole list of possible supplemental factors. And it would include all the disadvantages that we heard spoken to this morning so eloquently by people who have suffered them. Those factors should be considered. Those are obstacles that are overcome. Those should help people be admitted into the University. But that doesn't mean that it's morally right to award places in the University on the basis of race. So I agree with Regent Leach in that respect. So I support both of Regent Connerly's proposals.[54]

Regent Sue Johnson focused her remarks on the argument that affirmative action promoted group entitlement, rather than individual rights:

> I think what we're looking at is the concept that individuals have different abilities and it doesn't have anything to do with belonging to a race, it's

an individual matter and individual hard work. Does the University of California honor individual hard work as opposed to group membership? Now, I've felt for a long time that some of our race-based preferences are causing a sense of group entitlement or at least an emphasis or notions of group importance superseding almost anything else and causing a separateness. This is something I really regretted seeing. Others on the campuses, and I've talked to different students, tell me I'm off base, but I see it.[55]

Regent Johnson was interrupted by audience comments at that point. Throughout the day, Regents were disrupted by heckling when they deigned to comment on the culture or activities of students, as in the case of Connerly describing stigmas students faced, or Johnson referring to student separateness. After the students were gaveled to order, she concluded:

> At any rate, that is my perception and it's been grievous to me because as I told the students the other day, I'd like to just do away with all hyphenation and have us be not considered as part of a group. This is something I've held long before any political campaigns came along. This is something that I've kind of kept to myself, but since we are talking about this today, and since it's come before the board, I think it's important to vote our conscience and I will be voting for these new ideas and concepts of Regent Connerly.[56]

REGENT SAYLES

Regent Tom Sayles addressed the board from a unique position. He was an African American, appointed by Governor Wilson. Sayles had served as a member of Governor Wilson's administration, and yet he was opposed to Regent Connerly's proposals. During his remarks he presented a personal account of racial discrimination:

> Let me tell you a little bit about my life and who I am. I am obviously an African American and male. I was born and raised in south central Los Angeles, educated at Stanford and Harvard Universities, a lawyer. Had the privilege of serving the governor as a secretary of Business Transportation and Housing. I'm currently a corporate executive and I'm even a Regent. Someone described being a Regent as the closest thing to knighthood in America. Now having heard that over-generous description of who I am, probably some of you around this room are thinking, who is this guy, isn't he living proof that discrimination no longer exists in our society? And the answer is no. I can only tell you that despite the relatively modest success I've had in my life, it does not insulate even me, from racial insult and prejudice.

> This is a personal moment for me. I will tell you that a couple of weeks ago, I had my wife and my two children and we were looking for a new home. And I was in a neighborhood that would be described as upscale and I had my upscale car and my upscale clothes on. And the agent approached me. She was helping another couple. She walked away and said, "I'll be right with you sir." We were clearly within earshot and what she said to the other Caucasian couple is, "this is a great neighborhood, Whites and a few Asians live here." It was so I could hear that.
>
> So let me say to you that while these kinds of experiences are ongoing in my life and they are extraordinarily hurtful, I can handle myself; I'm battle hard and well equipped to defend myself, but we cannot say the same thing for the young men and women seeking to gain entrance to our universities. They simply do not have sufficient armor to protect them from the haunting specter of exclusion. Today when I was preparing for this meeting, I was tempted to bring with me the two men in this world that I love the most. My twelve-year-old son and my 80-year-old father. And that's because thinking about the two of them really solidified my decision to oppose the proposals put forth by my friend and colleague, Ward Connerly. Simply put, our current affirmative action program gives me reason to believe that the life experiences of my son and other minority children like him although undoubtedly touched by racism will involve opportunities for inclusion. On the other hand, the current proposal, particularly SP-1, gives me grave fear that my son and others like him will have life experiences much more akin to my father, where exclusion was the order of the day. In summary, I wish that I had the faith that some of my fellow Regents do, that we've come further, but we haven't and for those reasons I must oppose both proposals.[57]

REGENT LEVIN

The meeting was temporarily halted by the cheering for Regent Sayles's remarks. Afterward the board was addressed by another alumni representative, Regent Levin. She explained to the board why she could not support Regent Connerly and expressed her concern for the political implication of the process:

> My greater concern today, though, is with the process. I know we did begin this discussion some time ago and Regent Davies is correct in stating that. It's an issue that's been before this board for quite a while, we've tried to examine it and understand it and try to get the facts straight and that's not always easy to do in a bureaucracy of this size. But I really fear that it's come to a culmination today in a very unfortuitous manner. We have been thrust into the very center of a political campaign. I resent that and I appreciate the remarks and the counsel given us by Willie

Brown today asking us to remove ourselves from this. I think Regent Carmona has also spoken to that. This is not the appropriate place for us to be making this decision. It is a decision that needs to be made within the family of the University of California. Not in reaction to what is going on in certain political arenas at this time.[58]

Regent Levin concluded her remarks by declaring the UC Alumni Association's support for the position of the Office of the President:

> As stated in a letter from the Alumni Representatives to this Board, we hope that you will delay voting on this issue until we have had a chance to adequately and thoroughly discuss all the aspects of the issue including what we are doing right and what we are doing wrong. We stand in support of President Peltason's recommendations at this time. And as Yori Wada[59] so eloquently and gently stated, "affirmative action is the living symbol of the University of California and the peoples of this state." Let's attend to this issue with all the deliberation and time which it deserves. We must recognize our constitutional responsibility and not place the future of this great university at risk.[60]

REGENT NAKASHIMA

Again the meeting was disrupted by cheering for Regent Levin's remarks. After a long day of testimony and debate, the people in the auditorium opposed to Regent Connerly's proposals were increasingly restless and vocal. When order was restored, Regent S. Stephen Nakashima first denied there was a broader political linkage between SP-1 and SP-2 and the CCRI, and then described his own experiences with discrimination. As a young man, Regent Nakashima had been interned during World War II, and he spoke of affirmative action as a State intervention. Like many other Regents, Nakashima understood affirmative action as a State issue, although his interpretation was somewhat unique. Rather than seeing it as a State effort to redress inequality, Regent Nakashima saw his internment as an example of the State intervening to enforce unequal treatment, and he drew a parallel between that experience and the contemporary affirmative action contest at UC and across the nation.

> Secondly, to all the people in this audience, I'd like to say that you have no monopoly on discrimination. None of you went to an internment camp. You call it internment camp from the outside, but from the inside it's a concentration camp. In 1942 I was taken to Poston, Arizona. I was old enough, had finished two years of junior college and as a result I was a college-educated person and became a teacher and I taught in the high school and the elementary school there for one year. So I know what it

was like. My family, my parents and my brothers and sisters stayed in camp for the full three and a half years. Further, as Asians, we were subjected to the anti-miscegenation laws that did not come off the books until 1950 or '51. An Asian, a Japanese, could not marry a White. Neither could a White marry a Black. We had the Alien Land Law at that time where property could not be purchased by Japanese and it was directed directly at the Japanese because it says anybody ineligible for citizenship and the Japanese were the only ones ineligible for citizenship. Chinese could buy property, but not Japanese. So, don't think that you have a monopoly on discrimination and the problems that come with being a minority.[61]

Regent Nakashima also made the point that there was enough room in the UC system for all qualified students, and suggested that the problems with affirmative action only applied to Berkeley and UCLA. Regent Lee would also later make the point that all UC-eligible students were placed at one of the UC campuses, and, in an ironic twist, this was a point made on a number of occasions by the Office of the President. Nakashima's point that all UC campuses provided quality education is generally agreed upon, but it is also the case that UC Berkeley in 1994 received three times as many applications for admission as did UC Riverside. There was not complete agreement for Nakashima's view that there was equity in being admitted to a UC campus, as opposed to the UC campus of first choice.

REGENT KHACHIGIAN

Regent Meredith Khachigian faced unusual scrutiny as she prepared to speak to the board. Press accounts had suggested that she was one of the few undecided Regents prior to the votes,[62] yet in her comments she quickly dispelled that notion:

Affirmative action policy as currently practiced must be modified. I have heard many speakers say that a vote in favor of SP-1 and 2 is a turn backward. I see it as a move forward. To work toward a society based on individual rights and where rewards are based on individual success. The social effect of affirmative action carried out by legislative edict has created a whole new set of problems in that it stigmatizes minorities. Most of whom have arrived where they have in life because of individual merit, hard work and motivation, not because of preferential treatment. It is time that we look at people as individuals, not as members of an ethnic group that some government agencies decided need special favors in order to compete. Current affirmative action policy undermines the value of personal achievement, is demeaning and creates a cynical view that is unjustified. The current practice of affirmative action has created a stigma that a person belonging to a certain race or nationality got where he or she did simply because someone else decided to give them a break. Not that they earned that position on their own. A recent *Wall Street Journal* article stated, "Left to their own devices, most employers and most universities are going to continue to seek out minorities, not only as a good business practice, most Americans demand it. We disagree with those who say America is fundamentally a racist nation. As a nation, we're now a people that believe in equal opportunity for everyone regardless of race, ethnic group or gender. Redefining affirmative action won't change that."[63]

Regent Khachigian, like Regent Nakashima, invoked State intervention as a negative factor in achieving equality. As several Regents before her had done, she also made the "color-blind" argument that no individual should receive preference on the basis of race. She concluded with a firm commitment to ending affirmative action:

Although I deplore the politicizing of today's discussions I will cast my vote today in favor of SP-1 and 2.[64]

ADMISSIONS PREFERENCES FOR THE CHILDREN AND ALLIES OF REGENTS

An irony of the admission contest was that both Regent Khachigian and Regent Kolligian, outspoken opponents of preferences based on race, seemed to have few problems with preferences for individuals with connections to Regents. Less than two years after the Regents' votes, it would be reported that each had sought preferential treatment for their own children or children of their allies. In the spring of 1996, an article in the *Los Angeles Times* questioned how Kolligian could vote against preferences for underrepresented students but support them for his allies:

"I voted that way because I believe in equal rights," Regent Leo S. Kolligian, a Fresno attorney, said earlier this week about his vote to repeal affirmative action in admissions. "To me, when you give preferential treatment, you're not exercising equal rights. That's not the way I understand the Constitution to be." Yet four months before his vote, confidential records show, Kolligian leaned heavily on UCLA officials to admit the daughter of a Fresno-area builder who had been rejected with a 3.45 grade-point average, a 790 SAT score, and no high school honors classes—by the school's standard, an anemic academic record.

The *Times* article continued:

> The student was admitted and is currently enrolled at UCLA, records show. Meanwhile, the school turned thumbs down on more than 500 other students on their own appealed rejections who had better grades, SAT scores and honor classes than the Fresno applicant, records also show. Kolligian's intervention is all the more noteworthy considering that under current admissions policies, students from rural areas already receive special consideration. In all, the *Times*' investigation found that Kolligian had made 32 such requests to UCLA since he was appointed to the Board of Regents in 1985 by former Gov. George Deukmejian.

With regard to Regent Khachigian, the *Times* reported:

> Khachigian's case struck closer to home, documents show. Her daughter was rejected for the fall 1989 class although she had a 4.0 grade-point average. On March 24, 1989, records show, the Regent called UCLA to ask why and the request was given to John R. Sandbrook, the Chancellor's assistant at the time. Five days later, the rejection was reversed and the girl was offered admission with the fall class, records show. She opted instead to attend George Washington University.[65]

According to the *Times*, among the other Regents who had requested special admissions consideration for applicants were Governor Wilson, Regent Clark, and Regent Burgener, all of whom would vote to eliminate affirmative action at UC, and Regent Bagley.

REGENT MONTOYA

Regent Velma Montoya was also considered to be undecided prior to the meeting. Her remarks were concise and surprising to those who supported SP-1 and SP-2:

> Governor Wilson, Chairman Burgener, President Peltason, I do not favor admitting students based solely on their membership in a group. At the same time, I recognize that first, standardized tests and grades are highly imperfect indicators of future academic success, and second, our studies this spring have demonstrated that today minority students from disadvantaged communities, such as where I grew up in East Los Angeles, typically apply to the college with a lot fewer college enrichment classes than those from affluent non-minority communities. Mainly for these reasons, my view is that UC admissions policy should be that UC consider the applicant as a person, whole person including the applicant's

race, ethnicity and gender. This can provide valuable information that can be used in addition to other information, but not as the only information in the admissions decision. Thank you.[66]

REGENT GONZALES

Regent Gonzales, like Regent Carmona, questioned the details of Regent Connerly's proposals. She directly challenged his proposed alternatives to using race as a criterion, the use of disadvantage and dysfunction. She argued, as she had throughout the debate, that "color-blindness" was a construction of those who would avoid dealing with racism and that in fact, the opponents of affirmative action were offering no viable alternatives. She pointed to the persistence of racism in contemporary society:

> My biggest problem with both of the resolutions is that no one has convinced me to date that we live in a color or gender blind society. When I see Regent Connerly, I still see a Black man. I see a very bright, ambitious man. When you look at me, you still see a Hispanic woman. And I don't want to change that. Race and ethnicity, gender, are still important factors in this system, in this state and this country. Racism still exists and lives among us.[67]

In her closing remarks, Regent Gonzales advocated something akin to President Clinton's "mend it, don't end it" approach:

> We have a policy in place, an affirmative action policy in place. If it is being abused, let us address that. If there are really unqualified persons being admitted, let's change that. I too want those who are qualified to be admitted and only those who are qualified to be admitted. I want the best educated Asians, the best educated Hispanics, the best educated African Americans, the best educated Filipinos, the best educated Native Americans to graduate from our system. I support what many of my colleagues and many of you have said today, the pursuit of equal opportunity. And I want to make sure that that is the final outcome of our vote here today.[68]

FACULTY REPRESENTATIVE SIMMONS

Professor Daniel Simmons, a law professor at UC Davis and one of two faculty representatives to the board, spoke next. While Faculty Representative Simmons offered his personal experiences of admitting students to a UC professional school, he said little about shared governance or the appropriate role of the faculty and the Regents in determining admissions policy.

> First off, I pay my respect to Regent Connerly for his courage in raising these issues, the intellect he's brought to the debate and his true sincerity I believe, in advocating the position that he's advocating. My trouble is, I guess, is that the issue has gotten beyond what is appropriate for the University of California. It's become a football I suppose in presidential politics, and I think that that's a tragedy for the University. Last weekend, or at least the press account I saw Monday, portrayed the governor as attacking the University of California on national television. This morning we heard Assemblyman Richter blatantly insulting the administration of the University of California and on the other side we heard Senator Watson threatening the budget of the University of California. The tragedy in all of this is however this issue comes out, it is the University of California that is now seen at fault.[69]

Regent Simmons's remarks were remarkably restrained, in light of the passion expressed by the representatives of other university constituencies. The general sense of a passivity and distant quality to faculty efforts prior to the July meeting was reinforced by the comments of the faculty representative. Simmons also turned attention to the "pipeline" problem, the low numbers of UC-eligible African American students, and the effect of Regent Connerly's proposals on outreach efforts:

> Remember that there are only about 1,000 African Americans per year graduating from our high schools who are eligible for admission to the University of California. That is a tragedy, but the University of California doesn't have the funding to change that or fix it or probably even the expertise to do that. But if we do away with our ability to affirmatively reach out and bring those kids into the University, including maybe some who aren't UC eligible so we can pick some talent and undo the trouble created by their environment or their schooling or whatever, we're going to lose those kids. And enrollment in our professional schools in spite of what Regent Nakashima says, with which I agree a great deal because some of those kids may be going to other campuses, but enrollment of Hispanics and African Americans will disappear in our professional schools. I'm sorry and I hope I am wrong about this, but I've read too many admissions files and looked at these numbers too often to allow myself to be fooled into thinking otherwise.[70]

REGENT CONNERLY CHALLENGES THE INSTITUTIONAL CULTURE

Perhaps because of the number of challenges to the rather abstract concepts of "disadvantage" and "dysfunction," or the faculty representative's specific questions on what exactly was intended by the supplementary criteria that

SP-1 would substitute for race, Regent Connerly next asked for permission to respond. After that permission was granted by the Chair, Regent Connerly chided the university administration for its unwillingness to change, and issued a challenge to the Academic Senate. He pointed out that the language of his proposals was not definitive or prescriptive, but that it invited the faculty to come up with supplemental criteria, excluding race, that allowed an applicant's individual merit to be measured. This was something he suggested they would be unwilling to do unless forced by the passage of his proposals.

REGENT KOLLIGIAN

The next speaker, Regent Kolligian, began with some reflections on case law and the university's legal risk from offering preferences based on race:

> There is no question in my mind that this will be the most important issue that we will have to decide for the balance of this century. For those who believe that affirmative action in its current form should be continued or be postponed for some indefinite time, let me point out that there is a question I think we ought to keep in mind and that is its constitutionality, which we could be subjecting ourselves to a lengthy and expensive litigation. When unfair preferences are established to admit certain groups based on ethnicity or sex alone as under the present system that we have, it's discriminating, and we could be held to be operating illegally. In a very recent case on this subject decided by the U.S. Court of Appeals in *Brass v. California State Utilities Commission*, the court said, "anyone forced to compete on an unequal basis, that is one not receiving preferential treatment, could be a victim of illegal discrimination." But of course we say on this board that we are doing this to accomplish our goal, therefore it should be okay. In this regard, the court went on to say, "that a program is not immune from court scrutiny just because it is labeled to establish goals rather than quotas. We look to the economic realities of the program rather than the label attached to it." The courts in other cases have recently leaned toward finding against affirmative action and I do hope that we will escape such scrutiny by taking necessary action as soon as possible to avoid any kind of class action or other litigation against us.[71]

Kolligian offered his opinion that socioeconomic status, not race, was a worthy preference, particularly where applicants had overcome social or financial hardship. He concluded with a call for the Regents to be decisive, and back the governor:

> But this issue is for us to decide. We should take the lead and make the decision for the University of California just as we did in the apartheid

cases in South Africa. We didn't wait then, there is nothing to gain by waiting now. This university is the largest, most respected university in the world. Let's act like we deserve that distinction and take the lead and make this decision. The governor has already paved the way issuing his executive order, abolishing preferences in certain cases and has committed himself to this motion. We should support him and vote affirmatively on this motion.[72]

REGENT LEE

Next to speak was Regent David Lee, a businessman who found himself conflicted as the vote approached. His children had attended UC and urged him to preserve affirmative action.

In his remarks to the board, Lee reflected on his own family's experiences with education and discrimination:

When I was a kid, my family had to escape the communist People's Republic of China, the only reason was because my grandfather was a landowner. We were the people's enemy number one. And we escaped by boat to Korea. Then we went to Taiwan. Finally, we were very lucky that Argentina allowed us to emigrate over there. I can tell you, when we went there, it was very difficult, but at the same time we were given the opportunity to live there. I am very thankful to Argentina. For four years we were there. I was going to school, in high school, sometimes I had to work in my father's restaurant. For an Asian, for a Chinese over there, the only opportunity we had was to have a laundry or to have a restaurant. After I graduated from high school, I didn't want to work in a restaurant the rest of my life. Actually, I made a promise to myself I would never work in a restaurant for the rest of my life. So, with this background, I want you to understand, I'm against race, I just dislike people looking at me as a race, I like them to look at me as an individual. I'd like you to judge me as a person; don't look at me as my race. I'm hoping my children, some day, that people will look at them as what they are. Look at their personality. Look at their characters. What we have here, what I would like to ask is this. We as a governing board of this great university, we have the responsibility to give California residents' children equal opportunity to the UC system. When we all talk about equal, what does that mean? If you are poor, there is no color. There are a lot of Asians just as poor as Black as White, as Chicanos. And if there is opportunity, they need as much break as anyone. Therefore, I believe that if we really look, our job is to have the best school, the best students, the best faculty, we have to look at what is of quality. Now, we can put all the things in to justify whatever we want to do, but I dislike putting race as the dominating factor in the whole formula. With that I thank you for your attention.

He concluded:

> I want you to understand this, no matter what happens to today's debate, we have to look at this University, we've got to do everything possible to make it great and also to continue what it stands for, not only in this country, worldwide, this is the most famous university, and well known as the best public school worldwide.[73]

THE PASSAGE OF SP-2

After Regent Lee spoke, there was a call for closure of debate on SP-2. Understanding that they could still debate SP-1 further, the Regents unanimously passed the motion for closure. They then held a roll call vote on SP-2, Regent Connerly's proposal to eliminate affirmative action in UC employment and contracting. The vote passed by a 15–10 margin with Regents Burgener, Campbell, Clark, Connerly, Davies, del Junco, Johnson, Khachigian, Kolligian, Leach, Lee, Montoya, Nakashima, Watkins and Wilson voting "aye," while Regents Bagley, Brophy, Carmona, Davis, Eastin, Gomez, Gonzales, Levin, Peltason, and Sayles voted "no."

It is notable that the issue of employment and business practices never captured the public imagination in the way that admissions had. Although much of the audience reacted unhappily to the vote on SP-2, the audience and the board seemed to be pinning their hopes, and holding their reactions, until after the vote on SP-1.

THE BROPHY AMENDMENT TO SP-1

Regent Connerly then moved SP-1, which was seconded by Regent del Junco. Regent Brophy moved to amend SP-1 in order to forge a compromise around the concept of delaying the implementation of the proposal. He explained his amendment to his fellow Regents this way:

> Paragraph two is a brand new paragraph and it says, "The president, with the consultation of the Board of Regents and the Academic Senate, shall appoint a task force to evaluate the impact of the measures proposed in this resolution." That would include faculty, staff, students, the public and other involved people. "The task force would also evaluate other alternatives to current admissions practices." So we'll be sure what we're talking about. "The task force will report the results of its evaluation at the November, 1996 meeting of the Board."
>
> Now, here's what it means. It means that if we vote today and vote my amendment, then we will have an opportunity of 16 months between now

and the November meeting of 1996. We will vote this on as an amendment. But there is one twist to it. We will vote again, revisit the proposal at the Board meeting in November of 1996.[74]

Brophy also addressed the future of shared governance:

> This proposal also permits full consultation with the faculty, which has not been done until now. And the faculty has traditionally played the major role on advising on academic matters including admission policies. Reaffirming the principle of shared governance is especially important in the light of the significant sacrifices the faculty has made, they've hung in with us during this budget crisis taking no raises for three years and now we're short-cutting the shared governance performance on this particular issue by voting it out today or not voting it out today. It's my hope, and I know President Peltason shares it, that this proposal can bring most of us together and avoid the deep rifts between Regents and between Regents and others in our community.[75]

Regent Brophy had long been an acknowledged leader in California higher education governance, having served both as a state community college trustee and a trustee of the California State University system prior to joining the UC Regents. He also had been a leader in the state Republican Party, though he admitted that his stance on SP-1 and SP-2 cost him that status:

> I don't believe in political intrusion into the operation of public education whether it be K–12 or community colleges or universities or state colleges or whatever. And I stood against the governor on those things—not against the governor—I was his campaign chairman twice for senator in this part of the state, and I was with Reagan three times and Deukmejian twice, so I'm a good Republican. But the Republicans don't believe I'm a good Republican now because I didn't take the party line.[76]

ALL IN FAVOR

Brophy's remarks were followed by a great deal of parliamentary discussion of his amendment. Before the amendment could be voted on, Regent Levin substituted President Peltason's motion for the Brophy amendment. There was a motion call and a vote on the Peltason motion.

The motion was read to the board as follows:

> That the president be instructed to develop, in consultation with the Academic Senate, appropriate changes in undergraduate, graduate, and professional school policies governing admissions; these policies to take effect

on or before January 1, 1997 should state or federal law be changed to prohibit consideration of race, ethnicity, and/or gender. Further, that the president be instructed to increase, over a three-year period, the funds made available for student academic development activities. Funds for expansion of these activities would combine additional moneys obtained through the state budget and private moneys from employers and others with an interest in a well-trained, well-educated workforce.[77]

After nearly a year of deliberation and negotiation, this was the only alternative to Regent Connerly's proposals that the Office of the President would bring to a vote of the board. It was a proposal to preserve the status quo, unless the CCRI should become state law. In that event, UCOP and the Academic Senate would retain control over any modifications necessitated by the passage of the ballot initiative.

A roll call vote was taken and the motion was defeated 11–14, with Regents Bagley, Brophy, Carmona, Davis, Eastin, Gomez, Gonzales, Levin, Montoya, Peltason, and Sayles voting "aye," Regents Burgener, Campbell, Clark, Connerly, Davies, del Junco, Johnson, Khachigian, Kolligian, Leach, Lee, Nakashima, Watkins, and Wilson voting "no."

Regent Watkins then called for the question on the Brophy amendment. At that point audience members, including a contingent from the Coalition to Defend Affirmative Action by Any Means Necessary, began shouting and standing at their seats. Though Board Chair Burgener, Reverend Jackson, and others called for the protesters to sit down and let the meeting continue, their entreaties were to no avail. The protesters began singing "We Shall Overcome," and the Regents left the room. The protesters remained, awaiting the Regents' return.

THE OPEN MEETING LAW

At 8 p.m. the Regents reconvened in a private room above the auditorium. Their initial discussion revolved around whether they could conduct business out of the view of the public. Under the Bagley-Keene Open Meeting Act and the Brown Act, the Regents were allowed to conduct policy discussions and votes out of sight of the public if it was judged impossible or dangerous to conduct those discussions in public. Many of the Regents pushed for concluding their business in private, arguing that it would be impossible to continue in the main auditorium without further interruption. Reverend Jackson pressed for the Regents to return downstairs; Student Regent Gomez assured the Regents there would be a lawsuit if votes were taken in the private room. Regent Bagley (coauthor of the Open Meeting law) advised the Regents to return downstairs. Chair Burgener called for a vote of the Regents on where best to continue the meeting.

The following exchange took place, a conversation that revealed much about the group's attitudes concerning public access to policymaking:

Reverend Jackson: Can we have a chance to go back down and make an appeal to people down there to hear this process out?

Governor Wilson: You can do as you please, Reverend Jackson. I think we are obliged to do the public's business without further delay.

Regent Levin: Can you do the public business? Is this a violation?

Governor Wilson: No it isn't.

Regent Levin: Are you very sure?

Governor Wilson: Yes.

Reverend Jackson: Governor, can we go downstairs and make an appeal for order, to conduct that meeting before the public audience?

Governor Wilson: Reverend Jackson, we need to get on with the business. You, yourself have said it is chaotic. You have heard that there is no guarantee, indeed you said, and I thank you for your candor, that there is no guarantee that there will not be further disruptions because there's certainly no unanimity. I take that report at face value. I thank you for it. I think we are compelled to get on with the public's business.

Reverend Jackson: There's never any guarantees. The public is down there locked into a room. These are your students.

Governor: The public is 31 million people. This is a handful. Frankly, I think that they have indicated this afternoon that they can't conceive of anybody dealing with them in good faith. Most Californians can't.

Regent Burgener: I'm going to have counsel read the section, please Jim Holst read that.

General Counsel Holst: Governor Wilson, the Bagley-Keene Act says, "In the event any meeting is willfully interrupted by a group or group of persons so as to render the orderly conduct of such meeting unfeasible, and order cannot be restored by the removal of individuals who are willfully interrupting the meeting, the state body conducting the meeting may order the meeting room cleared and continue in session. My own observation at the moment is that I have a question of fact as to whether or not the meeting room is safe and whether or not anybody there who is disrupting the situation can be removed, so as to continue the meeting in a room where a maximum number of the public can be in attendance.

Reverend Jackson: I think we need to understand from those who are responsible for law enforcement there as to what the circumstances are.

Regent Gomez: I believe last month we had this whole thing put out before the Regents, on how we were to address these kinds of issues. The public was supposed to be warned three times, etc., etc., and I think we had a whole session on that, did we not? Does anybody not remember that? I wrote it all down.

Governor Wilson: Did the warnings contemplate an actual demonstration of the kind that's just occurred?

Gomez: They just talked about if there was public disruption, how they were to attend it and I'm just wondering if we followed those. That's all I'm asking.

Governor Wilson: I think with all respect, what you've just seen qualifies as a disruption.

Regent Gomez: Yes.

President Peltason: I would just suggest that we ask those who are not members of the Board to please take your seats so that the Board can deliberate and the Board needs to make a decision. I think the first decision is that whether or not, where they want to have that meeting and I think they've heard from their security officer and I think they ought to vote up or down and get on with the business.

Regent Bagley: The security officer seemed to indicate that we could safely return to the room.

Regent Gomez: Could we have the security officer state his opinion as to the safety of conducting this meeting in the originally scheduled room.

Governor Wilson: Let me point out that it isn't simply just a question of security. I don't think people are concerned particularly with their security. What we are a little tired of is being unable to complete the business of a duly noticed meeting. A public meeting, because it has been deliberately disrupted. That is what I think cannot be guaranteed, that we are not going to be disrupted again. I think that even though these are conscientious people, it is asking a good deal of them to simply ask them to continue a meeting that is now many hours long, one that has been disrupted. This contingency room was set up in anticipation of precisely the kind of disruption that would prohibit our going forward in that location. So I think that the time has come to do the public's business without further delay.

General Counsel Holst: I'd just like to say one more word, and that is with all due respect to the concerns that are expressed, that the test I think is whether or not that room can be made suitable both from a safety standpoint and from the standpoint of conducting orderly business. And the issue is if there are those there who are disrupting, can they be removed without an overwhelming effort. And if so, I believe the Bagley-Keene Act provision points to continuing the meeting in the room in which it was originally scheduled and more than that, the room in which the members of the public who are not disrupting have the maximum potential for being there.

Bagley: If we were to stay here, I think we ought to make a record, a finding of fact if you will, some kind of a record that we've observed what we've observed and we don't believe that we could continue to conduct, make some kind of record.

Regent del Junco: I think that we have to do what Bill said and number two, I think we have to understand that if we start removing people from that scene, we're going to provoke a serious problem. It's very provocative to go down there and start arresting these young students. This is our experience in the past.

Regent Burgener: I think Reverend, you're going to have to let us run our meeting now.

Reverend Jackson: UC students have a right to demand that the meeting be conducted in accordance with state law. Now if the legal counsel has stated that the room must be able to be, cannot be secured, then you are able to take alternate measures. The police officers already stated the room can be secured.

Regent Gomez: For the record, the public was never even instructed to sit down. Nobody even said would you please sit down.[78]

The Regents then held a vote on whether they felt the auditorium was secure enough for them to return there to conclude their public session. The vote was 14–11 in favor of staying in the contingency room, out of the public view.

CHANCELLOR YOUNG

The board resumed discussion of the Brophy amendment to delay implementation of the policy change, the discussion that had been interrupted by the audience outburst. Chair Burgener asked Chancellor Young of UCLA and Provost Massey to add their comments for the record. Chancellor Young, who had been chancellor at UCLA for over twenty-five years, spoke first:

As I said, I had planned not to speak, but I and my colleagues, the chancellors, decided that this was such an important issue for the University of California that we needed to put concisely and clearly before you our views on this matter even though you may have heard them before. As you consider your action today, it is important to start with an understanding of the public policy mission of the University of California. We believe, that is, the chancellors believe, that an essential element of that mission is the necessity to educate the next generation of leaders for a multi-cultural society. We have a duty to produce not just well educated professionals, but well educated professionals who can serve a diverse society and succeed in a multi-cultural environment. We also want to make it clear that we believe it is necessary to continue the excellence of the University of California. And we believe again that affirmative action does not as many have argued here today reduce excellence. A diverse student body serves all of its members better than one which is non diverse in its make up. It increases the excellence of the educational process.[79]

Chancellor Young then spoke at some length about the ways in which affirmative action benefited society, and the ways in which a diverse student body had improved the University of California. He concluded with a plea for moderation:

We should and can achieve diversity on our campuses while not violating the rights of individuals. We can properly take race, gender and ethnicity into account as long as we do not fall into the utilization of quotas or set asides or other deleterious kinds of actions in that process. If improper actions have been taken in the name of affirmative action, let us work together to modify or eliminate those actions as proposed by President Peltason and his recommendation to you today. But we urge you to vote today to retain the tools that will enable us to continue along the path to diversity for the good of the University of California and our society as a whole.[80]

PROVOST MASSEY

Provost Walter Massey followed Chancellor Young. A month prior to the votes, Provost Massey had announced he was leaving his position to take over as president of Morehouse College. His message embodied the philosophy espoused throughout the deliberations by the Office of the President, and his personal reflections on race. He also concluded with one of the strongest claims of the day for Regental deference to the recommendations of the administrators in the Office of the President and on the campuses, and he spoke directly to the question of a "stigma" from affirmative action:

It seems to me the primary difference of opinion is whether or not race matters in the United States. Unfortunately, race still matters in the United States. Having been raised in the rigidly segregated society of pre-60's Mississippi, I would attest that my desire and hope for a color-free society is as strong, as sincere as anyone's. If I believed that race-conscious programs of the type we have at this university were imperiling or even derailing that goal of a color-free society, I would be against them, but on the contrary I believe that these kinds of efforts are an important vehicle in helping us to create a society where race may not matter, at least as much as it does now.

Several speakers have spoken about the stigmatism that comes from affirmative action programs. The idea that affirmative action is a primary cause of White and other groups having particular views about the competency of Blacks is a bizarre concept. It certainly has little basis in American history. The notion that having a perception of advantage due to affirmative action is more stigmatizing than drinking from colored only fountains, being refused service at restaurants and stores, riding on the backs of buses, witnessing lynchings and beatings is a strange notion indeed. You may vote and it's fairly clear how you may vote today, but I assure you, however you vote, it will do little to stigmatize or lower the self esteem of most of us who are Black.

The other reason, and I will finish, I hope you will consider is that the leadership of this university whom you have asked to guide it, believes that these policies are in the best interest of the University of California. These policies do benefit underrepresented groups. They do contribute to the broader goals of the state of California to have an educated, diverse citizenry capable of working together to generate increased standards of living for all of its citizens. But these programs in a very narrow sense have been good for the University of California. Contrary to several assertions, measurable rates of quality such as time to degree, attrition, number of students attending graduate school, graduation rates, and the like have not decreased as diversity has increased. In fact they have been enhanced. The bar has not been lowered for students, but the bar has been raised for the university as a whole.

The chancellors, each and every one of them, all of the vice presidents, the faculty leaders and student leadership are committed to love and understand this university. Their arguments to you to continue these programs do not come from narrow, self-serving personal agendas, but out of the sincere concern and love for the University. And this group of leaders is not monolithic in their backgrounds or views on hardly any other issues. We are a diverse group. Women, Asian Americans, Black, White, and from various disciplinary backgrounds. I hope that you would agree with me, and I will be leaving, that as the governing board for this institution, that it should require an extraordinary degree of commitment to a different perspective and an extraordinary degree of certainty about the outcome to reject such a united recommendation from the leadership of the institution that you have chosen. Some of you no doubt have such a certainty of outcome and a commitment. I respect that point of view. But for those of you who may be uncertain, just a bit, I would hope that you would see fit to allow the university to retain these programs. Thank you.[81]

At the conclusion of Provost Massey's remarks, Regent Bagley moved the question on the Brophy amendment. A roll call vote was held, and the Brophy amendment failed by a vote of 14-10. Regents Bagley, Brophy, Carmona, Davis, Eastin, Gomez, Gonzales, Levin, Montoya, and Peltason voted "aye," while Regents Burgener, Campbell, Clark, Connerly, Davies, del Junco, Johnson, Khachigian, Kolligian, Leach, Lee, Nakashima, Sayles, Watkins, and Wilson voted "no."

THE PASSAGE OF SP-1:
THE END OF AFFIRMATIVE ACTION AT UC

After meeting for twelve hours, the Regents were finally ready for the vote on SP-1. Regent del Junco offered to move the question on SP-1. Regent Connerly, mindful of Regent Bagley's threat to call for reconsideration, which would have carried the matter over at least thirty days without resolution, offered the amendment that Regent Connerly, Regent Bagley, and Governor Wilson had drafted while the Brophy amendments were being discussed by the full board. The amendment essentially codified the university's commitment to outreach and other programs designed to help diversify the student body. The amendment, which was appended to both SP-1 and SP-2, read as follows:

> Believing California's diversity to be an asset, we adopt this statement: Because individual members of all of California's diverse races have the intelligence and capacity to succeed at the University of California, this policy will achieve a University of California population that reflects this state's diversity through the preparation and empowerment of all students in this state to succeed rather than through a system of artificial preferences.[82]

The full texts of SP-1 and SP-2 as amended[83] were then put up for a roll call vote. Regents Burgener, Campbell, Clark, Connerly, Davies, del Junco, Johnson, Khachigian, Kolligian, Leach, Lee, Nakashima, Watkins, and Wilson voted "aye." Regents Brophy, Carmona, Davis, Eastin, Gomez, Gonzales, Levin, Montoya, Peltason, and Sayles voted "no." Regent Bagley abstained. The amended text of SP-1 and SP-2 was therefore approved 14-10. The University of California had become the first university system in America to eliminate the use of race and gender as a consideration in admissions, hiring, or contracting. The board adjourned at 8:35 p.m.

One Regent recalled later going to dinner with some UC administrators after the votes, and described their reaction this way:

> We basically sat and cried because we saw that this was a great harm that was done to the University of California.[84]

Governor Wilson was reportedly angry that the delay in passing SP-1 had caused him to miss appearing live on the 11 p.m. evening news on the East Coast. He would more than make up for that in the morning when he would make appearances on nearly every national news program to herald the victory.

8

Aftermath

The reaction to the Regents' votes was swift in coming. Just days after the votes, White House chief of staff and former California congressman Leon Panetta stated that the federal government would reevaluate nearly $4 billion in funding to UC, and indicated that the government might withdraw that funding in light of the Regents' votes. Panetta's comment reflected a desire shared by many of the university's political allies, although the White House officially retrenched from Panetta's comments later in the week, asserting,

> Please be assured that the president is not interested in taking punitive action against the University of California for its ill-considered change in policy.

The letter, from White House counsel Abner Mikva also criticized the Regents for "using the University of California as a pawn in a political battle."[1]

FACULTY MOBILIZE

The votes also mobilized faculty activism. A petition calling for the Regents to rescind their votes was circulated on campuses and via the Internet. It was ultimately signed by over 1,800 faculty members and submitted to the Regents. The academic senates of each of the nine campuses also met in fall 1995 and voted overwhelmingly to call upon the Regents to rescind SP-1 and SP-2. The total vote of the nine campus academic senates was 593–37 in favor of requesting the Regents to rescind their votes. At the September meeting of the board, Faculty Representative Simmons presented a detailed report on shared governance. At the meeting in January 1996, over three hours of testimony were presented to the board by some twenty UC faculty, including Jerome Karabel.

In November 1995, the American Association of University Professors convened a commission to study the Regents' decision to end existing affirmative action policies. The AAUP report concluded the Regents had violated well-established principles of shared governance and urged the board to rescind the votes. The report noted the following:

In this case the issue was dealt with in a partisan political manner that appears to have promoted the interest of a particular candidate and party.[2]

STUDENT RESISTANCE

Students also showed renewed resistance in the wake of the Regents' votes, working to undo the Regents' actions on a number of levels. A group of students and student journalists from UC Santa Barbara filed a lawsuit against the Regents, hoping to persuade a state superior court that Governor Wilson and the Regents had violated the state's open meeting laws by discussing the issue in private prior to the July meeting. The lawsuit also contended that the Regents had further violated the law by voting outside of the public view after leaving the auditorium at the July meeting.

Throughout the fall semester after the vote, student organizations held protests at each of the UC campuses. Over 5,000 students rallied in October at UC Berkeley. On that day, many classes were effectively closed by a student-organized "affirmative action walk-out." Students blocked classrooms and administrative offices, and were arrested at nearly every campus and at protests outside the September and October Regents' meetings. A group of UC Irvine students received national attention for a hunger strike that lasted nearly three weeks. The hunger strikers led a protest rally at the governor's office in Sacramento and blocked the office of State Senator Bernie Richter, a leading proponent of efforts to eliminate affirmative action. During the December meeting of the Regents, fifty-nine students were arrested after they blocked a UC Berkeley administration building.

Much of the student effort was also directed at opposing the campaign to place the CCRI on the ballot. Each campus student association hosted "teach-ins" to organize student resistance to the CCRI and support for alternative ballot proposals.

CHANCELLORS RESIGN

Another significant set of changes occurred in the wake of the Regents' votes, as over the next eighteen months four chancellors resigned from their positions. None of the chancellors directly linked their resignations to the events surrounding SP-1 and SP-2. However, some observers suggested that Chancellor Chang-Lin Tien at Berkeley and Chancellor Charles Young at UCLA both left their campuses earlier than they might otherwise have done had they not taken particularly active roles in the defense of affirmative action. UC San Diego Chancellor Richard Atkinson was hired to replace the outgoing President Peltason, and Chancellor Karl Pister retired from his post at UC Santa Cruz. Taken together, it meant that within two years of the Regents' votes, nearly half of the chancellors had left their positions.

OFFICE OF THE PRESIDENT

The UC Office of the President was also the center of renewed conflict in the aftermath of the passage of SP-1 and SP-2. Incoming university President Atkinson had opposed SP-1 and SP-2, while serving as chancellor of UC San Diego. President Atkinson announced in January 1996 that the university might not be able to implement the new admissions policies mandated by SP-1 and SP-2 in the time frame provided for by Regent Connerly's measures. Governor Wilson and ten Regents promptly called a special meeting of the board with the intention of either forcing President Atkinson to comply with the letter of SP-1 and SP-2, or face dismissal.[3] Atkinson then retreated in letters to the board and the governor:

> There is no question in my mind that it is the constitutional duty of the Board to set policy for the University, and the role of the president is to implement that policy. I have a legal duty as well as a moral obligation to do so.[4]

The implications of this conflict for shared governance at the university were not lost on the faculty or the state legislature. UC Berkeley Professor Emeritus Charles Schwartz, one of the organizers of the faculty petition to rescind SP-1 and SP-2, described Atkinson's situation this way:

> In July, Connerly, with a little help from his friend, scored a resounding political victory. Since then, as the former chancellor and new president Dick Atkinson, along with his circle of advisors, must have been aware, Connerly has been sharp to respond to any challenge, coming from the faculty or from Regents who voted against him in July. And in so doing he has staked out the extreme position that there is no such thing as shared governance between Regents and faculty, and that while the Regents should consult fully with the faculty through the established channels of the Academic Senate, power and authority resides only with the Regents. What has now occurred, in this recent bout with Atkinson, is that Connerly has succeeded in forcing the president to acknowledge the absolute supremacy of the Regents over the administration.[5]

The Democrats in the state legislature were also quick to react, with the Chair of the Senate Committee on Higher Education scheduling hearings to evaluate the university's governance system. Lt. Governor Davis suggested,

The whole episode was an embarrassment to the University and Dick Atkinson. The Regents who backed the ban have shoved the University to the brink in order to advance their political agendas and run a very real risk of alienating and possibly losing our brand new president.[6]

THE WILSON CAMPAIGN FOR THE PRESIDENCY

In the wake of the Regents' votes, the Wilson campaign for the Republican presidential nomination received an initial infusion of attention and capital. Ten days after the votes, the *Los Angeles Times* reported the following:

> These are the days Wilson's campaign has been waiting for. For months it has been left to wallow in obscurity because of a series of setbacks, controversies and bad luck. Finally, Wilson enjoyed a politically therapeutic spotlight that portrayed him nationwide as the conservative point man challenging the forces of Clinton and Jesse Jackson. As a result, Wilson fund-raisers last week predicted a resurgence in their slumping effort to raise campaign money. And in key states such as Iowa and New Hampshire, organizers said the week could pay off in places where voters know very little about the California governor.[7]

It was not to be. The orchestration of the Regents' votes was the high water mark of the governor's presidential campaign, and over the ensuing months he failed to win a single primary before pulling out of the contest.

CCRI/PROPOSITION 209

One of the primary beneficiaries of the publicity and attention drawn by the Regents' deliberations over SP-1 and SP-2 was the campaign to place the CCRI on the California ballot. Less than a month after the Regents' votes, the CCRI, which a year earlier had failed to receive enough signatures to reach the ballot, was again filed. Within three months it had received nearly half of the 700,000 signatures needed to place the initiative on the ballot. The requisite signatures were received, thanks in no small measure to the installation of Ward Connerly as chair of the campaign.[8] The CCRI was soon thereafter placed on the November 1996 state ballot as Proposition 209. The initiative, which prohibited the use of race and gender in the operation of California public employment, public education, or public contracting, passed in November 1996, with 55% of the votes cast.

The passage of 209 was considered a significant victory for California governor Pete Wilson and the state Republican Party, and an equally significant blow to the state and national Democratic parties (Pusser, 2001; Chavez, 1998). Over the next two years a number of significant political events were shaped by the Regents' votes and Proposition 209, but not precisely as expected by those who orchestrated the Regents' votes. Key political actors in California that supported 209 suffered unprecedented losses in the November 1998 elections. Voters elected a Democratic governor for the first time in sixteen years, increased their majority in the State Senate and Assembly, and also claimed the lieutenant governorship, the attorney general's office, and the superintendent of instruction post. Under new governor Gray Davis, who opposed 209 and voted to preserve affirmative action as a UC Regent, Democrats placed the effort to increase access and diversity in the state's higher education systems near the top of their legislative agenda.

ADMISSIONS WITHOUT AFFIRMATIVE ACTION

An event that garnered considerable national attention from the higher education community, as a result of the Regents' votes, came two years later. In the summer of 1997, UC professional schools announced the composition of the first admissions classes at UC constructed without the use of race or gender as an admissions criterion. The decline in minority admits was startling. As one example, of the 792 offers of admission from UC Berkeley's school of law (Boalt Hall), 14 were extended to African Americans and 23 to Chicanos. This constituted a decrease of 81% in the number of African American admits and a drop of 48% in the number of Chicano admits (Guerrero, 2002; Pusser, 2001). Similar declines occurred across the system's law schools, and at the UC medical and business schools as well. The dean of Boalt, Herma Hill Kay, accompanied the release of the statistics with this comment:

> This dramatic decline in the number of offers of admission made to non-Asian minority applicants is precisely what we feared would result from the elimination of affirmative action at Boalt. When I testified before the Board of Regents in May of 1995, I opposed the proposed resolution banning affirmative action in admissions and explained that such a resolution would make an enormous difference in the composition of our student body. The students and faculty at Boalt Hall have obtained great educational benefit from the racial diversity of our student body. Moreover our minority graduates have made significant contributions to the legal profession. I deeply regret that Boalt's offers of admission to minority applicants have dropped so sharply. We must do everything we can to encourage those students of color who are admitted to Boalt Hall to accept our offers of admission.[9]

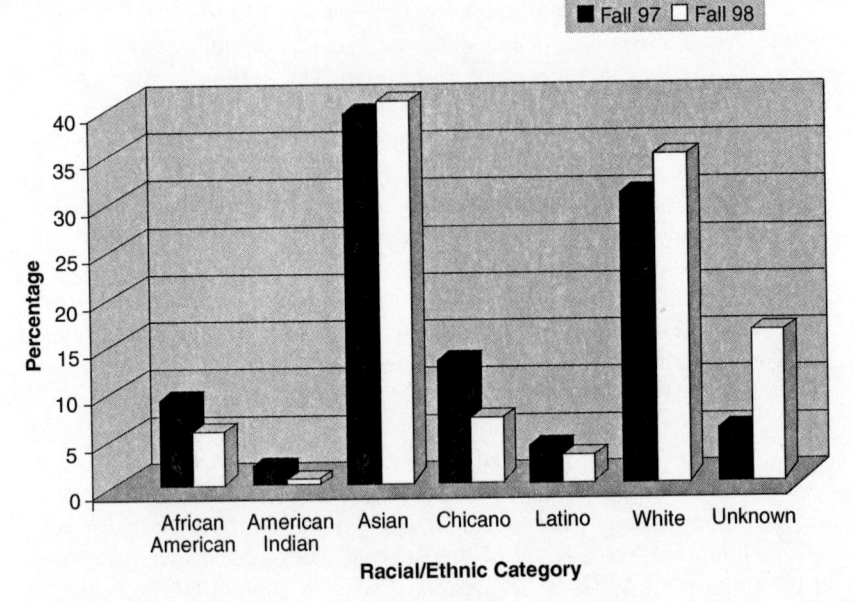

Figure 8.1. UC Berkeley Enrollment. (Source: UC Berkeley Office of Student Research Data Tables).

The bad publicity surrounding Boalt's admissions was just beginning. None of the fourteen African Americans admitted to Boalt in that first class after SP-1 and SP-2 chose to accept the offer of admission. The only African American who joined the admissions cohort for 1997 was a student who had been admitted a year earlier and deferred admission. The Boalt numbers and similar declines for the other UC professional schools recalled a remark Reverend Jackson made in his address to the Regents on the day of the votes. He had suggested that the "quota" the Regents should be concerned about was a "zero quota" of African American students in UC's professional schools that would result from the elimination of affirmative action. The UC professional school admissions numbers were reported across the nation and around the world.

A year later the system received another shock when the first UC undergraduate admissions cohort was selected without using race as a criterion in admissions (Figure 8.1). At the Berkeley campus, the number of admitted Chicano/Latino applicants fell from 1,266 in 1997 to 601 in 1998, a drop from 14% to 7% of the total admit cohort, while the African American numbers fell from 562 to 191, from 7% to 3% of the total admit cohort. At UCLA, Chicano/Latino admits dropped from 1,512 to 999, from 15% to

10% of the total admit cohort, and African American admits fell from 524 to 291, from 5% to 3% of the total admit cohort. The number of Asian Americans and Whites at both campuses increased substantially, as did the number of admitted students who declined to state their ethnicity. One experienced UC admissions officer suggested that most of those who did not declare a race were White or Asian American.[10] While the other UC campuses experienced declines, they were not as dramatic as those found at UC Berkeley and UCLA.[11]

The release of the undergraduate numbers again led to intense political debate and the convening of legislative committees to investigate the UC admissions process. While proponents of affirmative action took stances similar to Dean Kay's, opponents suggested that the declines demonstrated the degree to which the university had been using race as a factor in the admissions process.

WHAT THE REGENTS WROUGHT

As a result of the passage of SP-1, SP-2, and Proposition 209, a number of policy and process shifts have taken place with significant implications for California and other states. Three deserve particular attention: shifts in board confirmation dynamics, increased resource allocation for outreach based on educational disadvantage, and new methods for determining eligibility and admissions policy.

The shift in legislative attention to the confirmation dynamic began in earnest in 1997, when Governor Wilson nominated then chair of the Regents Tirso del Junco for a second twelve-year term. The subsequent challenge to del Junco has been linked to the Regents' votes on SP-1 and SP-2, to Proposition 209, and to an awakening on the part of the Senate Democrats to the importance of the Regents in broader state political contests (Chavez, 1998; Pusser, 2001, 2003). The question of whether the Republican Party had used the Regents to help advance its own political agenda, particularly the passage of Proposition 209, was at the heart of the confirmation hearing for Dr. del Junco.

While no witnesses had appeared in opposition to Dr. del Junco at his original confirmation hearing in 1986, more than a dozen witnesses representing a variety of interest groups opposed Dr. del Junco on the first day of the 1997 hearings. Witnesses at the del Junco hearings protested the Regents' votes on affirmative action, the role of Regents in passing Proposition 209, the apparent abrogation of shared governance on the board, and the politicization of the Regents. Dr. del Junco was called to account for all of those issues, and Senate Democrats prevented his renomination. What had once been a deferential and relatively invisible confirmation process had turned into an elaborate, contentious and very public battle.

The position of the Republicans on the Rules Committee was that citizen del Junco had a constitutional right to express himself away from the Regents in any way he saw fit, and that he could be also a nonpartisan figure in his role as a Regent. Committee Chair Lockyer summed up the Democrats' position this way:

> Dr. del Junco was a Regent when he chose to be Chair of the California Republican Party, when he chose to sign a lot of questionable attack mail pieces sent against my colleagues. Now, that wasn't somebody who had much regard for the non-political role of Regents. You know, I've had colleagues say to me in the Senate, "I've never met this guy. I don't know him. The only thing I know about him is when I was running for the Senate mail landed in my district, attacking me personally that was inaccurate, and it was signed by him as Chair of the Republican Party." So that's all I know about him. I'm voting no for that reason.

After a brief interuption, Senator Lockyer concluded:

> So the point is this, sir. You come to us and say, "don't be political." The politics started there, not here. That's the point. We don't need to debate it.[12]

Regent del Junco had a very different view of his confirmation hearing, describing it as a "political assassination," and calling for a return to a less contentious process.

> You know, theoretically you would like to have a system the way you have it now— if politics would not play a major role. By that I mean the type of politics that was brought upon me. In other words, you would allow for independent intellectual thinking. Because it's very important that the Regents feel free to express sincere opinions of what they think has to be done. The preservation of that constitutional right is so, so important.[13]

The shift to a contested confirmation dynamic continued through the remainder of Governor Wilson's term of office. Three Wilson nominees who had not been on the board at the time of the votes on SP-1 and SP-2 were forced off the board in 1997, when the Rules Committee chair refused to schedule hearings on their nominations prior to the expiration of their initial one-year appointments.[14] That led to these sentiments from Regent John Davies:

> Chairman Davies expressed his confidence that Governor Davis would appoint outstanding replacements for the outgoing Regents, but he also

pointed out that their departure represents a genuine loss for the University. He suggested that the failure on the part of the Senate to confirm appointments is a disturbing trend which should not continue, representing as it does a politicalization of appointments to the Board.[15]

After the election of Governor Gray Davis in November 1998, two more Wilson nominees were rejected by the Senate. Using the appointment power of Governor Davis and its solid control of the legislature, the California Democratic Party significantly reshaped the board. By the beginning of Governor Davis's second term (January 2003), only five Regents who had voted on SP-1 and SP-2 remained on the board. Of the eighteen appointed Regents on the board on January 1, 2003, seven were Democrats.

The long-term effects of SP-1 and SP-2 and Proposition 209 continue to shape California politics and its higher education policies. In the aftermath of the Regents' votes, the norms of confirmation dynamics and State Senate oversight of admissions policies, tuition prices, and labor negotiations have shifted, with the legislature taking an increasingly prominent role. Further, state Republican efforts to end affirmative action at the university and the party's role in the passage of Proposition 209 appear to have subsequently weakened its standing overall, as evidenced by the California Democratic Party's dramatic victories in 1998 (Chavez, 1998; Schrag, 1998b).

LEGISLATIVE POLICY RESPONSES

The decline in minority admissions to UC's undergraduate and professional programs also prompted strong reactions in the state capitol. In remarks prepared for a State Senate hearing on access, Senator Teresa Hughes wrote:

> If such enrollment numbers continue to persist, California will move toward a segregated society with non-college educated Blacks and Latinos filling the underclass and Whites and Asians disproportionately represented in middle and upper classes.[16]

The State Senate and Assembly Higher Education committees held hearings on a number of issues related to access, eligibility, admissions requirements, outreach, and coordination. The post–SP-1 and SP-2 challenge to increase diversity through outreach and intersegmental coordination was translated by the legislature into new legislation and increased financial commitments. Successful legislation included a bill that established regional academic partnerships between school districts and the three higher education segments to support K–12 school improvement. Funds were earmarked for students in high schools where the percentage of graduates enrolling in public universities was below the state average, and the bill required notification of the parents of all eighth grade students in those schools of the course prerequisites for university admission. Other bills provided $10 million in matching funds for school districts to provide low-income high school students with college admission test preparation, and funding to enable school districts to waive advanced placement examination fees for economically disadvantaged students. Legislation also created new summer academies to increase math and science training for high school students in disadvantaged communities. Increases in state funding included over $30 million for UC outreach programs (Pusser, 2001).

NEW APPROACHES TO ADMISSIONS CRITERIA

Along with their contribution to the passage of Proposition 209, and in shifting the political awareness of higher education in California, SP-1 and SP-2 have had another critical effect on California higher education: the reshaping of UC admissions criteria. As was the case with outreach, a number of factors, including the publication of CPEC's 1996 eligibility report and the drop in minority enrollments, also built legislative interest in the criteria shaping eligibility to UC.

Senator Teresa Hughes, chair of the California Senate's Select Committee on Higher Education Admissions and Outreach, concluded a series of hearings on state postsecondary admissions policies by proposing in 1998 that the University of California adopt a plan to admit each year a certain percentage of students from each high school in the state. While she was unable to pass a bill to admit the top 12.5% of each high school graduating class, her efforts led to the formation of a legislative coalition in favor of a plan that would endeavor to ensure that some percentage of the highest achieving students from each California high school would be offered admission to UC.[17]

In May 1998 the Regents received a proposal from the UC Board of Admissions and Relations that was described as "the most radical re-definition of eligibility criteria at the University of California in the last 30 years."[18] Under the proposal, the top 4% from each high school would be eligible for admission, provided they had completed certain prerequisites. When the plan was first presented, several Regents raised concerns over the need for such a transformation, whether it would affect the quality of university admissions classes, and whether these students would have sufficient academic preparation. One of the strongest endorsements of the proposal came from Regent Gray Davis.

In 1995, then Lieutenant Governor Davis had strongly opposed ending affirmative action at UC and had voted against both SP-1 and SP-2 as an ex officio Regent. He later became one of the state's most public opponents of Proposition 209. At the time that the 4% plan was under consideration by the board, he was one of several candidates for the Democratic Party's gubernatorial nomination. As Davis campaigned across the state, he publicly endorsed the 4% plan and promised to support its passage as governor. He pointed to the need to better distribute UC admission across the communities of the state, noting that approximately one-third of the state's nearly 900 high schools sent few, if any, students to UC.

Davis was elected governor in November 1998, by one of the largest margins in California history. As governor he became president of the Board of Regents. He was joined by a cohort of Democratic political allies that included the newly elected lieutenant governor, the state superintendent of instruction, and the Senate majority leader. He also faced the board as the man who would be responsible for appointing new Regents, and taking those nominations to a State Senate Rules Committee controlled by his fellow Democrats. It was in that context that he joined UC President Richard Atkinson to publicly encourage other Regents to support the 4% plan for admissions to the university. In March 1999 that plan was passed by the board with one dissenting vote. In the spring of 2001 the Regents endorsed a dual-admission path to increase admission of students from all California high schools through a transfer program offered at California's community colleges. Despite these initiatives, the effects of SP-1 and SP-2 are still clear in the admissions process at UC's flagship campuses, Berkeley and Los Angeles. The admit rate for African American applicants at UC Berkeley dropped from 50.1% for fall 1995 to 28.4% for fall 2000. The admit rate for Chicano students at Berkeley dropped from 61.5% in fall 1995 to 27.3% for fall 2000. Similarly, at UCLA, the admit rate for African American applicants fell from 47.7% in fall 1995 to 22.0% in fall 2000. The admit rate for Chicano students at UCLA dropped from 54.9% in fall 1995 to 25.0% in fall 2000.[19] The predictions of a precipitous decline in underrepresented admissions at the flagship campuses made by UCOP during the battle over SP-1 and SP-2 had been borne out.

OUT OF THE ASHES

On May 16, 2001, two months shy of six years after the Regents of the University of California voted to end the use of race and gender in admissions, contracting, and hiring, they gathered again to address SP-1 and SP-2. They discussed Regents Item RE-28, Future Admissions, Employment and Contracting Policies—Resolution Rescinding SP-1 and SP-2. The passage of SP-1 and SP-2 had done more than shift UC admissions policy; it had been a critical factor in the subsequent passage of Proposition 209. Under 209,

RE-28 was essentially symbolic, as the Regents had no power to rescind the fact of the vote, or the effect of the vote.

Eight Regents who voted on SP-1 and SP-2 were still on the board. The principle author of RE-28, Regent Judith Hopkinson, an appointee of Governor Davis, was new to deliberations over affirmative action on the board, but in a twist worthy of O. Henry, she was assisted in crafting RE-28 by Regent Ward Connerly.

The meeting to consider RE-28 was oddly reminiscent of the voting over SP-1 and SP-2, with a charitably revisionist turn. Students rallied loudly outside the auditorium. Democratic state legislators demanded the repeal and threatened the university's budget if the Regents did not act. Regent Bagley suggested that the passage of SP-1 and SP-2 "may have produced unintended consequences in the form of putting the University at the forefront of a national movement against affirmative action." He also expressed the hope that the passage of RE-28, which he had championed for the past six years, would "be more than a symbolic action in that it would send a message to the world that the University is not a sponsor of a national movement, and to future Boards of Regents to reject all who would use the University for or against ideological political causes."[20] The Civil Rights Movement was again invoked, this time by Lieutenant Governor and ex officio Regent Cruz Bustamante, as he read a letter of support from the NAACP and invoked *Brown v. Board of Education.*

Regent Bob Hertzberg was quoted as saying, rather optimistically, that "he believed that in adopting RE-28 the Regents would effectively extricate the Board from the arena of politics." Regent Davies restated his belief that the Regents were correct to pass SP-1 and SP-2, and his intention to vote to repeal it. He also endorsed the concept of removing political influences on the board. Regent Lee again explained his votes in favor of SP-1 and SP-2. He then expressed his support for the repeal of the policies, because they "reaffirmed the University's position that race and national origin should not be considerations for admission."[21]

Regent Johnson, who had voted for SP-1 and SP-2, suggested that the votes would "redeem" the university in the eyes of the public and restore "the institution's established and historic role of the faculty to address admissions issues."[22]

More than one Regent thanked Regent Connerly for his efforts on the repeal, and expressed the general consensus that repeal of SP-1 and SP-2 would send a message that underrepresented students were welcome at the university.

Audience comments on the issue were once again divided, as a number of groups that had battled over SP-1 and SP-2 weighed in again. One audience member "urged the supporters of affirmative action not to bow to the wishes of Regent Connerly. He stated that to amend the ban on affirmative action begrudgingly would be worse than to let it stand."[23] He represented the Coalition to Defend Affirmative Action by Any Means Necessary.

At the end of the day, Regent Connerly was on the winning end of the vote again. After making clear his belief that race should have no place in the actions of government, and that Proposition 209 had ensured equal opportunity under California constitution, he joined the other Regents in a unanimous vote to rescind SP-1 and SP-2.

9

The End and the Beginning

The contest over affirmative action at UC reveals a great deal about the contemporary politics of higher education organization and governance. As a complex and multilayered public contest over an important policy, one in which the preferences and strategies of a wide variety of interests were revealed, it offers answers to the question, "How should we understand contested policymaking in higher education?" The analysis of this contest suggests that contemporary higher education policy is made in a dynamic that moves well beyond our understanding of bureaucratic expertise, interest articulation, and organizational culture, as the contest encompassed far more than the institution itself. While those elements are part of the process, so are broader forces, driven by political actors, interest groups, and the State itself. Key to understanding this contest is acknowledging the instrumental and symbolic value in broader political contests of control over policymaking for a public university. While theories that account for the emergence of public political institutions explain much of the contemporary policy environment in higher education, it is also imperative to recognize the important role of resistance by those who are disenfranchised in a pluralist policy dynamic.

THE LIMITATIONS OF INTEREST-ARTICULATION MODELS

In its earliest stages, the contest unfolded in ways that were in keeping with understandings from the interest-articulation and institutional-cultural frames of higher education organizational behavior. The struggle over SP-1 and SP-2 was shaped early on by a public challenge by Regent Connerly to his fellow Regents to become more effective in their role as overseers and policymakers at the university. In keeping with longstanding norms of administrative articulation of demands for changes in university policy, President Peltason responded by attempting to preserve the leadership role of the university's administration in planning and analysis. When the Cooks brought the question of fairness in UC affirmative action to Regents Burgener and Connerly, and subsequently through them to the board, the contest over affirmative action was effectively divided into two struggles. One was over the question of whether the university should continue to use affirmative action. The other question, which was fought most intensely in the early months of the contest, was over who should decide whether the university should continue to use affirmative action.

ADMINISTRATION AS AN INTEREST GROUP

This case offers another significant challenge to the interest-articulation model. While institutional leaders in higher education are certainly called upon to mediate and articulate competing interests and demands, it is also the case that they have a stake in the outcome of a conflict, and interests that may shape how they approach the broader contest. The pursuit of an administration's own agenda, as potentially distinct from their efforts to use expertise and authority to mediate demands and shape policy, was an issue addressed by Baldridge (1971; Riley and Baldridge, 1977), that has rarely been addressed in research on higher education since. Baldridge proposed that the legitimacy of bureaucratic expertise was sufficient to overcome resistance that might grow out of the perception of self-interested behavior by the administration. That proposition cannot be supported by an analysis of this case. The Regents' perception of administrative self-interest on the part of UCOP and campus leaders was a key factor in the UC affirmative action contest. Whether or not the systemwide and campus leaders had a distinct interest of their own, many of the Regents expressed the belief that administrative actors did pursue their own agenda. That belief shaped the way the Regents perceived information they received over the course of the contest, and it was a factor in Regent Connerly's success in building a board coalition to eliminate affirmative action.

COMPLEXITY

Another limitation of contemporary models of postsecondary policymaking became apparent as the case unfolded. The process of articulation, of spanning boundaries in the interests of mediation and compromise, is more effective when fewer interest groups are involved, and the parties are closer to the institution. The UC administration is generally called upon to shape policy within the institution, or between the institution and the state of California. When the administration has been involved in national and international policy arenas, it has generally done so as the legitimate voice of the institution, with the backing of the Regents.[1]

As the contest over affirmative action at UC unfolded, it became increasingly complex and was increasingly contested by actors at some distance from the university. From an initial letter written by a San Diego couple to a local member of the Regents, the scope of the contest grew to encompass every constituency within the university and a vast array of advocates, including the president of the United States. The administration's ability to mediate and persuade participants with that degree of legitimacy and authority is quite limited. Research on higher education governance and policymaking has generally modeled contests with less conflict and fewer powerful actors involved. Further, a key aspect of the public university policy process is negotiation between the higher education institution and members of the state legislature. This negotiation is shaped by the constraints on the university as a nonprofit, nonpartisan public entity. In interviews and in their behavior throughout the contest, UC administrators were reluctant to appear to be seen as public political actors by, for example, issuing public opinions on the gubernatorial appointment process. A number expressed frustration that they were enmeshed in a very public political battle over institutional policy, while their responses needed to be made in a cautious, apolitical, often behind-the-scenes manner.

That frustration aside, administrative efforts to mediate interests and work politically to resolve the conflict were evident. Those efforts were driven by a desire to preserve and protect the university and need to be acknowledged as such.

THE CONTRIBUTIONS OF POSITIVE THEORY

The analysis of this contest also brings to the fore the utility of positive theories of institutions for understanding higher education governance and decision making. The PTI framework helps illustrate interest group efforts to shape the structure and process of institutions in order to influence the allocation of the costs and benefits of institutional action. Those efforts were manifest at UC in three specific areas: (1) the long-term structuring of the board through gubernatorial appointments; (2) the structuring of institutional rules and regulations to shape access to the policy agenda; and (3) the use of the institution as an instrument in a broader struggle for the control of political and economic benefits.

Confirmation Dynamics

On the first point, the contest over affirmative action at UC suggests that the structuring of governing boards is a key and under-studied element of the institutional decision-making process. While there are a number of descriptive accounts of board composition and a well-developed normative literature on effective trusteeship, the political dynamic of board appointments has only recently been explored.[2] In this case, the long-term structuring of the membership of the Board of Regents was one of the most important factors in eliminating UC's affirmative action policies. A remarkable paradox in contemporary higher education governance is that a crucial element of the policymaking process, board appointments, has not been particularly contested. As the UC case demonstrates, prior to the affirmative action contest the California State Senate made little use of its power to confirm or reject appointments to the Board of Regents. This in turn enabled a succession of Republican governors to "stack the deck" so that by 1994 when the contest over affirmative action arrived at the board, it was greeted by an extremely partisan set of Regents.

Then California State Senate Majority Leader Bill Lockyer[3] suggested that the Regents' votes on SP-1 and SP-2 motivated the Rules Committee, under his guidance, to begin active oversight of gubernatorial appointments. He described the shift this way:

> I can tell you why we started to be critical, and that is there was a view in my caucus, a pretty pronounced one, that we had rubber-stamped gubernatorial appointees too easily, and secondly that there were matters of significant philosophical disagreement that deserved some comment and that we needed to join the issues. Those were two needs. Then there was the question of faculty shared governance and things of that sort. So as Pro Tem, I felt that it was important to assert our coequal status and not just always roll over for the governor's appointees.[4]

A number of normative propositions have been advanced in literature on trusteeship in recent years that suggest trustees should have postsecondary expertise and, after appointment, considerable autonomy. In this case it is clear that the appointment process did not demand nominees with specific expertise in higher education or governance. What it did demand was that most nominees have a relationship, personal or political, with the governor. This in turn raises significant questions about the degree of autonomy they could demonstrate on the board.

Given UC's constitutional status, the fundamental route for political actors to directly influence UC policymaking (in contrast to the considerably more indirect budget negotiation) is through the nomination and confirmation of Regents. This contest suggests that the confirmation dynamic is increasingly politicized and increasingly contested, a shift that may have significant implications for future policy contests in higher education.

Agenda Control

A powerful benefit of Governor Wilson's close relationship with the appointed Regents was his concurrent influence over the board agenda. Agenda setting played a central role in the outcome of this contest, as the partisan nature of the board limited the ability of the Office of the President or the proponents of UC's affirmative action policies to shape debate. This became apparent near the outset of the conflict, when Regents Brophy and Gonzales failed in their procedural attempt to end Regent Connerly's request for an investigation of UC's affirmative action policies by forcing an early committee vote.

Over the course of the contest, Regent Connerly was able to bring the issue of ending affirmative action to the board agenda, put the proponents of affirmative action on the defensive, and bring his proposals to a vote of the full board without facing a significant parliamentary challenge. Despite Regent Connerly's contention that his proposals could have garnered committee approval on the way to a full board vote, the nature of the proposals themselves and the significance of the contest would have been declared much earlier, and Connerly would have faced a more difficult tactical challenge.

Once challenged by Connerly, the Office of the President chose to take a moderate approach and to present a thorough review of affirmative action. That put an effective end to the efforts of some Regents to contest Connerly's push to place the issue on the Regents' agenda. When interviewed on this point, UC President Peltason suggested that UCOP should not engage in efforts to tactically control the agenda. He stressed the importance of the administration's maintaining its role as provider of expertise and information throughout the contest.[5] This serves as another reminder of the importance of institutional norms of governance, and the ways they interact with interest group challenges, in the contemporary policymaking process.

THE INSTRUMENTAL VALUE OF UC POLICY

The struggle over affirmative action at UC also points to the heightened visibility and symbolic importance of higher education policymaking. That visibility makes public universities attractive sites of contest for external political actors and interest groups. As a key site of the allocation of public costs and benefits, the university is an important political institution. Such issues as UC labor policies and environmental practices have great salience in the state and for the major political parties and their constituents.

Given that the university has periodically been the object of significant challenges from external political forces, a deeper understanding is called for. The rapid increase in the national significance of political struggles over elementary-secondary education over the past two decades should serve as a harbinger of what is likely to occur in higher education. One of the longest-serving UC Regents suggested that given the success of using the university as a battleground for a broader attack on affirmative action, the next contest might well be fought over the use of the university medical centers for training physicians who might later perform abortions.[6] He noted somewhat regretfully that any number of groups or political actors might challenge UC medical center policies before the Board of Regents in order to garner attention and support for state legislation, or political ambition.[7]

THE GOVERNOR'S PRESIDENTIAL ASPIRATIONS

A political theoretical approach to postsecondary governance also points to the importance of political gain for individuals that may emerge from contests over institutional control. In order to understand the UC affirmative action contest, it is essential to acknowledge the value of a flagship land grant university in the broader agenda of a state's governor. The data in this case reveal a widely shared perception that the UC contest was sustained in large measure by Governor Wilson's campaign for the Republican presidential campaign. Regent William Bagley, a former California Assembly member and longtime Wilson ally, put it this way:

> Had Pete not been involved, had the governor not been involved, we would have never passed the resolution. The governor got involved because he was running for president. The governor used my university as a forum to run for president.[8]

This case adds to our understanding of the short-term and long-term politics of gubernatorial intervention. In the short run, it appears extremely difficult to resist the power, visibility, and authority that a governor brings to a policy contest. However, it is not clear that the immediate gains in attention and control that accrue to a governor through intervention are lasting gains. In the UC case, Governor Wilson's success at the board level did not translate into a presidential nomination. Further, the organized resistance engendered by Wilson's attack on affirmative action in SP-1 and SP-2 and in Proposition 209 can be seen as instrumental in the widespread electoral repudiation of the governor's party in the November 1998 elections. One beneficiary of that repudiation was Regent Gray Davis. As lieutenant governor and ex officio Regent, Davis had been a strong proponent of affirmative action at UC. To the surprise of most analysts, in 1998 he became the first Democrat elected governor of California in twenty years. However, the role of the campaign to pass SP-1 and SP-2 in the subsequent passage of Proposition 209 cannot be overlooked. Proposition 209 altered the California Constitution and significantly limited the ability of the university to use race as a factor in policymaking.

INTEREST GROUP COMPETITION

The influence of interest group competition was also manifest throughout the contest. The active intervention by the state and national political parties, legal and public interest foundations, state and national women's organizations, and labor unions are just a few examples. Groups representing a wide variety of coalitions also actively lobbied the Regents for and against affirmative action.

UC Santa Cruz Chancellor Karl Pister suggested that the interest group pressure was, if not a new phenomenon, indicative of a resurgence of interest group intervention in higher education policymaking:

> My first reaction would be that it's a consequence of a much broader societal phenomenon because if I look beyond higher education and just look at the public education in California, K–12, the degree of political intervention in K through 12 is just astounding today. Witness the state Board of Education's behavior on the math standards and God knows what's going to happen on the science standards when they come up before the state board. Education indeed is part of the larger issue. Our society is often being driven by political design, by which issues make people identify either with left or right or whatever camps you want to use to explain it.[9]

This case suggests that gains available to political parties and other political actors contending for control of UC's affirmative action policy ratcheted the level of interest group commitment and intervention beyond the limit of the UC administration's ability to negotiate a solution. This process required more than interest group intent. That those groups were able to use a long-term advantage in board appointments and a powerful governor to overwhelm the university's administration points to the importance of longer-term struggles over the composition of institutional decision-making structures for understanding postsecondary policymaking.

CULTURAL AND SYMBOLIC INFLUENCES

This contest also points to the continuing utility of cultural and symbolic perspectives on institutional organization and policymaking. Meyer and Rowan's (1977) model of organizations as complex bundles of enacted rules, social relationships, and shared beliefs is evident in the UC organizational structure and its public discourse. Cultural beliefs and symbols shaped this case in powerful ways, particularly in regard to the strategies of various university constituencies. The Office of the President held a very different set of beliefs about the appropriate exercise of authority than the Regents did. Regent Connerly emphasized the point, when he suggested that UCOP operated under an "illusion of control" and that universities in general were notoriously out of touch with the norms of society.[10]

The Regents' understanding of their own authority to make university policy under the California constitution collided with the Academic Council's belief that faculty control of admissions policy had been codified in the Regents' own standing orders for over fifty years. Representatives of labor organizations at the university expressed frustration at being unable to form an effective coalition with the Office of the President or the campus chancellors to advocate for their shared goal, preservation of affirmative action. Labor leaders interviewed were not surprised at this lack of collaboration, given their sense of deeply entrenched UC institutional norms regarding organized labor at the university.

One of the strongest elements of the University of California's institutional culture, its powerfully entrenched, fragmented, and hierarchical organization, also played a role as the contest unfolded. Despite the various internal constituencies' strong support for existing affirmative action policies, that support was lodged in a house divided. As the conflict expanded to include organized opposition to affirmative action from well-coordinated interest groups, particularly the state and national Republican parties and conservative policy institutes, the university could not respond with a similarly coordinated effort to preserve affirmative action.

Some Regents believed that the insular and closely held beliefs of the system and campus leadership about affirmative action and access policies were so strong that those leaders were unable to recognize the legal implications of UC admissions practices. The same Regents felt the administration had turned affirmative action into a holy grail. While most Regents respected the administration's fervor, many did not share the same policy goals.

The symbolic importance of the university had great influence throughout the contest on another, more positive dimension. A number of Regents who were opposed to affirmative action were also quite reluctant to oppose the Office of the President, or to engage in a controversial contest, for fear that it would hurt the reputation and quality of the institution. Regents used such phrases as "my university under siege," or "I hated to bring this grief on this great university," as if the university were a person or a friend. Some Regents thought of the university as a family and expressed reluctance to fight in public or to turn the family against itself. While many Regents' beliefs about the reputation, history, and symbolism of the university made them reluctant to pursue the conflict over affirmative action policy, those feelings were weighed against their loyalty to their political peers and the governor. Ultimately, the governor prevailed.

THE CONTESTED STATE PERSPECTIVE

An analysis of the contest over affirmative action at UC also reaffirms the value of State theoretical perspectives on the organization and governance of higher education. The issues of resistance and contest, marginalization, public resource allocation, and the redress of inequality recurred throughout the conflict. The University of California was conceptualized by a number of participants in the conflict over affirmative action as a site where historical inequities in the distribution of public resources could be redressed. Students, labor organizers, administrators, Regents, and members of the legislature made reference to this aspect of the contest over SP-1 and SP-2. The increasing tension between the intense competition for the economic and status benefits of admission to elite public higher educational institutions and the role those institutions have played as centers of social democratization was also apparent throughout the debate.

The selective public institution, with its zero-sum admissions process, is a relatively new phenomenon. Until the early seventies, both UC Berkeley and UCLA admitted a high percentage of the eligible students who applied.[11] At the time of the votes on SP-1 and SP-2, UC Berkeley received over 20,000 applications for fewer than 3,500 slots. That increase has been accompanied by a change in the perception of the benefits of higher education, from a communal public benefit that could expand to meet demand to an increasingly individual benefit, with limited access at the elite levels, and zero-sum allocation (Marginson, 1997; Schrag, 1998b). The perception of greater benefits for individuals attending elite public institutions increased demands for access and redress of historical inequities by traditionally underrepresented students. At the same time, the perceived returns for attendance at elite publics emboldened advocates for students with the highest academic indexes, who argued they deserved spaces on the most selective campuses.

Regent Tirso del Junco suggested that the competition for scarce resources had just begun, with resistance from the state's middle class bound to increase:

> The other question is the socioeconomic; that is, as we give more and more scholarships and get more and more funds for the racial/ethnic groups and the financially deprived, you are in effect increasing the demands upon the middle class and affluent. So, from an economic point of view, yes we are affecting those people. Are those people going to say one of these days, "Hey, enough is enough"?[12]

Then chair of the State Senate Higher Education Committee, Tom Hayden, described how the shift in perception of the economic benefits of higher education influenced the affirmative action contest:

Affirmative action was invented in the 1960's during a time of job and educational expansion. But as jobs and educational opportunities have contracted, and personal incomes gone flat, affirmative action ignites a student scramble over shrinking opportunities.[13]

RACE AND CLASS IN THE CONTESTED STATE

A fundamental argument advanced by Regent Connerly and others seeking to end UC affirmative action policies was that, in some cases, advantage in admissions, hiring, and contracting was being given solely on the basis of race. They further argued that race no longer necessarily imparted disadvantage. The underlying presumption, occasionally overtly expressed in the debate, was that a "level playing field" had been achieved, where racial discrimination was not a significant factor. Consequently, so the argument went, there was no longer a need to redress inequality through preferences based on race. A related problem, according to the opponents of affirmative action, was the inappropriate awarding of preferences to economically privileged individuals on the basis of their racial/ethnic group status. These presumptions and the leaps of logic that ensue have been challenged in recent work on race, class, and discourse in educational conflict (Chang, 2001, 2002).

Most Regents opposed to using race in admissions and hiring were willing to countenance preferences based on other forms of disadvantage, primarily lower socioeconomic status. Those Regents did not register significant concern over the admissions simulation prepared by the Office of the President, which showed that the use of SES in place of race would greatly reduce the number of traditionally underrepresented students on UC's flagship campuses. Accepting the shift from race to SES required a belief that there is no racial effect or legacy that transcends SES. However, within socioeconomic strata, UC's own data indicated disparities in test scores and college attendance by students of different ethnic and racial backgrounds.[14]

Whether the desire to substitute SES for race indicated a commitment to a different form of equity on the part of the Regents or simply an effort to offer something to fill the vacuum left by the elimination of race as a criterion is unclear. An analysis of the broader context suggests that should students from lower socioeconomic brackets begin to displace students in higher socioeconomic brackets who have higher academic rankings, there may eventually be challenges to admissions preferences for the economically disadvantaged.

The conflict at UC also demonstrates that contests over race and socioeconomic class will be increasingly linked in the higher education policy arena. A number of proponents justified their demands to preserve affirmative action with language that invoked both the redress of racial discrimination and the redress of income inequality. Nancy Barreda, a student from UC Irvine, made one of the strongest public statements on the day of the votes, with her allusions to jobs often associated in California with immigrant labor. She proclaimed, to chants and applause that nearly caused the Regents to shut down the meeting,

> We don't want to pick your fruit, to be your maids, to be your busboys, to do your laundry and tend your gardens. Unfortunately, some of our parents have taken those jobs to give us a better chance. We too are Americans, and it is a shame that we have to fight constantly to remind those in power who seem to ignore that fact. Affirmative action was the first time we were provided access into these institutions. We will not forget those who sacrificed in the past so that we could have a chance today. We will not stand by while you take away affirmative action, we will not stand by and watch you destroy our right to access.[15]

Arthur Fletcher, formerly of the U.S. Civil Rights Commission, and one of the authors in the mid-sixties of a landmark urban affirmative action hiring plan, told the Regents that racial inequality could not be redressed without minority capital accumulation and that higher education was key to that process:

> Down through our history Americans have had a difficult time making sure that minorities as a whole and African Americans in particular participate in the economy of this country. We under-girded that economy with slave labor, but we were not supposed to own anything, and I can produce for you 54 laws that are on the statute books that denied us the opportunity to hold any of America's wealth.[16]

Similarly, Boalt Hall graduate Eva Paterson addressed the Regents and questioned the state's commitment to using higher education to produce greater equality:

> I was at Third Baptist Church yesterday with Reverend Jackson, hundreds of Black and Brown kids came into that auditorium. I looked in their faces and I went, I wonder if all of you know that you are basically going to deny these kids education. My understanding is that at certain universities in this system, the percentage of African Americans will go from four to two percent. I looked those babies in the eye and I went, what that means is that you will not be able to find a job, we are building prisons for you, you are going to be homeless, we will put you on welfare and then we will cut welfare so that you cannot even live.[17]

Cheryl Hagen, the chair of the university's largest organized labor organization, the UC Council of Staff Assemblies, linked the issue of access to high-quality jobs at UC to an unequal distribution of power. She informed the board,

> The reasons for racism and sexism are rooted in issues of economics, political power, social order and psychological factors. The question has never been whether or not minorities and women should be accepted and treated as equals, it has been a question of whether or not power is to be shared, and on what basis. The issue of power seeps through and permeates all thought when it comes to any movement within our society. There is nothing inherently wrong in the good-old-boy methodology. It works. It is only problematic because for faculty positions and senior staff positions within the University of California, women and minorities have not had the same access.[18]

Race, social class, and access were melded in quite a different way by the proponents of SP-1 and SP-2 when they suggested affirmative action gave preference to wealthy applicants from underrepresented groups over less affluent Whites and Asian Americans. This issue also underpinned the argument by Governor Wilson and Regent Connerly that in the admission process, whatever the family wealth of a student from an underrepresented group, he or she would receive a supplemental ranking equivalent to a less financially well-off White or Asian American student. Given its attention to income inequality, a contested State perspective will be increasingly useful as universities move from racial/ethnic criteria to factors based on socioeconomic disadvantage.

From a State theoretical perspective, the State itself is an actor in a broader struggle for resources and authority. A number of the actors in the UC contest acknowledged State intervention in the struggle over affirmative action, but they differed in their perception of whether the State should intervene at all, and whether that intervention would be a positive force. Several Regents expressed irritation with President Clinton's call to "mend not end" affirmative action on the eve of the Regents' votes, and by the intimation prior to the vote that the Office of Civil Rights would review UC's federally funded contracts should the Regents pass SP-1 and SP-2.

Proponents of affirmative action also warned opponents about the risk to state and federal funding should the Regents vote to eliminate affirmative action. John Vasconcellos, chairman of the Assembly Budget Committee and a state politician with a great deal of influence over UC's annual appropriation, wrote this in a letter to the Regents the day after the votes:

> You have committed the most destructive act in modern California history. The Board has profaned its sacred trust as trustees of what once was

California's great public university. You have absolutely forfeited your right to govern what was the world's most prestigious university by engaging in a blatant political act.[19]

He concluded the letter with these words of warning on the budget:

How dare you rush to judgment—according to no public interest timetable—to join the desperate effort of a presidential candidate to jump-start his non-start campaign. How pathetic! How dare you pervert this public board of regents of this public university by a narrow vote, a political power play. If you want to join Pete Wilson's campaign committee, have the integrity to resign the public position of trust you have violated. I am asking Legislative Counsel to draft legislation that will provide adequate vouchers to UC students to obtain their education at institutions whose trustees are committed to education—not politics.[20]

Regent Khachigian maintained in her testimony that the State was partly responsible for the failure of affirmative action programs. Regent Nakashima, in his explanation of why he was voting to eliminate affirmative action, recalled his internment during World War II as an example of State-sponsored discrimination. California Assemblyman Nao Takasugi also testified to the board about his time in an internment camp:

Let us be clear today what we are discussing with UC's special preferential admissions policy, it is nothing more or less than State mandated discrimination based on race, the same discrimination that locked me and my family away in a prison of injustice in Gila River, Arizona.[21]

THE DISAPPEARANCE OF GENDER

Just as the shift from race to socioeconomic status as a component in admissions policy raises a number of significant issues, so does the relative absence of gender from the conflict over affirmative action at UC. Over the past forty years, there has been a rapid gain in the percentage of women attending higher education institutions, and the University of California in particular. In fact, the ascendance of women has resulted in some campuses admitting freshman classes in which nearly 60% of those admitted were women. This disproportionate representation was so taken for granted that the use of gender in undergraduate admissions at UC was rarely discussed during the Regents' deliberations over affirmative action, and its prohibition under SP-1 and SP-2 received only a little more commentary than did the elimination of religion as a criterion. However, a number of interest groups did lobby the Regents on behalf of the presevation of gender as a criterion in hiring and contracting.

While the gains made by women, particularly White women, in UC staff positions and on the faculty over the previous two decades were noted in UCOP's reports on hiring and contracting, they were little discussed by the board. Regents Eastin and Levin, two of only six women on the twenty-six-member board at the time of the votes, did raise the importance of women faculty as role models, as did students who spoke to the board. On the whole, gender was nearly entirely sublimated by race and ethnicity in the deliberations. In part this neglect can be attributed to the fact that hiring and contracting policies were also sublimated by admissions policies as the focus of the contest, and so the issue of women's underrepresentation in the tenured faculty ranks, for example, was less discussed than it might otherwise have been.

In interviews, a number of Regents equated the relatively large numbers of undergraduate women student admits with the absence of discrimination on the basis of gender. The lack of discussion of gender in UC admissions has significant implications, as there is no evidence that the proportional representation of women in UC's undergraduate cohort indicates a lack of discrimination. Considerably more women might be admitted if the university were to take gender discrimination into consideration, but redress has traditionally been based on underrepresentation. Those traditions were altered to some degree by challenges brought through the Office of Civil Rights by another disproportionately represented group, Asian students at UCLA. Those challenges led to changes in UC admissions policies on some campuses that subsequently led to an increase in Asian American admissions. Similarly, a shift from race to disadvantage as a criterion for admission to UC may impact the gender balance in entering cohorts.

RESISTANCE AND CHANGE

One of the more powerful findings from this case was the importance of resistance by actors with limited voting power in the policy contest. Most research on higher education policymaking has focused on pluralist processes, or the relationship between institutions and actors who control significant resources. In this case student resistance, through rallies and protests, cross-campus alliances, and the invitation to Jesse Jackson to address the board on students' behalf, led to a significant shift in the contest.

It was also resistance on the part of students, in coalition with community groups and labor organizations, that helped shift the board confirmation dynamic in the aftermath of the votes. This shift was manifest in the organized resistance to the renomination of Regent Tirso del Junco in 1997. While the Office of the President was constrained from taking a position on the nomination, and no faculty members or faculty representatives appeared, an unprecedented number of witnesses appeared to testify against the renomination and to encourage the Senate Democratic leadership to join them in rejecting del Junco. UC employee union representatives appeared in concert with representatives of state and local unions unaffiliated with the university, while for the first time present and former Regents testified against the confirmation of one of their own. Student representatives and representatives of various community, legal, and activist coalitions also testified against del Junco. Subsequent protests at the state capitol, and testimony before the Senate Rules Committee, would also contribute to the rejection of a number of nominees in the aftermath of the elimination of affirmative action.

Future consideration of higher education policymaking and governance will need to incorporate research into the nature of emerging political alliances between internal university constituencies and external political institutions and interest groups. These alliances will have significant consequences for historical norms of governance and policymaking. Renewed activism in the wake of the Regents' votes, combined with the increased strength and visibility of coalitions of student and labor organizations formed during the affirmative action contest, were instrumental in the subsequent successful efforts to provide domestic partner benefits for UC employees and in the unionization of UC graduate students.[22] Students working with legislative leaders also contributed significantly to the enactment by the Board of Regents of the 4%-admissions plan and other shifts in admissions requirements. These changes, along with significantly increased outreach funding, were unexpected outcomes of the struggle, engendered by constant pressure from students, community groups, labor organizations, and others who were not able to vote on the Board of Regents or in the administrative councils at the university.

INSTITUTIONAL AUTONOMY AND SHARED GOVERNANCE

Two comments on the Regents' votes perhaps best summed up the board's division over the issue of shared governance and policymaking. Regent Brophy, addressing the board on the day after the votes, stated:

> That permits me to say what I intend to say, and that is, if there was ever a violation of shared governance it occurred during the affirmative action votes yesterday.[23]

Regent Connerly maintained a quite different perspective:

> Only the Board of Regents governs. There is nothing in the California Constitution that states that the faculty has any role in governing UC.[24]

The contest over affirmative action sheds considerable light on the question of institutional autonomy in governance and policymaking. This issue arose on a number of occasions, in suggestions from various actors involved in the policy deliberations that the institutional right to self-governance had been violated. It also came to the fore when Regent Connerly stated his belief that UC policy was public policy, and that public policy should be made through a democratic political process, with the university open to that process.

The framers of the California constitution held yet another view on institutional autonomy. Inherent in their vision was the belief that higher education was a unique public commodity, so distinct from the vast majority of state policies, laws, and regulations that they designated the university a "public trust."[25] They also sought to insulate that public trust, to a nearly unprecedented degree, from the California legislature. What the contest over affirmative action at UC demonstrates, like the loyalty oath controversy and the dismissal of President Kerr, is that insulating the university from the legislature hardly puts the institution above political intervention. It can be argued that insulating the university from legislative intervention has rendered the institution particularly vulnerable to politically opportunistic governors and challenges from a variety of interest groups. In the twenty years prior to the Regents' votes on affirmative action, a succession of Republican governors had filled the board with highly loyal and partisan nominees. The State Senate, despite Democratic control for the past quarter century, failed to contest the nominations. Contesting gubernatorial nominations is never without political cost, and in the calms between UC policy storms the senatorial norm has been to defer to the governor.

As this case demonstrates, while the State Senate can make corrections in its own approach to political contest over a state institution, the university is in a different situation. The protection that the university and its internal constituencies have historically relied upon has not been a constitutional protection but an institutional cultural norm, shared governance. Shared governance is an institutional compact, to the extent that faculty roles and responsibilities are elucidated in the Regents' bylaws and standing orders. The norm of shared governance suggests that the Regents consult with faculty and the administration in governing the university and adopting policy. What became clear throughout the contest was that shared governance is a political terrain. The right to share in governance must be contested by the various internal and external university constituencies. The power of those various constituencies, their ability to organize and form coalitions, becomes central to its implementation.

UC Santa Cruz Chancellor Karl Pister expressed the problem this way:

> It all seems a little bit complicated by the university's autonomous status which, when I first entered the realm of research and governance, I was sure was entirely a blessing. But now, in some ways it strikes me there

is a political battle raging which the university can't avoid, but on the other hand the university is entirely constitutionally constrained from and/ or ostensibly removed from. So obviously we don't have a huge lobbying staff. The university is a political player to the extent that it can leverage reputation and so forth. It seems to me if the legislature is increasingly gridlocked and policy is made by ballot initiatives, I don't believe the university as an entity can even take particularly public stands on most initiatives. I think there have been some controversies over chancellors who even attempted to take personal stances.[26]

Ironically, the university's autonomous status, with its contingent reliance on shared governance, leaves the institution remarkably little recourse against partisan efforts by its own governing board. While it is true that as a nonprofit public trust the university cannot actively espouse partisan political causes, it could certainly do more in the broader political economy to facilitate the defense of its own policies and to support and coordinate the efforts of those within and external to the institution who support those policies.

COLLECTING THE NAILS FROM THE ASHES

The contest over affirmative action at the University of California offers both a powerful reminder of what is useful about the ways we understand organizational decision making in higher education and a challenge to improve our understanding of the political dimension of those models. The case affirms the utility of many elements of the prevalent frameworks for understanding organizational behavior in higher education. Yet taken together, those analytical frames fail to explain the decision reached in this contest. The argument here is not that political contests and challenges to public universities are appropriate or inappropriate, only that they are poorly understood.

By acknowledging the many ways in which the instrumental value of the university drove this contest, and that the contest was waged in many ways beyond a pluralist process, we find the essential elements for a revision of the models that have long shaped our understanding of higher education policymaking. A public university is a political institution, with great salience, visibility, and instrumental value. By accepting that, we can turn attention to the ways that long-term political action shapes the organization and governance of public higher education.

While the prolonged and often bitter struggle at UC was waged over affirmative action policies at one university, it was also a conflict over the role of elite public universities in the wider society. That the University of

California would no longer use race and gender as criteria in admissions, hiring, and contracting was decided by the Regents' votes. With the passage of Proposition 209, those prohibitions were extended to all of California's public institutions. Yet the question of who belongs in elite public universities, of how the costs and benefits of those institutions should be distributed, and of who should make those essential decisions, will be contested for generations to come.

Appendix 1. SP-1 as Amended and Passed

UNIVERSITY OF CALIFORNIA BOARD OF REGENTS POLICY ENSURING EQUAL TREATMENT: ADMISSIONS

WHEREAS, Governor Pete Wilson, on June 1, 1995, issued Executive Order W-124-95 to "End Preferential Treatment and to Promote Individual Opportunity Based on Merit"; and

WHEREAS, paragraph seven of that order requests the University of California to "take all necessary action to comply with the intent and the requirements of this executive order," and

WHEREAS, in January, 1995, the University initiated a review of its policies and practices, the results of which support many of the findings and conclusions of Governor Wilson, and

WHEREAS, the University of California Board of Regents believes that it is in the best interest of the University to take relevant actions to develop and support programs which will have the effect of increasing the eligibility rates of groups which are underrepresented in the University's pool of applicants as compared to their percentages in California's graduating high school classes and to which reference is made in section four.

NOW, THEREFORE, BE IT RESOLVED AS FOLLOWS

<u>Section 1</u> The President, with the consultation of the Board of Regents, shall appoint a task force representative of the business community, the University, other segments of education, and organizations currently engaged in academic "outreach." The responsibility of this group shall be to develop proposals for new directions and increased funding for the board of Regents to increase the eligibility rate of those currently identified in section four. The final report of this task force shall be presented to the Board of Regents within six months after its creation.

Section 2 Effective January 1, 1997, the University of California shall not use race, religion, sex, color, ethnicity or national origin as a criterion for admission to the University or to any programs of study.

Section 3 Effective January 1, 1997, race, religion, sex, color, ethnicity or national origin shall not be a criterion for admissions in exception to UC-eligibility requirements.

Section 4 The President shall confer with the Academic Senate of the University of California to develop supplemental criteria for consideration by the Board of Regents which shall be consistent with section one. In developing such criteria, which shall provide reasonable assurances that the applicant will successfully complete his or her course of study, consideration shall be given to individuals who despite having suffered disadvantage economically or in terms of their social environment (such as an abusive or otherwise dysfunctional home, or a neighborhood of unwholesome or anti-social influences), have nonetheless demonstrated sufficient character and determination in overcoming obstacles to warrant confidence that the applicant can pursue a course of study to successful completion, provided that any student admitted under this section must be academically eligible for admission.

Section 5 Effective January 1, 1997, not less than fifty (50) percent and not more than seventy-five (75) percent of any entering class on any campus shall be admitted solely on the basis of academic achievement.

Section 6 Nothing in section two shall prohibit any action which is strictly necessary to establish or maintain eligibility for any federal or state program, where ineligibility would result in a loss of federal or state funds to the University.

Section 7 Nothing in section two shall prohibit the University from taking appropriate action to remedy specific documented cases of discrimination by the University, provided that such actions are expressly and specifically approved by the Board of Regents or taken pursuant to a final order of a court or administrative agency of competent jurisdiction.

Section 8 The President of the University shall periodically report to the Board of Regents detailing progress to implement the provisions of this resolution.

Section 9 Believing California's diversity to be an asset, we adopt this statement: Because individual members of all of California's diverse races have the intelligence and capacity to succeed at the University of California, this policy will achieve a UC population that reflects this state's diversity through the preparation and empowerment of all students in this state to succeed rather than through a system of artificial preferences.

Appendix 2. SP-2 as Amended and Passed

UNIVERSITY OF CALIFORNIA BOARD OF REGENTS POLICY ENSURING EQUAL TREATMENT: BUSINESS PRACTICES AND EMPLOYMENT

WHEREAS, Governor Pete Wilson, on June 1, 1995, issued Executive Order W-124-95 to "End Preferential Treatment and to Promote Individual Opportunity Based on Merit," and

WHEREAS, paragraph seven of that order requests the University of California to "take all necessary action to comply with the intent and the requirements of this executive order," and

WHEREAS, in January, 1995, the University initiated a review of its policies and practices, the results of which support many of the findings and conclusions of Governor Wilson.

NOW THEREFORE, BE IT RESOLVED AS FOLLOWS:

Section 1 Effective January 1, 1996, the University of California shall not use race, religion, sex, color, ethnicity, or national origin as a criterion in its employment and contracting practices.

Section 2 The President of the University of California is directed to oversee a system-wide evaluation of the University's hiring and contracting practices to identify what actions need be taken to ensure that all persons have equal access to job competitions, contracts and other business and employment opportunities of the University. A report and recommendations to accomplish this objective shall be presented to the Board of Regents before December 31, 1996.

Section 3 Nothing in section one shall prohibit any action which is strictly necessary to establish or maintain eligibility for any federal or state program, where ineligibility would result in a loss of federal or state funds to the University.

<u>Section 4</u> Nothing in section one shall prohibit the University from taking appropriate action to remedy specific, documented cases of discrimination by the University, provided that such actions are expressly and specifically approved by the Board of Regents or taken pursuant to a final order of a court or administrative agency of competent jurisdiction.

<u>Section 5</u> Believing California's diversity to be an asset, we adopt this statement: Because individual members of all of California's diverse races have the intelligence and capacity to succeed at the University of California, this policy will achieve a UC population that reflects this state's diversity through the preparation and empowerment of all students in this state to succeed rather than through a system of artificial preferences.

Notes

CHAPTER 1. BURNING DOWN THE HOUSE: THE POLITICS OF HIGHER EDUCATION POLICY

1. The text of the proposals is attached as appendices 1 and 2.

2. The director of admissions of one of the system's largest campuses commented on the day after the votes: "I never thought it would pass." Bill Villa in Alice Dembner, "Educators Fear UC Action will Set Trend," *Santa Barbara News Press,* July 22, 1995, pp. A1 & A14.

3. See Duryea, 1981; Marginson, 1997; Pusser, 2001, 2003; Rhoades, 1992, 1996; Slaughter and Leslie, 1997; John Levin, 2001; Apple, 1982; Clark, 1996.

4. See Hurtado and Nava, 1997; Breneman, 1995; Jessop, 1990; Labaree, 1997; Henry Levin, 2001; Pusser, 2002; Slaughter, 1993; Conkey, 1996; Bowen, 1980.

5. See Gitlin, 1987; Kerr, 2001.

6. See Tolbert and Hero, 1996; Chavez, 1998; Klinkner, 1996.

7. See Howard, 1997; Lemann, 1999.

8. The chair and vice-chair of the UC Academic Council sit as non-voting members of the board.

9. For a more detailed analysis of multidimensional models, see Berger and Milem, 2000; Pusser, 2003. For the development of the political frame in higher education more generally, see Baldridge, 1971; Riley and Baldridge, 1977; Hardy, 1990, 1996; Millett, 1984; Pfeffer and Salancik, 1978; Bolman and Deal, 1997; Blau, 1973; Cohen and March, 1974; McConnell, 1981; Weick, 1976.

10. See Shafritz and Hyde, 1987; Moe, 1991; Pusser, 2003; Dixit, 1996.

11. See Moe, 1996; Niskanen, 1971; Wilson, 1989; Kraatz and Zajac, 1996.

12. See Kingdon, 1984; McCubbins, Noll and Weingast, 1987; Moe, 1991; Milgrom and Roberts, 1992; Horn, 1995; Mashaw, 1990; Chubb and Moe, 1990; Youn and Arnold, 1997; Masten, 1993; Williamson, 1995.

13. See Shepsle, 1986; Arrow, 1974; Olson, 1965; Moe, 1991; Masten, 1995.

14. See Calvert, McCubbins and Weingast, 1989; Bendor, 1988; Hill, 1985; Williamson, 1985; Moe, 1984.

15. See McCormick and Meiners, 1988; Masten, 1995; DiMaggio and Powell, 1983.

16. See Kingdon, 1984; Hammond and Hill, 1993; Weingast and Marshall, 1988; Olson, 1965; Parsons, 1997; Wilson, 1989; Mintzberg, 1979.

17. See Ordorika, 2003; Slaughter, 1990; Pusser, 2003.

18. Here *pluralist* refers to contests in which a majority or plurality of legitimate votes by an electorate or governing board is used to determine an issue or election.

19. See March and Olsen, 1995; Carnoy and Levin, 1985; Hobbes, 1968; Locke, 1955; Dahl, 1956.

20. See Marx, 1867; Gramsci, 1971; Bowles and Gintis, 1976, 1990; Aronowitz, 1981; Willis, 1981; Giroux, 1981; Freire, 1973; Aronowitz and Giroux, 1993.

21. See Carnoy and Levin, 1985; Jessop, 1990; Slaughter, 1988; Labaree, 1997.

22. Labaree, 1997, p. 42.

23. See Weir, Orloff, and Skocpol, 1988; Skocpol, 1992; Jessop, 1990; Domhoff, 1990.

24. Mann, 1993, p. 54.

25. Wirt and Kirst, 1972, p. 1.

26. See Slaughter, 1988, 1990, 1993; Rhoades and Slaughter, 1997; Slaughter and Leslie, 1997.

27. These data are drawn from the Profile of the University University of California Office of the President, various years.

28. State of California, Department of Finance, Current Population Survey Report: various years. Sacramento, CA.

29. See UC Means Business, the Economic Impact of the University of California: A report by the University of California Office of the President. University of California Office of the President, 1996. Oakland, California.

CHAPTER 2. THE UC GOVERNANCE AND DECISION-MAKING STRUCTURE: HISTORY AND CONTEXT

1. These events are recounted in exceptional detail in Douglass, 2000.

2. Gilman, in Douglass, 1992b, p. 60.

3. For an illuminating fictional account of this period in California history, see Frank Norris's *The Octopus: A Story of California* (Cambridge, MA: R. Bentley, 1971).

4. Douglass, 2000, p. 64.

5. California Constitutional Convention 1879, in Debates and Proceedings of the Constitutional Convention of the State of California, 1878–79, quoted in Douglass, 2000, p. 65.

6. California Constitution Article IX, section IX, quoted in Douglass, 2000, p. 69.

7. For an excellent history of the establishment of the University of California and the role of the constitutional convention in that process, see Douglass, 1992a; 2000, and Douglass in Skrentny, 2001.

8. Gardner, 1967; Stadtman, 1970; Schrag, 1998b; Hofstadter and Metzger, 1955; Fitzgibbon, 1968; Berdahl, 1971; Smelser, 1974; Clark, 1983, 1972.

9. Brown, 30 OPS Attorney General 162, 1957.

10. Regents' meetings include both open and closed sessions. Closed-session items include all labor negotiations, personnel contracting, and matters of national security.

11. California Constitution, Article IX Revision, 1974.
12. These data are compiled from the Centennial Record of the University of California and the archives of the California State Senate Rules Committee.
13. At a number of junctures in the contest over affirmative action at UC the issue of the class and gender status of the Regents was raised. A number of commentators suggested that the composition of the board did not appropriately reflect the population of California. See <u>UC Regents of the People? Legion of Critics Think Not</u>, Lisa Lapin, *Sacramento Bee,* July 26, 1992, p. A1 and A18.
14. California Constitution, Article IX, section f.
15. See Stadtman, 1970; Coons, 1968; Fitzgibbon, 1968; Douglass, 2002.
16. Chief Justice Gibson, in Gardner, 1967, p. 242.
17. For the history of this movement see Douglass, 1995; Fitzgibbon, 1968; Stadtman, 1970.
18. <u>Report of the Committee on Academic Freedom and Tenure</u>, December 1915, pp. 6–29. Washington, D.C.: American Association of University Professors.
19. Dean Ewald Grether, in Fitzgibbon, 1968, p. 26.
20. Standing Orders of the Regents of the University of California, Section 105.1 and 105.2.
21. *Tolman v. Underhill,* 39 Cal. 2d 708, quoted in Gardner, 1967, p. 242.
22. Fitzgibbon, 1968, p. 86.
23. See Karabel, 1996; Kerr and Gade, 1989; and Douglass, 1995; AAUP, 1996; Ferrier, 1930.
24. *Cooper v. Ross,* in Rabban, 1990, p. 281.
25. See Berdahl, 1971; Heilbron, 1973; Kerr and Gade, 1989; Douglass, 2000, 1996; and Karabel, 1996; Burrell and Morgan, 1979.
26. See Heilbron, 1973; Kerr and Gade, 1989; Douglass, 1995; Schwartz, 1996; Karabel, 1996.
27. The definitive work on the topic is John Douglass's *The California Idea and American Higher Education* (2000).

CHAPTER 3. THE CONTEXT SHAPING THE AFFIRMATIVE ACTION CONTEST AT UC

1. See <u>*UC Staff Development and Affirmative Action, Report to the Regents*</u>, June 15, 1995, Associate Vice-President Lubbe Levin.
2. Brown, letter to Hitch, July 2, 1973, in Richardson, 1996, p. 187.
3. Brown, letter to Haughabook, June 28, 1973, in Richardson, 1996, p. 187.
4. For analyses of *Bakke* see Rabban, 1990; and Ball, 2000.
5. <u>*Freshman admissions at Berkeley: A policy for the 1990s and beyond.*</u> Berkeley, CA: Committee on Admissions and Enrollment, Berkeley Division, Academic Senate, University of California, by Jerome Karabel, Chair, 1989.
6. Donald Werner, "College Admissions, Shaky Ethics," <u>*New York Times*</u>, June 1, 1988, p. A1.
7. U. S. Department of Education Office for Civil Rights Docket # 09-89-6003.

8. Data drawn from the chart "Average SAT Scores by Parental Income and Race/Ethnicity," New Directions for Outreach: Report of the University of California Outreach Task Force, Executive Summary, p. 11. UC Office of the President, Oakland, CA.

9. Source: Annual Report on Undergraduate Admissions and Enrollments, Statistical Overview, Fall 1994, p. 19. UC Office of the President, Oakland, CA.

10. See Schrag, 1998 for a detailed analysis of the effects of Proposition 13.

11. Source: Eligibility of California's 1996 High School Graduates for Admission to the State's Public Universities. California Postsecondary Education Commission Report 97–9. December, 1997.

12. Ibid.

13. A number of individuals influenced the context despite not having voting authority. The nonvoting faculty representatives and those members who left the board prior to the votes: faculty representatives (nonvoting), Arnold L. Leiman, vice chairman of the Academic Council (1993–1995); Daniel Simmons, chairman of the Academic Council (1993–1995); Regents who left the board just prior to July, 1995, Willie Brown, Democrat, ex officio Speaker of the Assembly 1980–1994, replaced by Doris Allen, Speaker of the Assembly, June 1995; David Flinn, president, Alumni Associations of UC, chair of the Special Committee on Affirmative Action Policies, left board July 1, 1995; Peter Preuss, vice president, Alumni Associations of UC, left board July 1, 1995; Terrence Wooten, Student Regent, left board June 30, 1995, replaced by Ed Gomez. Regents joining the board in 1995, Jess M. Bravin, Student Regent Designate from July 1, 1995 through June 30, 1996 while Ed Gomez served as Student Regent; Richard Russell, vice president of the UC Alumni Associations.

14. These data are derived from UCOP data and Senate Rules Committee documents.

15. Regent Leach was appointed U.S. Ambassador to France in 2001.

16. Interview with Ward Connerly, March 27, 1998, Sacramento, California.

17. State senate confirmation of UC Regents was established in 1972 by a state constitutional amendment, Measure 5.

18. California Senate Rules Committee Hearing Transcript, June 1, 1986, p. 4.

19. California Senate Rules Committee Hearing Transcript, June 27, 1984, p. 30.

20. California Senate Rules Committee Hearing Transcript, February 28, 1994, p. 14.

21. California Senate Rules Committee Hearing Transcript, June 23, 1997, p. 85.

22. For an excellent account of the role of ballot initiatives in California politics, see Schrag, 1998.

23. See Tolbert and Hero, 1996; Chavez, 1998.

24. For the definitive study of the campaign to pass Proposition 187, see Chavez, 1998.

25. Data from Chavez, 1998, p. 38 and p. 39.

26. Chavez, 1998, p. 38.

27. For detail on the development of the text of Proposition 209, see Chavez, 1998.

28. William Rusher, *National Review*, November 1, 1993, p. 55, in Chavez, 1998, p. 23.

29. Patrick Buchanan, in Chavez, 1998, p. 111.

30. Thomas Wood, in Chavez, 1998, p. 24.
31. Wayne Johnson, in Chavez, 1998, p. 24.

CHAPTER 4. INTEREST ARTICULATION AND THE ILLUSION OF CONTROL

1. Charles Schwartz, *Budget Report #12,* unpublished ms., August 7, 1994, Berkeley, CA.
2. Connerly, in Charles Schwartz, *Budget Report #12,* p. 3, unpublished ms., August 7, 1994, Berkeley, CA
3. Gubernatorial nominees to the Board of Regents initially serve for one year as "Regent Designate." At the conclusion of the year they stand for Senate confirmation to a 12-year term.
4. This chain of events was presented in an interview with Regent Ralph Carmona, April 21, 1998.
5. Ward Connerly, letter to Chair Leach et al. December 21, 1993.
6. Jack Peltason to Connerly et al. January 4, 1994. Italics in original.
7. "A Worried Generation of College Students," *Los Angeles Times* Op-Ed January 9, 1994, p. M4.
8. Charles Schwartz, *Budget Report #12,* p. 3, August 7, 1994.
9. This issue was addressed by Democrats at the Senate Rules Committee confirmation hearing for Regent nominee Lester Lee on February 24, 1994.
10. A number of those interviewed were under the impression that Leland Stanford was also rejected as a Regent nominee in 1887. While the record is not entirely clear, it appears Stanford withdrew prior to rejection.
11. Lance Williams, "A Glimpse into UC's Inner Sanctum," *San Francisco Examiner,* March 20, 1994, p. A1.
12. Cook, in Richard Bernstein, "Moves Under Way in California to Overturn Higher Education's Affirmative Action Policy," *New York Times,* January 25, 1995, p. B7.
13. Cook, Ellen and Jerry E. Cook "Race and UC Medical School Admissions." July 1, 1994, p.3. Unpublished ms.
14. The Cooks in their letter and their report use the term "affirmative action applicants" to refer to the group of students that UC designates "underrepresented."
15. Cook and Cook, "Race and UC Medical School Admissions."
16. Deputy General Counsel Morrison, letter to Regent Burgener, July 12, 1994. Archives, Office of the Secretary of the Regents, Oakland, CA.
17. Ibid.
18. Ibid.
19. Ibid.
20. Regents Connerly and del Junco suggested in interviews that UC was violating *Bakke* at the time.
21. Deputy General Counsel Morrison to Regent Burgener, July 12, 1994. Archives, Office of the Secretary of the Regents.
22. Ibid.

23. Ibid.
24. Ibid.
25. Cook and Cook, "Race and UC Medical School Admissions."
26. Deputy General Counsel Morrison, letter to Regent Burgener, July 12, 1994.
27. The Deputy General Counsel in his reply to Regent Burgener used the term "minority" in place of the more common UC admissions identifier of "underrepresented."
28. Cook and Cook "Reply to the Morrison Report." August, 12, 1994.
29. Jerry Cook, in Chavez, 1998, p. 33.
30. Interview with Ward Connerly, March 27, 1998.
31. Interview with Jess Bravin, May 6, 1998.
32. Connerly, in Chavez, 1998, p. 34.
33. Ralph Carmona, in Chavez, 1998, p. 49.
34. Interview with Richard Russell, May 27, 1998, Los Angeles, California.
35. Jack Peltason, remarks to the Committee on Educational Policy and Special Committee on Affirmative Action Policies, November 17, 1994.
36. Deputy General Counsel Gary Morrison, remarks for the board, November 17, 1994.
37. U.S. Department of Education, Office of Civil Rights, Docket #09-89-6003 p. 1.
38. Deputy General Counsel Gary Morrison, remarks for the board, November 17, 1994.
39. Text of the opinion, *Hopwood et al. v. State of Texas*, March 19, 1996.
40. Deputy General Counsel Gary Morrison, remarks for the board, November 17, 1994.
41. Vice-President. Hopper, remarks prepared for meeting of the Regents, November 17, 1994.
42. Dr. Ralph Purdy in minutes of the joint meeting of the Committee on Educational Policy and Special Committee on Affirmative Action Policies, November 17, 1994. Office of the Secretary of the Regents.
43. Dr. Michael Drake, prepared remarks to the Regents, November 17, 1994.
44. Interview with Ralph Carmona, April 21, 1998.
45. Regent Connerly, from minutes of the joint meeting of the Committee on Educational Policy and Special Committee on Affirmative Action Policies, November 17, 1994. Office of the Secretary of the Regents.
46. Ibid.
47. Regent Tirso del Junco, from minutes of the joint meeting of the Committee on Educational Policy and Special Committee on Affirmative Action Policies, November 17, 1994. Office of the Secretary of the Regents.
48. Ibid.
49. Regent Leo S. Kolligian, from minutes of the joint meeting of the Committee on Educational Policy and Special Committee on Affirmative Action Policies, November 17, 1994. Office of the Secretary of the Regents.
50. Regent John Davies, from minutes of the joint meeting of the Committee on Educational Policy and Special Committee on Affirmative Action Policies, November 17, 1994. Office of the Secretary of the Regents.

51. Regent David B. Flinn, from minutes of the joint meeting of the Committee on Educational Policy and Special Committee on Affirmative Action Policies, November 17, 1994. Office of the Secretary of the Regents.
52. Interview with Chancellor Emeritus Karl Pister, June 1, 1998.
53. Deputy General Counsel Morrison, to Regent Burgener, July 12, 1994, p. 2.
54. Regent Kolligian, from minutes of the joint meeting of the Committee on Educational Policy and Special Committee on Affirmative Action Policies, November 17, 1994. Office of the Secretary of the Regents.
55. Regent David B. Flinn, from minutes of the joint meeting of the Committee on Educational Policy and Special Committee on Affirmative Action Policies, November 17, 1994. Office of the Secretary of the Regents.
56. Student Regent Wooten, from minutes of the joint meeting of the Committee on Educational Policy and Special Committee on Affirmative Action Policies, November 17, 1994. Office of the Secretary of the Regents.
57. Interview with Ward Connerly, March 27, 1998.
58. Vice President Hopper, from minutes of the joint meeting of the Committee on Educational Policy and Special Committee on Affirmative Action Policies, November 17, 1994. Office of the Secretary of the Regents.
59. Interview with Ward Connerly, March 27, 1998.
60. Peter Schrag, "UC's Hodgepodge Defense of Race Policy." *Orange County Register*, May 26, 1995.
61. Interview with Dr. Tirso del Junco, May 26, 1998.
62. Interview with Regent William T. Bagley, June 1, 1998, San Francisco, California.
63. Interview with Ward Connerly, March 27, 1998.
64. John Boudreau "Effort to Outlaw Affirmative Action Promoted in California: Civil Rights Groups See Initiative as Political-Cultural Grenade." *Washington Post* December 27, 1994, p. 3, in Chavez, 1998, p. 40.
65. Chavez, 1998, p. 40.
66. *San Jose Mercury News*, January 19, 1995.
67. Interview with Ed Gomez, April 22, 1998, Riverside, California.
68. President Jack Peltason "Statement on the University of California's Affirmative Action Programs and Policies." Prepared remarks, January 19, 1995.
69. Jack Peltason, remarks to the UC Regents Special Committee on Affirmative Action Policies, meeting transcript, January 19, 1995. Emphasis added.
70. Ibid.
71. Ibid.
72. Alice Gonzales, remarks to the UC Regents Special Committee on Affirmative Action Policies, meeting transcript, January 19, 1995.
73. John Davies, remarks to the UC Regents Special Committee on Affirmative Action Policies, meeting transcript, January 19, 1995.
74. Roy Brophy, remarks to the UC Regents Special Committee on Affirmative Action Policies, meeting transcript, January 19, 1995.
75. Interview with President Emeritus Jack Peltason, May 27, 1998, Irvine, California.

76. Generally the committee chair is first to speak to an item and then recognizes other Regents as they request to speak to the board.

77. Ward Connerly, remarks to the UC Regents Special Committee on Affirmative Action Policies, meeting transcript, January 19, 1995.

78. Ibid.

79. Ibid.

80. President Peltason, remarks to the UC Regents Special Committee on Affirmative Action Policies, meeting transcript, January 19, 1995.

81. Ibid.

82. Ibid.

83. Burgener, remarks to the UC Regents Special Committee on Affirmative Action Policies, meeting transcript, January 19, 1995.

84. Davies, remarks to the UC Regents Special Committee on Affirmative Action Policies, meeting transcript, January 19, 1995.

85. Leiman, remarks to the UC Regents Special Committee on Affirmative Action Policies, meeting transcript, January 19, 1995.

86. Connerly, remarks to the UC Regents Special Committee on Affirmative Action Policies, meeting transcript, January 19, 1995.

87. Nakashima, remarks to the UC Regents Special Committee on Affirmative Action Policies, meeting transcript, January 19, 1995.

88. Khachigian, remarks to the UC Regents Special Committee on Affirmative Action Policies, meeting transcript, January 19, 1995.

89. Eastin, remarks to the UC Regents Special Committee on Affirmative Action Policies, meeting transcript, January 19, 1995.

90. Carmona, remarks to the UC Regents Special Committee on Affirmative Action Policies, meeting transcript, January 19, 1995.

91. Flinn, remarks to the UC Regents Special Committee on Affirmative Action Policies, meeting transcript, January 19, 1995.

92. See Chavez, 1998, p. 49.

93. According to Chavez, a Gallup/CNN poll from March of 1995 showed 55% in favor of affirmative action, with 63% opposing quotas (1998, pg. 275).

94. Chavez, 1998, p. 49.

95. Wilson, address to the Republican party convention. February 25, 1995. Sacramento, CA. Governor's Office Transcript.

96. California Assembly Bill ACA 2 was introduced by Assemblyman Richter in an effort to place the language of CCRI on the state ballot. It failed at the committee level.

97. Peltason, prepared remarks to the joint Committee on Educational and Policy Special Committee on Affirmative Action Policies, March 16, 1995.

98. Flinn, minutes of the joint Committee on Educational and Policy Special Committee on Affirmative Action Policies, Regents' meeting, March 16, 1995. Office of the Secretary of the Regents, Oakland, CA.

99. "Diversity: an Introduction to the University of California's Policies and Programs," March 1995, UCOP.

100. Regents' Undergraduate Admissions Policy of May 1988, UCOP.

101. "Diversity: an Introduction to the University of California's Policies and Programs," University of California Office of the President. March 1995.

102. Ibid.
103. Ibid.
104. The phrase "academic development" is used here to describe formal UC programs that are part of broader university efforts to increase diversity, more often referred to as "outreach."
105. Galligani, minutes of the Committee on Educational Policy Special Committee on Affirmative Action Policies, Regents' meeting, March 16, 1995. Office of the Secretary of the Regents, Oakland, CA.
106. The Puente Program is an outreach program directed at increasing transfer of Latino/Chicano students from 2-year to 4-year schools.
107. Minutes, Regents' meeting, March 16, 1995.

CHAPTER 5. THE NEW POLITICS OF GOVERNANCE

1. Stephanopoulos in Chavez, 1998, p. 50.
2. Richter and McManus, in Chavez, 1998, p. 51.
3. Dole, *Congressional Record*, March 15, 1995, in Chavez, 1998, p 52.
4. Wilson, from Lesher and Stall, *Los Angles Times*, March 24, 1995, in Chavez, 1998, p. 52.
5. Ellis, *Los Angeles Times*, April 7, 1995.
6. Ward Connerly, "UC Must End Affirmative Action," *San Francisco Chronicle*, May 3, 1995, p. A19.
7. Interview with Chancellor Emeritus Charles Young, May 19, 1998, San Jose, California.
8. Amy Wallace, "Affirmative Action Dispute Halts Meeting of UC Regents." *Los Angeles Times*, May 19, 1995, p. A1 & A29.
9. Statistical Summary of Students and Staff, University of California fall 1994, Office of Information Systems, University of California Office of the President.
10. Ibid.
11. Data drawn from <u>Statistical Overview 1994</u>, UCOP, Student Academic Services, p. 19. A subsequent UC report, <u>The Use of Socio-Economic Status in Place of Ethnicity in Undergraduate Admission, Occasional Paper 5</u>, showed that for all 1994 Freshmen applicants to UC, 70% of Chicano/Latino applicants had parental income below $50,000, 66.6% of African American applicants were below that level, and 56.5% of Asian American applicants had parental income below $50,000. Of white applicants, 29.7% reported parental income below $50,000. UCOP, Office of the Assistant Vice President Student Academic Services. May, 1995.
12. Associate Vice President Galligani, <u>Slide Presentation on Undergraduate Admissions Policies and Practices</u>, presented to the joint Committee on Educational Policy, Special Committee on Affirmative Action Policies, May 18, 1995.
13. Ibid.
14. Ibid.
15. Ibid
16. Ibid.
17. Ibid.

18. Vice Chancellor Doby, remarks to the joint meeting of the Committee on Educational Policy and the Special Committee on Affirmative Action Policies, May 18, 1995.

19. Professor Phillip Curtis, "Freshman Selection for the College of Letters and Sciences at UCLA," a presentation to the joint meeting of the Committee on Educational Policy and the Special Committee on Affirmative Action Policies, May 18, 1995.

20. Ibid.

21. Ibid.

22. Regent Velma Montoya, remarks to the Regents, author's meeting transcript, July 20, 1995.

23. Regent Leo Kolligian, remarks to the Regents, author's meeting transcript, July 20, 1995.

24. Professor Phillip Curtis, "Freshman Selection for the College of Letters and Sciences at UCLA," a presentation to the joint meeting of the Committee on Educational Policy and the Special Committee on Affirmative Action Policies, May 18, 1995.

25. The White and Asian applicants in that case would have received an intensive reading. Approximately 25% of students who received intensive readings were subsequently admitted.

26. Curtis, presentation to the board, May 18, 1995.

27. Interview with Ward Connerly, March 27, 1998.

28. Interview with Dr. Tirso del Junco, May 26, 1998.

29. Report on Graduate and Professional School Admissions, May 10, 1995, prepared by UCOP for joint meeting of the Committee on Educational Policy and the Special Committee on Affirmative Action Policies, May, 18, 1995, p. 2.

30. Ibid, p. 4.

31. Ibid.

32. Vice Chancellor Claudia Mitchell-Kernan, minutes, joint meeting of the Committee on Educational Policy and the Special Committee on Affirmative Action Policies, May 18, 1995.

33. Ibid. p. 3.

34. For an analysis of affirmative action at Boalt Hall, see Guerrero, 2002.

35. <u>Statement of Faculty Policy Governing Admission to Boalt Hall</u>, May 6, 1993, p. 6–7.

36. <u>Admissions Policy Statement and Task Force Report</u>, p. 24–25, Boalt Hall, August 31, 1993.

37. Ibid.

38. Ibid.

39. Dean Herma Hill Kay, presentation to the Committee on Education Policy and Special Committee on Affirmative Action, May 18, 1995.

40. Interview with Dr. Tirso Del Junco, May 26, 1998.

41. Regent Watkins and Vice Chancellor Doby, minutes, Committee on Education Policy, Special Committee on Affirmative Action Policies, Office of the Secretary of the Regents. May 18, 1995.

42. Robert Laird, minutes, Committee on Education Policy, Special Committee on Affirmative Action Policies, Office of the Secretary of the Regents. May 18, 1995.

43. Dean Herma Hill Kay, minutes, Committee on Education Policy, Special Committee on Affirmative Action Policies, Office of the Secretary of the Regents. May 18, 1995.

44. Annual Report on Affirmative Action and Graduate and Professional School Admissions, UCOP, May, 1995.

45. The Use of Socio-Economic Status in Place of Ethnicity in Undergraduate Admissions: A Preliminary Report on the Results of a Computer Simulation. UCOP, Office of the Assistant Vice President Student Academic Services, May, 1995.

46. Movimiento Estudiantil Chicano de Aztlan.

47. Interview with Edward Gomez, April 22, 1998. The Coalition to Defend Affirmative Action by Any Means Necessary (BAMN) has maintained a presence in contemporary protests over affirmative action and other social issues. They appear to have originated in Detroit, Michigan, and while it is not entirely clear who leads the organization, there is little evidence they have served as agent provocateurs.

48. Generally, those members of the public wishing to speak to the board must notify the board secretary in advance of the meeting. For the meetings held early in 1995, in order to enable more public comment this provision was occasionally not enforced.

49. Amy Wallace, "Affirmative Action Dispute Halts Meeting of UC Regents." *Los Angeles Times*, May 19, 1995, p. A1 & A29.

50. Interview with Ed Gomez, April 22, 1998.

51. UCOP Report of Communications Received, June 16, 1995.

52. Governor Pete Wilson, Executive Order W-124-95.

53. Ronald Reagan quoted in Wilson, Executive Order W-124-95.

54. Governor Wilson to Regent Leach, June 1, 1995, p. 1.

55. Ibid.

56. Governor Wilson, Opposing Quotas and Preferential Treatment. Fact Sheet, June 1, 1995.

57. Governor Wilson, Open Letter to the People of California, June 1, 1995.

58. Ibid.

59. Virginia Ellis, "Wilson to Order Cuts in Affirmative Action." *Los Angeles Times*, May 28, 1995, p. A1.

60. B. Drummond Ayres Jr., "California's Wilson Vows to Cut Back Affirmative Action." *New York Times*, June 1, 1995, p. A1.

61. Ibid.

62. Tom Brokaw, *NBC Nightly News,* June 12, 1995.

63. *Adarand v. Pena,* June 12, 1995.

64. Ibid.

65. Phil Gramm, in Judy Keen, "Affirmative Action Takes New Turn for 1996 Race." *USA Today*, June 13, 1995, p. 5A.

66. Ibid.

67. Terry Colvin, in Suzanne Espinoza Solis, "UC Medical Admissions Challenged." *San Francisco Chronicle*, June 9, 1995, p. A22.

68. Ward Connerly, in Suzanne Espinoza Solis, "UC Medical Admissions Challenged." *San Francisco Chronicle*, June 9, 1995, p. A22.

69. David Flinn, minutes, joint meeting of the Committee on Educational Pollicy and Special Committee on Affirmative Action Policies, June 15, 1995.
70. Interview with Roy Brophy, March 27, 1998.
71. President Jack Peltason, minutes, joint meeting of the Committee on Educational Policy and Special Committee on Affirmative Action Policies, June 15, 1995.
72. Vice Chancellor Mitchell-Kernan, from minutes, Committee on Educational Policy, Special Committee on Affirmative Action Policies, June 15, 1995. Office of the Secretary of the Regents, Oakland, CA.
73. Assistant Vice President Lubbe Levin, speaking notes, <u>University of California Staff Diversity and Affirmative Action</u>, Board of Regents Meeting June 15, 1995.
74. Ibid.
75. Director Umscheid, minutes, Committee on Education Policy, Special Committee on Affirmative Action Policies, June 15, 1995. Office of the Secretary of the Regents, Oakland, CA.
76. Ibid.
77. Ibid.
78. Ward Connerly, minutes, Committee on Education Policy, Special Committee on Affirmative Action Policies, June 15, 1995. Office of the Secretary of the Regents, Oakland, CA.
79. Daniel Simmons, minutes, Committee on Education Policy, Special Committee on Affirmative Action Policies, June 15, 1995. Office of the Secretary of the Regents, Oakland, CA.
80. Provost Massey, minutes, Committee on Education Policy, Special Committee on Affirmative Action Policies, June 15, 1995. Office of the Secretary of the Regents, Oakland, CA.
81. Ward Connerly, minutes, Committee on Education Policy, Special Committee on Affirmative Action Policies, June 15, 1995. Office of the Secretary of the Regents, Oakland, CA.
82. Daniel Simmons, minutes, Committee on Education Policy, Special Committee on Affirmative Action Policies, June 15, 1995. Office of the Secretary of the Regents, Oakland, CA.
83. Howard Leach, minutes, Committee on Education Policy, Special Committee on Affirmative Action Policies, June 15, 1995. Office of the Secretary of the Regents, Oakland, CA.
84. Connerly and Kennedy, minutes, Committee on Education Policy, Special Committee on Affirmative Action Policies, June 15, 1995. Office of the Secretary of the Regents, Oakland, CA.
85. Ward Connerly, letter to the Regents, December 21, 1993.
86. Interview with Karl Pister, June 10, 1998.
87. Edward Gomez, minutes, Committee on Education Policy, Special Committee on Affirmative Action Policies, June 15, 1995. Office of the Secretary of the Regents, Oakland, CA.
88. Meredith Khachigian, minutes, Committee on Education Policy, Special Committee on Affirmative Action Policies, June 15, 1995. Office of the Secretary of the Regents, Oakland, CA.

89. Sayles and Mitchell-Kernan, minutes, Committee on Education Policy, Special Committee on Affirmative Action Policies, June 15, 1995. Office of the Secretary of the Regents, Oakland, CA.
90. Delaine Eastin, minutes, Committee on Education Policy, Special Committee on Affirmative Action Policies, June 15, 1995. Office of the Secretary of the Regents, Oakland, CA.
91. Ward Connerly, minutes, Committee on Education Policy, Special Committee on Affirmative Action Policies, June 15, 1995. Office of the Secretary of the Regents, Oakland, CA.
92. Karl Pister, minutes, Committee on Education Policy, Special Committee on Affirmative Action Policies, June 15, 1995. Office of the Secretary of the Regents, Oakland, CA.
93. Walter Massey, minutes, Committee on Education Policy, Special Committee on Affirmative Action Policies, June 15, 1995. Office of the Secretary of the Regents, Oakland, CA.
94. Minutes, Committee on Education Policy, Special Committee on Affirmative Action Policies, June 15, 1995. Office of the Secretary of the Regents, Oakland, CA.

CHAPTER 6. NATIONAL CONTEST AND CONFLICT

1. Interview with Jack Peltason, May 29, 1998.
2. Interview with Charles Young, May 19, 1998.
3. Interview with Edward Gomez, April 22, 1998.
4. Susan Yoachum "Wilson Predicts UC Regents Will End Race-Based Admissions." *San Francisco Chronicle*, July 7, 1995.
5. Ibid.
6. Tim W. Ferguson, "Affirmative Action's California Battle Lines." *Wall Street Journal*, July 13, 1995, p. A19.
7. Interview with Daniel Simmons, April 21, 1998.
8. Interview with Ralph Carmona, April 21, 1998.
9. Interview with Daniel Simmons, April 21, 1998.
10. Ellen Cook, letter to the Regents, July 17, 1995.
11. David Flinn, letter to the Regents, June 19, 1995.
12. The University of California Academic Council is a representative body of the UC Assembly of the Academic Senate.
13. Daniel Simmons, letter to Jack Peltason, June 20, 1995.
14. Ward Connerly, letter to Clair Burgener, June 30, 1995.
15. Ibid.
16. Professor Davis was earlier dismissed from her post as lecturer at UCLA by the UC Regents in 1970.
17. Ralph Carmona, letter to the Regents, June 30, 1995.
18. Ibid.
19. Ward Connerly, letter to the Regents, July 5, 1995.
20. Ibid.

21. The titles SP-1 and SP-2 were arbitrary designations for Regent Connerly's proposals, created by the Office of the Secretary of the Regents. See appendices 1 and 2.
22. Connerly, proposal to the Board of Regents, July 5, 1995.
23. Ibid.
24. Ibid.
25. Jack President Peltason, letter to the board, July 10, 1995.
26. Jack Peltason, proposal for action item, July 10, 1995.
27. UCOP, Rationale for Recommendation, July 10, 1995.
28. "Statement of the President, Chancellors, and Vice Presidents of the University of California," July 10, 1995.
29. Interview with Karl Pister, June 10, 1998.
30. Ibid.
31. Ward Connerly, letter to the Regents, June 12, 1995.
32. Ibid.
33. The Student Regent is not the official representative of UC students. Students are represented by individual campus associations, and by the federation of all campus student associations, the University of California Student Association (UCSA).
34. Interview with Edward Gomez, April 22, 1998.
35. UC Student Association, Resolution on Affirmative Action to the Regents of the University of California. July 17, 1995.
36. Ward Connerly, in James Richardson, "UC Regent Submits Plans: Racial Preferences Would be Barred in Admisison, Hiring." *Sacramento Bee*, July 6, 1995, p. A5.
37. Ward Connerly, in Laura Kurtzman, "UC Admissions Policy Called Illegal." *San Jose Mercury News*, July 6, 1995, p. 3B.
38. James Holst in James Richardson, "UC Regent Submits Plans: Racial Preferences Would be Barred in Admisison, Hiring." *Sacramento Bee*, July 6, 1995, p. A5.
39. Edward Epstein, "4 Regents Hit UC Chief Over Race: Public Criticism is Prelude to Key Vote." *San Francisco Chronicle*, July 15, 1995, p. A1.
40. Regents Campbell, del Junco, Kolligian and Lee, letter to Peltason, July 13, 1995.
41. Ibid.
42. William Bagley, in Edward Epstein, "4 Regents Hit UC Chief Over Race: Public Criticism is Prelude to Key Vote." *San Francisco Chronicle*, July 15, 1995, p. A1.
43. Dario Caloss, quoted in Senator Tom Campbell press release, July 17, 1995, p. 2.
44. Senator Tom Campbell press release, July 17, 1995.
45. Ibid.
46. Walter E. Massey to the Regents of the University of California, July 18, 1995.
47. Produced by the Office of Undergraduate Admissions UC Berkeley as presented in the *Berkeleyan* September 9-22, 1992, Volume 21, #3. For an excellent review of the creation of this matrix and the evolution of the UC Berkeley admissions policies, see Office of the Assistant Vice Chancellor Admissions and Enrollment,

Report to the UC Regents on Berkeley's Admissions Policies Processes and Outcomes, November 8, 2001, UC Berkeley.

48. Governor Wilson, in Amy Chance, "UC Admission Goals Create 'Patent' Bias, Wilson Says." *Sacramento Bee*, July 17, 1995, p. A1.

49. Jesse Jackson, in April Allison, Ray Delgado, and Dexter Waugh, "Protestors Seek Arrest to No Avail." *San Francisco Examiner*, July 21, 1995, p. A14.

50. Governor Wilson, in Dave Lesher, "Governor Wilson's Alternative to Affirmative Action." *Los Angeles Times*, July 17, 1995, p. A3.

51. Ibid.

52. Susan Yoachum, "Wilson Predicts UC Regents Will End Race-Based Admissions." *San Francisco Chronicle*, July 17, 1995, p. A1.

53. Text of address to the Employers Group, July 18, 1995, Office of the Governor. Emphasis in original.

54. William H. Honan, "Regents Prepare for Storm on Affirmative Action." *New York Times*, July 19, 1995, p. B7.

55. Ward Connerly, in Honan, *New York Times*, July 19, 1995, p. B7.

56. William Jefferson Clinton in Paul Richter, "Clinton Declares Affirmative Action is Good for America." *Los Angeles Times*, July 20, 1995, p. A1.

57. Ibid.

58. Pete Wilson, in Paul Richter, "Clinton Declares Affirmative Action is Good for America." *Los Angeles Times*, July 20, 1995, p. A1.

CHAPTER 7. CONTEST, RESISTANCE, AND DECISION

1. Scott Kamena, "Behind the Scenes Look at Regents' Meeting." *Berkeley Counterpoint*, Vol. 2, #3, October 1995, p. 1.

2. Ibid.

3. Pete Wilson, author's transcript from audiotapes of Regents' meeting, July 20, 1995 provided by the University of California. Hereafter, speakers' comments transcribed from these audiotapes will be designated "author's transcript, July 20, 1995."

4. Ibid.

5. Rob Morse, "Send Pete Wilson to the Principles Office." *San Francisco Examiner*, July 21, 1995, p. A1.

6. Pete Wilson, author's transcript, July 20, 1995.

7. Assemblyman Brown was an ex officio Regent while Speaker of the Assembly.

8. Willie Brown, author's transcript, July 20, 1995.

9. Reverend Jesse Jackson, author's transcript, July 20, 1995.

10. Ibid.

11. The rhetorical linkage of efforts to end affirmative action with the Civil Rights movement of the 1960s by Regent Connerly and the governor would be picked up by other Regents and would continue well into the campaign for the passage of Proposition 209 in 1996. Late in that campaign a television advertisement promoting 209 that used the image and words of Dr. King's speech at the

march on Washington would backfire and cause the campaign to pull the advertisements (Chavez, 1998).

12. Reverend Jackson, author's transcript, July 20, 1995.
13. Ibid.
14. Ibid.
15. Ibid.
16. Ibid.
17. Author's transcript, July 20, 1995.
18. Colleen Sabatini, author's transcript, July 20, 1995.
19. Ed Center, author's transcript, July 20, 1995.
20. York Chang, author's transcript, July 20, 1995.
21. Ralph Armbruster, author's transcript, July 20, 1995.
22. Ward Connerly, author's transcript, July 20, 1995.
23. Jack Peltason, author's transcript, July 20, 1995.
24. Pete Wilson, author's transcript, July 20, 1995.
25. Ibid.
26. Ibid.
27. The alumni representatives and Student Regents first serve an apprenticeship on the board as "designates" during which time they cannot vote. Student Regent Gomez was designate while Student Regent Wooten was on the board. Alumni Representative Russell was designate while Representatives Carmona and Levin were on the board.
28. Richard Russell, author's transcript, July 20, 1995.
29. The Bagley-Keene Act required public business and votes to be held in public sessions.
30. Interview with William Bagley, June 1, 1998.
31. Richard Russell, author's transcript, July 20, 1995.
32. William Bagley, author's transcript, July 20, 1995.
33. Ibid.
34. Gray Davis, author's transcript, July 20, 1995.
35. Howard Leach, author's transcript, July 20, 1995. See also, minutes, The Regents of the University of California, July 20, 1995.
36. Interview with William Bagley, June 1, 1998.
37. Interview with Richard Russell, May 27, 1998.
38. Delaine Eastin, author's transcript, July 20, 1995.
39. Ibid.
40. Chang-Lin Tien, author's transcript, July 20, 1995.
41. Ibid.
42. Ibid.
43. Ralph Carmona, author's transcript, July 20, 1995.
44. Robert Laird, author's transcript, July 20, 1995.
45. Ralph Carmona, author's transcript, July 20, 1995.
46. Pete Wilson, author's transcript, July 20, 1995.
47. Chang-Lin Tien, author's transcript, July 20, 1995.
48. This exchange is from the author's transcript, July 20, 1995.
49. Jack Peltason, author's transcript, July 20, 1995.
50. Chang-Lin Tien, author's transcript script, July 20, 1995.

51. This exchange is from the author's transcript, July 20, 1995.
52. Interview with David Lee, May 12, 1998.
53. John Davies, author's transcript, July 20, 1995.
54. Ibid.
55. Sue Johnson, author's transcript, July 20, 1995.
56. Ibid.
57. Tom Sayles, author's transcript, July 20, 1995.
58. Judith Levin, author's transcript, July 20, 1995.
59. Yori Wada was a former Regent who had earlier addressed the board as an invited speaker.
60. Judith Levin, author's transcript, July 20, 1995.
61. S. Stephen Nakashima, author's transcript, July 20, 1995.
62. Lance Williams et al., "Wilson Pleads for 'Fairness.'" *San Francisco Examiner*, July 20, 1995, p. A1.
63. Meredith Khachigian, author's transcript, July 20, 1995.
64. Ibid.
65. Ralph Frammolino, Mark Gladstone, and Amy Wallace. "Some Regents Seek UCLA Admissions Priority for Friends." *Los Angeles Times*, March 22, 1996, p. A3.
66. Velma Montoya, author's transcript, July 20, 1995.
67. Alice Gonzales, author's transcript, July 20, 1995.
68. Ibid.
69. Daniel Simmons, author's transcript, July 20, 1995.
70. Ibid.
71. Leo Kolligian, author's transcript, July 20, 1995.
72. Ibid.
73. David Lee, author's transcript, July 20, 1995.
74. Roy Brophy, author's transcript, July 20, 1995.
75. Ibid.
76. Interview with Roy Brophy, March 27, 1995.
77. Jack Peltason, motion to the Regents, author's transcript, July 20, 1995.
78. Author's transcript, July 20, 1995.
79. Charles Young, author's transcript, July 20, 1995.
80. Ibid.
81. Walter Massey, author's transcript, July 20, 1995.
82. Ward Connerly, amendment to SP-1 and SP-2, author's transcript, July 20, 1995.
83. See appendices 1 and 2.
84. Author's notes, 1998.

CHAPTER 8. AFTERMATH

1. Lance Williams, "Affirmative Action Decision Unpopular but it Won't Cost." *San Francisco Examiner*, July 28, 1995, p. A1.
2. American Association of University Professors, Report of the Commission on Governance and Affirmative Action Policy, AAUP: Washington, D.C., May 29, 1996, p. 1.

3. Peter Schmidt, "U. of California Chief Won't Delay Ban on Race Preferences." *Chronicle of Higher Education*, February 9, 1996, p. A29.

4. Richard Atkinson, letter to Governor Wilson, January 29, 1996, quoted in Pamela Burdman, "Regents Let UC Chief Off Hook: Conciliatory Letters Appease Critics." *San Francisco Chronicle* January 30, 1996, p. A1.

5. Charles Schwartz, *Aftermath #3*, unpublished ms., February 12, 1996.

6. Peter Schmidt, "U. of California Chief Won't Delay Ban on Race Preferences." *Chronicle of Higher Education*, February 9, 1996, p. A29.

7. Dave Lesher, "Affirmative Action Raises Wilson Profile." *Los Angeles Times*, July 31, 1995, p. A23.

8. See Connerly, 2000; Chavez, 1998.

9. UC Berkeley Office of Public Information, news release, May 14, 1997.

10. Bert Eljera "UC Admits More APAs, Fewer Other Minorities." *AsianWeek* April 9–15, 1998, p. 1.

11. See UCOP, Information Digests, 1996–2000. Oakland, CA.

12. *Senate Rules Committee Hearing Transcript*, June 23, 1997, p. 85.

13. Interview with Tirso del Junco, May 26, 1998. Los Angeles, California.

14. Gubernatorial nominees serve a year on the board prior to their confirmation hearings. At the end of that period they must be confirmed by the State Senate to continue their full terms.

15. Minutes, The Regents of the University of California, January 15, 1999.

16. Senate Select Committee on Higher Education Admissions and Outreach, Transcript. February 5, 1998, Sacramento, California.

17. For more on guaranteed admission plans, see Hurtado and Washington Cade, 2001; Horn and Flores, 2003.

18. Keith Widaman, Senate Select Committee on Higher Education Admissions and Outreach Transcript, February 5, 1998, p. 103.

19. See UCOP, Admissions Facts and Figures, 2001, UCOP Information Digest 2001. Oakland, California.

20. Minutes, The Regents of the University of California, May 16, 2001.

21. Ibid.
22. Ibid.
23. Ibid

CHAPTER 9. THE END AND THE BEGINNING

1. One notable exception was the stance that President Kerr took in 1967 that led to Kerr's dismissal.

2. See Kerr and Gade, 1989; Chait, 1995; Ingram, 1995; Jones and Skolnik, 1997; Pusser, 2003.

3. Senator Lockyer was elected Attorney General of California in 1998.

4. Interview with Bill Lockyer, March 20, 1998.

5. Interview with President Emeritus Jack Peltason, May 27, 1998, Irvine, California.

6. The contest over the training of obstetrician-gynecologists in public university medical centers has already begun. See Ben Baez and Sheila Slaughter. "Academic Freedom and Federal Courts in the 1990s: The Legitimation of the Conservative Entrepreneurial State," in John Smart and William Tierney, eds. *Handbook of Theory and Research in Higher Education* (Bronx, NY: Agathon Press, 2001, pp. 73–118).

7. Interview with William Bagley, June 1, 1998.

8. Ibid.

9. Interview with Karl Pister, June 10, 1998.

10. Interview with Ward Connerly, March 27, 1998. In his book *Creating Equal: My Fight Against Race Preferences* (San Francisco: Encounter Books, 2000) Regent Connerly presents in detail his perspective on affirmative action.

11. Of the nearly 9,000 applicants to UCLA's undergraduate college in 1980, some 80% were UC eligible, and nearly all eligible applicants were admitted. See UCLA Freshman Admission in the 1990s: A Decade of Rapid Change July 21, 1990.

12. Interview with Tirso del Junco, May 26, 1998.

13. Tom Hayden, Closing Doors: Affirmative Action and Downsizing at the University of California, a statement presented to the Regents of the University of California, July 20, 1995.

14. UCOP, Statistical overview, fall 1994 applicants, May 1995.

15. Nancy Barreda, remarks to the Regents, author's transcript, July 20, 1995.

16. Arthur Fletcher, remarks to the Regents, author's transcript, July 20, 1995.

17. Eva Paterson, remarks to the Regents, author's transcript, July 20, 1995.

18. Cheryl Hagen, remarks for the Regents, July 20, 1995.

19. John Vasconcellos, letter to Chair Burgener, July 21, 1995.

20. Ibid.

21. Nao Takasugi, remarks to the Regents, author's transcript, July 20, 1995.

22. In November 1997, after a divisive contest, the Regents voted 13–12 to provide domestic partner benefits to UC employees. In March 1999, despite significant administrative opposition, UCLA graduate students voted to create a union affiliation for teaching assistants.

23. Roy Brophy, remarks to the Regents of the University of California, July 21, 1995. Because discussion of the votes of the board on the previous day was not an agenda item, Regent Brophy spoke from the audience as part of the public comment session.

24. Ward Connerly, in Jerome Karabel "University Governance and the Crisis at UC." Testimony before the California State Senate Select Committee on Higher Education. February 20, 1996 p. 3.

25. Article IX, Constitution of the State of California.

26. Interview with Karl Pister, June 1, 1998.

Bibliography

AAUP. 1996. *Report of the Commission on Governance and Affirmative Action Policy.* May 29, 1996. Washington, DC: AAUP.

AAUP. 1995. *Policy Documents and Reports* 1995 Edition. Washington, DC: AAUP.

Apple, Michael. 1982. *Education and Power.* Boston: Routledge and Keegan Paul.

Aronowitz, Stanley. 1981. *The Crisis in Historical Materialism: Class, Politics and Culture in Marxist Theory.* New York: J.F. Bergin.

Aronowitz, Stanley and Henry Giroux. 1993. *Education Still under Siege.* Second Edition. Westport, Conn.: Bergin and Garvey.

Arrow, Kenneth J. 1974. *The Limits of Organization.* New York: Norton.

Atkinson, Richard C. 1996. *Transcript of California State Senate Fiscal Retreat.* University of California at Berkeley, UC Office of the President, February 3.

Baldridge, J. Victor, David V. Curtis, George P. Ecker and Gary L. Riley. 1983. "Alternative Models of Governance in Higher Education." In *ASHE Reader in Organization and Governance in Higher Education,* ed. Robert Birnbaum. Lexington, Mass.: Ginn Custom.

Baldridge, J. Victor. 1971. *Power and Conflict in the University: Research in the Sociology of Complex Organizations.* New York: J. Wiley.

Ball, Howard. 2000. *The Bakke Case: Race, Education and Affirmative Action.* Lawrence: University Press of Kansas.

Bendor, Jonathan. 1988. "Formal Models of Bureaucracy: A Review Essay." *British Journal of Political Science* 31:353–395.

Bensimon, Estela M. 1989. "The Meaning of 'Good Presidential Leadership': A Frame Analysis." *Review of Higher Education* 12:107–123.

Berdahl, Robert. 1971. *Statewide Coordination of Higher Education.* Washington, DC: ACE.

Berger, Joseph B., and Jeffrey F. Milem. 2000. "Organizational Behavior in Higher Education and Student Outcomes." In *Higher Education: Handbook of Theory and Research,* Volume XV, ed. John Smart. New York: Agathon Press.

Blau, Peter M. 1973. *The Organization of Academic Work*. New York: Wiley.

Bolman, Lee, and Terrence E. Deal. 1997. *Reframing Organizations: Artistry, Choice and Leadership*. Second Edition. San Francisco: Jossey Bass.

Bourdieu, Pierre. 1977. "Cultural Reproduction and Social Reproduction." In *Power and Ideology in Education*, eds. Jerome Karabel and A. H. Halsey. New York: Oxford University Press.

Bowen, Howard R. 1980. *The Costs of Higher Education*. San Francisco: Jossey-Bass.

Bowles, Samuel, and Herbert Gintis. 1976. *Schooling in Capitalist America*. New York: Basic Books.

Bowles, Samuel, and Herbert Gintis. 1990. *Democracy and Capitalism*. New York: Basic Books.

Breneman, David W. 1995. *A State of Emergency? Higher Education in California*. San Jose: California Higher Education Policy Center.

Burrell, Gibson, and Gareth Morgan. 1979. *Sociological Paradigms and Organisational Analysis: Elements of the Sociology of Corporate Life*. London: Heinemann.

Calvert, Randall, Mathew D. McCubbins, and Barry R. Weingast. 1989. "A Theory of Political Control and Agency Discretion." *American Journal of Political Science* 33:588–611.

Carnoy, Martin, and Henry M. Levin. 1985. *Schooling and Work in the Democratic State*. Stanford: Stanford University Press.

Chait, Richard P. 1995. *The New Activism of Corporate Boards and the Implications for Campus Governance*. Washington, DC: Association of Governing Boards of Universities and Colleges.

Chang, Mitchell J. 2001. "The Positive Educational Effects of Racial Diversity on Campus." In *Diversity Challenged: Evidence on the Impact of Affirmative Action*, eds. G. Orfield and M. Kurlaender. Cambridge, MA: Harvard Education Publishing.

Chang, Mitchell J. 2002. "Preservation or Transformation: The Real Educational Discourse on Diversity?" *The Review of Higher Education* 25(2):125–140.

Chavez, Lydia. 1998. *The Color Bind: California's Battle to End Affirmative Action*. Berkeley: University of California Press.

Chubb, John E., and Terry Moe. 1990. *Politics, Markets and America's Schools*. Washington, DC: Brookings Institution.

Clark, Burton R. 1972. "The Organizational Saga in Higher Education." *Administrative Science Quarterly* 17:178–184.

Clark, Burton R. 1983. *The Higher Education System: Academic Organization in Cross-National Perspective*. Berkeley: University of California Press.

Clark, Burton R. 1996. "Complexity and Differentiation: The Deepening Problem of University Integration." In *Emerging Patterns of Social Demand and University Reform: Through a Glass Darkly*, eds. D. Dill and B. Sporn. Oxford: Pergamon.

Cohen, Michael D., and James G. March. 1974. *Leadership and Ambiguity: The American College President*. New York: McGraw Hill.

Conkey, Margaret, Troy Duster, Louise Fortmann, Jerome Karabel, Kristin Luker, Stanley Prussion and Lawrence Wallick. 1996. *University Governance, Political Intrusion, and the UC Board of Regents*. Unpublished ms., for the UCB Chapter of the Systemwide Faculty Committee to Rescind SP-1 and SP-2. January 14.

Connerly, Ward. 2000. *Creating Equal: My Fight Against Race Preferences*. San Francisco: Encounter Books.

Coons, Arthur. 1968. *Crisis in California Higher Education*. Los Angeles: Ward Ritchie.

Dahl, Robert. 1956. *A Preface to Democratic Theory*. Chicago: University of Chicago Press.

DiMaggio, Paul J., and Walter W. Powell. 1983. "The Iron Cage Revisited: Institutional Isomorphism and Collective Rationality in Organizational Fields." *American Sociological Review* 48:147–160.

Dixit, Avinash. 1996. *The Making of Economic Policy: A Transaction Costs Politics Perspective*. Cambridge: MIT Press.

Domhoff, William G. 1990. *The Power Elite and the State*. New York: Aldine.

Douglass, John Aubrey. 1992a. "Creating a Fourth Branch of State Government: The University of California and the Constitutional Convention of 1879." *History of Education Quarterly* 32:31–71.

Douglass, John Aubrey. 1992b. *Politics and Policy in California Higher Education: 1850 to the 1960 Master Plan*. PhD Dissertation, UC Santa Barbara.

Douglass, John Aubrey. 1995. "Shared Governance: Shaped by Conflict and by Agreement." *Notice* (November). Volume 20 #2, p. 3–6. UC Academic Senate.

Douglass, John Aubrey. 2000. *The California Idea and American Higher Education: 1850 to the 1960 Master Plan*. Palo Alto: Stanford University Press.

Douglass, John Aubrey. 2001. "Anatomy of Conflict: The Making and Unmaking of Affirmative Action at the University of California." In *Color Lines: Affirmative Action, Immigration, and Civil Rights Options for America*, ed. J. D. Skrentny. Chicago: University of Chicago Press.

Duryea, Edward D. 1981. "The University and the State: A Historical Overview." In *Higher Education in American Society*, eds. P. Altbach and R. Berdahl. Buffalo: Prometheus Books.

Eley, Lynn W. 1964. "The University of California at Berkeley: Faculty Participation in the Government of the University." *AAUP Bulletin* (Spring) pp. 5–13.

Favish, Alan J. 1996. "From Bakke to the UC Regents Vote, the California Civil Rights Initiative and Hopwood." *University of West Los Angeles Law Review* 27:353–377.

Ferrier, William. 1930. *Origin and Development of the University of California*. Berkeley: Sather Gate Book Shop.

Fitzgibbon, Russell H. 1968. *The Academic Senate of the University of California*. University of California. Oakland: Office of the President.

Fredrickson, George. 1997. *The Comparative Imagination: On the History of Racism, Nationalism and Social Movements*. Berkeley: University of California Press.

Freire, Paulo. 1973. *Pedagogy of the Oppressed*. New York: Seabury Press.

Garcia, Mildred. 1997. "The State of Affirmative Action at the Threshold of a New Millenium." In *Affirmative Action's Testament of Hope*, ed. Mildred Garcia. Albany: SUNY Press.

Gardner, David P. 1967. *The California Oath Controversy*. Berkeley: University of California Press.

Giroux, Henry A. 1981. *Ideology, Culture and the Process of Schooling*. Philadephia: Temple University Press.

Gitlin, Todd. 1987. *The Sixties: Years of Hope, Days of Rage*. New York: Bantam Books.

Gramsci, Antonio. 1971. *Selections from Prison Notebooks*. New York: International Publishers.

Guerrero, Andrea. 2002. *Silence at Boalt Hall: The Dismantling of Affirmative Action*. Berkeley: The University of California Press.

Gumport, Patricia J., and Brian Pusser. 1995. "A Case of Bureaucratic Accretion: Context and Consequences." *The Journal of Higher Education Volume 66 #5* (September/October):493–520.

Hammond, Thomas H., and Jeffrey S. Hill. 1993. "Deference or Preference? Explaining Senate Confirmation of Presidential Nominees." *Journal of Theoretical Politics* 5:23–59.

Hardy, Cynthia. 1990. "Putting Power into University Governance." In *Higher Education: Handbook of Theory and Research*, ed. John C. Smart. New York: Agathon Press, p. 393–426.

Hardy, Cynthia. 1996. *The Politics of Collegiality: Retrenchment Strategies in Canadian Universities*. Montreal: McGill Queen's University Press.

Heilbron, Louis H. 1973. *The College and University Trustee*. San Francisco: Jossey-Bass.

Heller, Donald E., ed. 2001. *The States and Public Higher Education Policy: Affordability, Access, and Accountability*. Baltimore: Johns Hopkins University Press.

Hill, Jeffrey S. 1985. "Why So Much Stability: The Role of Agency Determined Stability." *Public Choice* 46:275–287.

Hobbes, Thomas. 1968. [1651]. *Leviathan*. New York: MacPherson.

Hofstadter, Richard, and Walter Metzger. 1955. *The Development of Academic Freedom in the United States*. New York: Columbia University Press.

Horn, Catherine and Stella Flores. 2003. "Percent Plans in College Admission: A Comprehensive Analysis of Three State's Experiences." Report from The Civil Rights Project at Harvard University, Cambridge, Massachusetts.

Horn, Murray J. 1995. *The Political Economy of Public Administration*. London: Cambridge University Press.

Howard, John R. 1997. "Affirmative Action in Historical Perspective." In *Affirmative Action's Testament of Hope,* ed. Mildred Garcia. Albany: SUNY Press.

Hurtado, Sylvia, and Heather Washington Cade. 2001. "Time for Retreat or Renewal? Perspectives on the Effects of *Hopwood* on Campus." In *The States and Public Higher Education Policy: Affordability, Access and Accountability*, ed. Don Heller. Baltimore: Johns Hopkins University Press.

Ingram, Richard T. 1995. *Effective trusteeship: A guide for board members of independent colleges and universities*. Washington, DC: Association of Governing Boards of Universities and Colleges.

Jessop, Bob. 1990. *State Theory: Putting the Capitalist State in Its Place*. Cambridge: Polity Press.

Jones, Glen A., and Michael L. Skolnik. 1997. "Governing Boards in Canadian Universities." *The Review of Higher Education* 20:277–295.

Karabel, Jerome. 1989. *Freshman admissions at Berkeley: A policy for the 1990s and beyond*. Berkeley, CA: Committee on Admissions and Enrollment, Berkeley Division, Academic Senate, University of California, by Jerome Karabel, Chair.

Karabel, Jerome. 1996. "University Governance and the Crisis at UC." *California State Senate Select Committee on Higher Education* 20 (February):1–10.

Kerr, Clark. 2003. *The Gold and the Blue: A Personal Memoir of the University of California, 1949–1967: Volume II: Political Turmoil*. Berkeley: University of California Press.

Kerr, Clark. 2001. *The Uses of the University (5th ed.)*. Cambridge, MA: Harvard University Press.

Kerr, Clark, and Marian L. Gade. 1989. *The Guardians: Boards of Trustees of American Colleges and Universities*. Washington, DC: AGB.

Kingdon, John W. 1984. *Agendas, Alternatives, and Public Policies*. Boston: Little, Brown.

Klinkner, Philip A. 1996. *Midterm: The Elections of 1994 in Context*. Boulder, Colo.: Westview Press.

Kraatz, Matthew, and Edward J. Zajac. 1996. "Exploring the Limits of the New Institutionalism: The Causes and Consequences of Illegitimate Organizational Change." *American Sociological Review* 61:812–836

Labaree, David F. 1997. "Public Goods, Private Goods: The American Struggle over Educational Goals." *American Educational Research Journal* 34 (Spring):39–81.

Lemann, Nicholas. 1999. *The Big Test: The Secret History of the American Meritocracy.* New York, NY: Farrar, Straus and Giroux.

Levin, Henry M. 2001. *Privatizing education.* Boulder, CO: Westview Press.

Levin, John S. 2001. *Globalizing the Community College: Strategies for Change in the Twenty-first Century.* New York: Palgrave Press.

Locke, John. 1955. [1690]. *On Civil Government.* Chicago: Regnery.

Mann, Michael. 1993. *The Sources of Social Power,* Volume II. Cambridge: Cambridge University Press.

March, James G., and Johan P. Olsen. 1995. *Democratic Governance.* New York: Free Press.

Marginson, Simon. 1997. *Markets in Education.* Cambridge: Cambridge University Press.

Marx, Karl. 1867. *Capital,* Volume I. New York: Modern Library.

Mashaw, Jerry. 1990. "Explaining Administrative Process: Normative, Positive and Critical Studies of Legal Development." *Journal of Law, Economics and Organization* 6:267–298.

Masten, Scott E. 1993. "Transaction Costs, Mistakes, and Performance: Assessing the Importance of Governance." *Managerial and Decision Economics* 14:199–129.

Masten, Scott E. 1995. "Old School Ties: Financial Aid Coordination and Governance of Higher Education." *Journal of Economic Behavior and Organizations* 28:23–47.

McConnell, T. R. 1981. "Autonomy and Accountability: Some Fundamental Issues." In *Higher Education in American Society*, eds. P. G. Altbach and R. O. Berdahl. Buffalo: Prometheus.

McCormick, Robert E., and Roger E. Meiners. 1988. "University Governance: A Property Rights Perspective." *Journal of Law, Economics and Organization* 31:423–442.

McCubbins, Matthew D., Roger G. Noll, and Barry R. Weingast. 1987. "Administrative Procedures as Instruments of Political Control." *Journal of Law, Economics and Organization* 3:243–277.

McDonough, Patricia M. 1997. *Choosing Colleges: How Social Class and Schools Structure Opportunity.* Albany: SUNY Press.

Metzger, Walter P. 1990. "The 1940 Statement of Principles of Academic Freedom and Tenure." *Law and Contemporary Problems* 53:3–78.

Meyer, John W., and Brian Rowan. 1977. "Institutionalized Organizations: Formal Structure as Myth and Ceremony." *American Journal of Sociology* 83:340–363.

Milgrom, Paul, and John Roberts. 1992. *Economics, Organization, and Management.* New York: Prentice Hall.

Miller, Gary, and Terry Moe. 1983. "Bureaucrats, Legislators, and the Size of Government." *American Political Science Review* 77:297–322.

Millett, John David. 1962. *The Academic Community: An Essay on Organization.* New York: McGraw-Hill.

Millett, John David. 1984. *Conflict in Higher Education: State Government Coordination Versus Institutional Independence.* San Francisco: Jossey-Bass.

Mills, Nicolaus. 1994. *Debating Affirmative Action: Race, Gender, Ethnicity, and the Politics of Inclusion.* New York: Delta Press.

Mintzberg, Henry. 1979. *The Structuring of Organizations.* Englewood Cliffs: Prentice Hall.

Moe, Terry. 1984. "The New Economics of Organization." *American Journal of Political Science* 28:739–777.

Moe, Terry. 1991. "Politics and the Theory of Organization." *Journal of Law, Economics and Organization* 8:237–254.

Moe, Terry. 1995. The politics of structural choice: Toward a theory of public bureaucracy. In Oliver E. Williamson (Ed.). *Organization Theory: From Chester Barnard to the Present and Beyond.* (p. 116–153). Oxford, United Kingdom: Oxford University Press.

Moe, Terry. 1996. *The Positive Theory of Public Bureaucracy.* New York: Cambridge University Press.

Niskanen, William A. 1971. *Bureaucracy and Representative Government.* Chicago: Aldine-Atherton Press.

Olson, Mancur. 1965. *The Logic of Collective Action: Public Goods and the Theory of Groups.* Cambridge, Mass.: Harvard University Press.

Ordorika, Imanol. 2003. *Power and Politics in University Governance.* London: Routledge Falmer.

Parsons, Michael D. 1997. *Power and Politics: Federal Higher Education Policymaking in the 1990s.* Albany: SUNY Press.

Parsons, Talcott. 1960. *Structure and Process in Modern Societies.* Glencoe, Ill.: Free Press.

Pfeffer, Jeffrey, and Gerald R. Salancik. 1978. *The External Control of Organizations: A Resource Dependence Perspective.* New York: Harper & Row.

Pusser, Brian. 2003. "Beyond Baldridge: Extending the political model of higher education governance." *Educational Policy, 17(1),* 121–139.

Pusser, Brian. 2002. "Higher education, the emerging market and the public good." In P.A. Graham & N. Stacey (Eds.), *The knowledge economy and postsecondary education.* (p. 105–125). Washington, DC: National Academy Press.

Pusser, Brian, and Dudley J. Doane. 2002. "Public Purpose and Private Enterprise." *Change* 5 (33):19–25.

Pusser, Brian. 2001. "The Contemporary Politics of Access and Diversity Policy." In *The States and Public Higher Education: Affordability, Access, and Accountability*, ed. Donald E. Heller. Baltimore: Johns Hopkins University Press.

Rabban, David M. 1990. "A Functional Analysis of 'Individual' and 'Institutional' Academic Freedom under the First Amendment." *Law and Contemporary Problems* 53:227–302.

Rhoades, Gary. 1992. "Beyond "the State": Interorganizational Relations and State Apparatus in Post-secondary Education." In *Higher Education: Handbook of Theory and Research*, ed. John C. Smart. New York: Agathon, p. 84–142.

Rhoades, Gary. 1996. "Reorganizing the Faculty Workforce for Flexibility: Part-Time Professional Labor." *Journal of Higher Education* 67:626–659.

Rhoades, Gary, and Sheila Slaughter. 1997. "Academic Capitalism, Managed Professionals, and Supply-Side Higher Education." *Social Text* 51:9–38.

Richardson, James. 1996. *Willie Brown: A Biography.* Berkeley: University of California Press.

Riley, Gary L. & J. Victor Baldridge. 1977. *Governing academic organizations: New problems, new perspectives.* Berkeley, CA: McCutchan.

Schrag, Peter. 1998a. "Gray Davis: Will There Be Affirmative Reaction?" *Sacramento Bee* November 18:B6.

Schrag, Peter. 1998b. *Paradise Lost: California's Experience, America's Future.* New York: New Press.

Schwartz, Charles. 1991. "A Look at the Regents of the University of California." Unpublished ms. October 1.

Schwartz, Charles. 1996. "Aftermath #3." Unpublished ms. January 4.

Scully, Caitlin M. 1987. "Autonomy and Accountability: The University of California and the State Constitution." The Hastings Law Journal 38:927–955.

Shepsle, Kenneth A. 1989. "Studying Institutions: Some Lessons from the Rational Choice Approach." *Journal of Theoretical Politics* 1:131–147.

Skocpol, Theda. 1992. *Protecting Soldiers and Mothers.* Cambridge: Harvard University Press.

Skrentny, John D. 2001. *Color lines: Affirmative action, immigration, and civil rights options for America.* Chicago, IL: University of Chicago Press.

Slaughter, Sheila. 1988. "Academic Freedom and the State." *Journal of Higher Education* 59:241–265.

Slaughter, Sheila. 1990. *The Higher Learning and High Technology: Dynamics of Higher Education Policy Formation.* Albany: SUNY Press.

Slaughter, Sheila. 1993. "Retrenchment in the 1980s: The Politics of Prestige and Gender." *Journal of Higher Education* 64:250–282.

Slaughter, Sheila, and Larry L. Leslie. 1997. *Academic Capitalism.* Baltimore: Johns Hopkins University Press.

Smelser, Neil J. 1974. "Growth, Structural Change and Conflict in California Public Higher Education, 1950–1970." In *Public Higher Education in California,* eds. Neil J. Smelser and Gabriel Almond. Berkeley: University of California Press.

Stadtman, Verne. 1970. *The University of California 1868–1968.* New York: McGraw Hill.

Strauss, Anselm L., and Juliet Corbin. 1994. "Grounded Theory Methodology: An Overview." In *Handbook of Qualitative Research,* eds. Norman K. Denzin and Yvonna S. Lincoln. Thousand Oaks, Calif.: Sage Publications.

Tolbert, Caroline J., and Rodney E. Hero. 1996. "Race/Ethnicity and Direct Democracy: An Analysis of California's Illegal Immigration Initiative." *The Journal of Politics* 58:806–818.

Van Alstyne, William. 1990. "Academic Freedom and the First Amendment in the Supreme Court of the United States: An Unhurried Historical Review." *Law & Contemporary Problems,* 53, 79–154.

Weber, Max. 1947. *The Theory of Social and Economic Organization.* Glencoe, Ill.: Free Press.

Weick, Karl E. 1976. "Educational Organizations as Loosely Coupled Systems." *Administrative Science Quarterly* 21:1–19.

Weingast, Barry R., and William J. Marshall. 1988. "The Industrial Organization of Congress; or, Why Legislatures, Like Firms, Are Not Organized as Markets." *Journal of Political Economy* 96:132–163.

Weir, Margaret, Ann Orloff, and Theda Skocpol. 1988. *The Politics of Social Policy in the United States.* Princeton: Princeton University Press.

Williamson, Oliver E. 1985. *Economic Organization: Firms, Markets, and Policy Control.* New York: New York University Press.

Williamson, Oliver E. 1995. *Organization Theory: From Chester Barnard to the Present and Beyond.* New York: Oxford University Press.

Willis, Paul E. 1981. *Learning to Labor.* New York: Columbia University Press.

Wilson, James Q. 1989. *Bureaucracy: What Government Agencies Do and Why They Do It.* Cambridge: Basic Books.

Wirt, Frederick M., and Michael W. Kirst. 1972. *Political and Social Foundations of Education.* Berkeley: McCutchan Publishing.

Youn, Ted I. K., and Gordon B. Arnold. 1997. "What Does the Reform of Undergraduate Curriculum Tell Us about the Political Order in Academia?" Paper presentation to the Association for the Study of Higher Education, Albuquerque, N.M., November.

Zusman, Ami. 1986. "Legislature and University Conflict: The Case of California." *The Review of Higher Education* 9:397–418.

Index

AAUP. *See* American Association of University Professors

academic admissions criteria: academic indexes, 34–36; advanced placement/honors courses, 91, 92–93; affirmative action, after revocation of, 201–3, 206–7; affirmative action, general, 24, 27–30, 33, 34–36, 49–62 (passim), 75, 95–96, 98, 129, 201–3, 205; color-blind, 60, 61, 62, 157; diversity and, 28, 56, 57, 59, 60, 75–76, 78–79, 89, 97–98, 100, 114, 125, 159, 160, 164–65, 176, 192–93, 230; diversity matrix and, 92–93, 95, 115, 126, 170, 171, 173, 174–75; gender and, 1, 16, 17, 25, 28, 42, 84, 106, 107, 128, 146, 201, 223–24 (*see also* SP-1); GPA (grade-point average), 30, 49, 50, 57, 60, 75, 81, 91, 92, 95, 98, 102; high school graduates, 33–34, 88, 92, 169–70, 206, 229; LSAT scores, 30, 100; medical school, 1, 26, 27–30, 49, 50–65; qualitative criteria and, 57, 59–60; race/ethnicity and, 1, 16, 17, 24, 25, 27–36, 34–35, 49–64, 70–77, 88–89, 91–96, 107, 114, 125–40 (passim), 145–96 (passim) (*see also* SP-1); religious beliefs and, 17, 25, 130, 230; retention and graduation rates and, 92, 95–96, 101; SAT scores, 31, 91, 96, 103; socioeconomic status and, 27, 30–36, 56, 59, 93, 94, 95, 103–4, 137–38, 219–23; test scores, general, 50, 51, 57; UC academic senate, 13, 14, 18–19, 23, 91–92

Academic Council of the University of California, 20, 122, 125, 126, 159, 189

academic development programs: faculty and staff hiring, 111; general, 78, 79, 81, 131, 189; primary and secondary education, 129, 132, 169, 205–6; targeted outreach, 79, 81–82, 84, 114, 125, 128–30 (passim), 153, 170, 203, 205–6, 229

academic freedom: affirmative action and, 21; autonomy without, 21; general, 9–10, 20; General Declaration of Principles, 18; loyalty oath, 18, 19–20

academic senate. *See* senate, UC academic

access: California Master Plan, 24; constitutional law, 30; cultural capital, 31; employment/contracts, 112, 231; general, 2, 3–4; legislative policy responses, 205; president, UC position, 79, 80, 90; *Proposition 13*, 33–34; *Proposition 187*, 43; Regents' deliberations, 34, 60–61, 72, 75, 79, 90, 100, 101, 112, 124, 150, 152, 155, 161, 189, 201; socioeconomic factors, 2, 30–31, 33–34, 150, 189; State theory, 8

263

Adarand Constructors v. Pena, 108–10, 112–13

administration: affirmative action admissions debate, 49–53, 55–61, 63–70, 76, 79–80, 87–92, 96–99, 102, 103–4, 108–11, 113–15, 118, 119, 130–34, 137–38, 159–62, 172, 180, 199–200, 212, 213, 215, 224; affirmative action, faculty/staff hiring, 107–10, 111–12, 114–17, 199–200; diversity issue, 59, 62–63, 67–69, 79–81; fairness of affirmative action, 50, 64, 70, 76, 88, 90–91; institutional culture, 96, 217–18; interest articulation, 4, 45–47, 49–53, 55–61, 63–64; Regents' relations with, 14, 20, 45–48, 53, 55–56, 60–61, 63–64, 67, 68–70, 76, 79, 87–92, 96–99, 103, 108–11, 113–18, 119, 130–37, 159–62, 172, 180, 187, 224. *See also* president, UC

admission tests. *See* LSAT; MCAT; SAT; test scores

affirmative action, general: academic admissions criteria and, 24, 27–30, 33, 34–36, 49–62 (passim), 75, 95–96, 98, 129, 201–3, 205–7; academic freedom and, 21; African American admissions, 33, 52, 55, 81, 93, 95–96, 107, 128, 130, 155, 158, 172, 203, 221; African American faculty and staff hiring, 111; African Americans, historical context, 26, 81, 148–49; American Indian admissions, 52, 93, 103; Asian Americans, impact on, 29, 30, 49, 52, 71, 74–75, 81, 93, 94, 96, 103, 109, 127, 137–38, 170, 201, 203, 205, 224; Berkeley admissions, 29, 91, 96, 126, 138, 139, 140, 159, 160–61, 162, 180, 201–3, 219, 221; *Brown v. Board of Education*, 25; California Civil Rights Initiative (CCRI), 41, 43–44, 54, 66–67, 69, 71–72, 77, 79, 84–85, 110, 114, 131, 133, 136, 160, 167, 198, 200–1, 203, 205, 206, 207–8, 209; caucasian admissions, 29, 48–52, 71, 75, 77, 80, 93, 94, 96, 127, 138, 170, 203, 205; chancellors' position, 1, 62, 132–33, 164–65, 192–94; Clinton administration position, 2, 83–84, 141–42, 175, 197, 213, 222; constitutional law, state, 27, 28, 30, 146 (*see also* Supreme Court, California); constitutional law, U.S., 26, 27, 28, 93, 126, 162 (*see also* Supreme Court, U.S.); contractors, federal law, 26–27, 108–10, 112–13, 124–25; contractors, UC, 25, 112–13, 124, 128; Davis, UC at, admissions, 11, 26–28, 48–51, 58–59, 159, 169; ex officio Regents, 63, 209 (*see also specific ex officio Regents, listed on page 37*); faculty position, admissions, 73–74, 81, 91, 119, 121–22, 123, 162, 197–198, 199; faculty hiring, 27, 107–10, 111–12, 114–17, 197–98, 199 (*see also* SP-2); federal court decisions, 10, 58 (*see also* Supreme Court, U.S.); federal programs, 25–27, 30, 108–10, 112, 124–25, 221; federal 1994 midterm elections, 41–42; graduate admissions/degrees, general, 24, 201–3; historical context, 1–3, 11, 25–44, 55, 56, 59, 72, 73–74, 89, 107–8, 161, 162, 168–69, 230; inequality as basis, 26, 150–51, 155, 221; institutional factors, 1, 26, 75, 76, 84, 155, 212, 213, 225–27; interest articulation, 45–82, 211–12; Latino/Latina admissions, 47, 48, 52, 80, 81, 96, 115–17, 128, 130, 202–3; Latino/Latina faculty and staff hiring, 111, 115; law school admissions, 30, 97–103, 201–2; mass media coverage, 85, 108, 110, 120–21, 135–41 (passim), 143, 170, 171, 196, 200, 213; medical school admissions, 1, 26, 27–30, 49, 50–57, 58, 59, 61, 62–65; national politics, 2–3, 29, 42, 53, 55, 65–67, 72, 73, 77, 83–84, 108–10, 120–21, 133, 138–42, 147–50, 201; political factors, 1–2, 3, 37–

44, 73, 111, 133–34, 136–37, 143–96 (passim), 197–98, 203–6, 211, 213–14; president, UC, 1, 46–47, 53, 55–56, 60–61, 67, 68, 72, 78–79, 111, 118, 130–37, 159–62 (*see also* "*UCOP*" *infra*); Regents, after rejection of, 197–210; Regents' debate, 1–3, 19, 33–34, 37, 41, 52–57, 60–65, 69–82, 85–106, 110–96 (passim), 200, 212, 216, 220; Regents' debate, faculty and staff hiring, 27, 107–10, 111–12, 114–17; Regents' debate, graduate programs, 1, 24, 27–30, 49, 50–57, 97–103; Regents, historical context of affirmative action, 25, 33–34, 36–41, 73–74, 89, 161, 162, 168–69, 230; Regents' perceptions of quotas, 50, 58, 59, 61, 62–65, 124–25; senate, UC academic, 1, 19, 129, 131; socioeconomic status and, 27, 30–36, 56, 59, 93, 94, 95, 103–4, 137–38, 219–23; State Assembly, 27, 65, 205; student activism/protests, 78, 85–86, 104–5, 119–20, 126–27, 138, 139, 143–45, 151–56, 170, 189, 198; student associations, 1, 27, 105, 120, 134–35, 153; students' attitude, affirmative action based on, 57, 59–60; Supreme Court, U.S., general, 25, 26, 27–29, 159 (*see also UC Regents v. Bakke*); targeted outreach, 79, 81–82, 84, 114, 125, 128–30 (passim), 153, 170, 203, 205–6, 229; taxation and, 145–46; UCLA policies, 91, 91–95, 96, 98, 126, 159, 180, 202–3; UCOP position, 49–53, 55–61, 63–70, 76, 79–80, 87–92, 96–99, 102, 103–4, 108–11, 113–15, 118, 119, 130–34, 137–38, 159–62, 172, 180, 199–200, 212, 213, 215, 224; UCOP position on fairness, 50, 64, 70, 76, 88, 90–91; UCOP position on staff/faculty hiring faculty/staff hiring, 107–10, 111–12, 114–17, 199–200; Wilson, Pete, 2, 42–43, 54–55, 77, 95, 106–7, 110, 119, 120–21, 127, 128, 133, 134, 135, 136, 138–39, 142, 144, 145–46, 151, 153, 158, 160–62, 163, 165, 169, 170–77, 187, 188, 189, 196, 200–1, 214–15. *See also* academic development programs; quotas; SP-1; SP-2

"Affirmative Action and Graduate and Professional School Admissions," 97–99

African Americans: admissions applicants, overview, 33, 86–87, 88; affirmative action, historical context, 26, 81, 148–49; affirmative action admissions, 33, 52, 55, 81, 93, 95–96, 107, 128, 130, 155, 158, 172, 203, 221; affirmative action, faculty and staff hiring, 111; graduate admissions/degrees, general, 98–99; socioeconomic status and race, 103

agendas and agenda controls: Board of Regents, 41, 53, 55, 64, 65, 68, 69, 72, 141, 148, 214–15; personal political, 5, 7, 40, 77, 194, 200, 201, 203, 214–15, 216

alumni: affirmative action, general, 1; Regent representatives, 34, 37, 55, 60, 63, 76, 114, 118, 122, 127–28, 130–31, 133, 212, 213 (*see also* Carmona, Ralph; Levin, Judith; Russell, Richard); UC governance structure, 16, 76

American Association of University Professors (AAUP): *General Declaration of Principles*, 18; Regents' vote, reaction to, 197–98; *Statement of Principles on Academic Freedom and Tenure*, 21; *Statement on the Relationship of Faculty Governance to Academic Freedom*, 23

American Indians: admissions applicants, overview, 86; affirmative action admissions, 52, 93, 103; graduate admissions/degrees, 98, 109; socioeconomic status, 103

Asian Americans: admissions applicants, overview, 86, 87, 88, 95; affirmative action, impact on, 29, 30, 49, 52, 71, 81, 93, 94, 96, 103, 109, 127, 137–38, 170, 201, 203, 205, 224; gender and, 224; graduate admissions/degrees, 99, 109; graduation rates, UC, 92; medical school admissions, 33, 49, 57, 60, 61
Atkinson, Richard, 199–200, 207
autonomy: academic freedom lacking, 21; affirmative action and, 21, 225–27; funding and, 13, 16, 21; loyalty oath, 18, 19–20; Regents' appointment/confirmation, 214, 226; student protests, 20; UC governance, legal and historical context, 16, 17–21, 225–27. *See also* academic freedom

Bagley, William, 37, 54, 117, 137, 164–66, 187, 189, 190–91, 195, 216
Bagley-Keene Open Meeting law, 189, 192
Bakke. *See UC Regents v. Bakke*
Berkeley, University of California at: academic admissions requirements, 34–36, 98; affirmative action admissions, 29, 91, 96, 126, 138, 139, 140, 159, 160–61, 162, 180, 201–3, 219, 221; Chancellor Tien, 75, 138, 162, 170–77, 198; graduate admissions/programs, 98, 99–103, 201–2, 221–22; student protests, 198, 221
Berkeley Revolution of 1920, 18–19, 20
black. *See* African Americans
Board of Regents of the University of California: admissions policy control, general, 61–62, 95–96; academic senate and, 13, 14, 18–19, 91–92, 188–89; access to opportunity issues, 34, 60–61, 72, 75, 79, 90, 100, 101, 112, 124, 150, 152, 155, 161, 189, 201; affirmative action, debate/votes,

general, 1–3, 19, 33–34, 37, 41, 52–57, 60–65, 69–82, 85–106, 110–96 (passim), 200, 212, 216, 220; affirmative action, faculty and staff hiring, 25, 27, 107–10, 111–12, 114–17, 124–25, 128, 222; affirmative action, gender-based, 1, 42, 89, 115, 116, 127, 131, 148, 149, 151, 153, 156, 181, 183, 185, 188, 193, 201, 223–24, 228; affirmative action, graduate degrees, 1, 24, 27–30, 49, 50–57, 97–103; affirmative action, historical context, 25, 33–34, 36–41; affirmative action rescinded, aftermath, 197–210; agendas and agenda control, 41, 53, 55, 64, 65, 68, 69, 72, 141, 148, 214–15; alumni Regents, 34, 37, 55, 60, 63, 76, 212, 213 (*see also* Carmona, Ralph; Levin, Judith; Russell, Richard); American Association of University Professors on vote, 197–98; appointments/confirmations, 4, 13–14, 15–17, 34, 36–41, 45, 46–47, 63, 203–5, 213–14, 226; *Bakke,* 1, 26, 27–30, 49, 50–51, 56–58, 61, 126, 127, 136, 162–63, 206; budgetary control, 45, 46, 64, 81–82; California Civil Rights Initiative (CCRI), 41, 43–44, 54, 66–67, 69, 71–72, 77, 79, 84–85, 110, 114, 131, 133, 136, 160, 167, 198, 200–1, 203, 205, 206, 207–8, 209; California Master Plan for Higher Education, 24; children and allies of, admissions preferences for, 181–82; chancellors, relations with, 47, 62, 63, 162, 164–65, 170–77, 192–94, 198–99; composition, 17, 37–41, 46, 75, 135, 149–50, 188, 203–7; constitutional/legislative basis and historical context, 13–19 (passim); Cook, Jerry and Ellen, input, 48–54, 63, 89–90, 103, 110, 123, 125, 128, 211–12, 213; curricula policies, 13, 23; Democratic Party members, 37–41, 46, 75, 203–

4, 205, 206–7; diversity of Board, 17, 30, 55, 62–63, 79–80, 146, 163, 177, 179–80, 186–87, 223; ex officio, 13–14, 15, 16, 37, 63, 209; faculty representation/relations, 1, 14, 19, 20, 22–23, 37, 73–74, 81, 115, 119, 121–22, 125, 183–84, 197–98; institutional culture, 96, 217–18; interest articulation, 45–46, 52–57, 60–65; interest group input, 26, 83, 122–24; Jackson, Jesse, addresses, 120–21, 133, 138–39, 141, 147–51, 168, 169, 189, 190, 192; Kerr, Clark, removal, 20; loyalty oath, 18, 19–20; president, UC, relations with, 14, 20, 45–48, 53, 55–56, 60–61, 67, 68, 72–73, 74, 78–79, 86, 91, 92, 188–89, 111, 118, 130–37, 229, 230 (*see also "UCOP..." infra*); public comment/presence at meetings, 74–75, 78, 79, 86, 114, 122–24, 144, 151–56, 189–92, 208, 223, 224–25; public comments on racism, 124, 147, 148–49, 150, 152, 154, 155, 156, 223; racism, Regents' reflections on, 168–69, 178, 183, 178–80, 183, 186–88; shared governance, 18, 19–20, 22–23, 24, 55, 62, 64, 160, 188–89, 197–98; socioeconomic diversity of Board, 17, 30, 31, 45–46; State Assembly and, 13, 37, 61, 65, 70–71, 123, 146, 169, 184; State Senate and, 13, 15–16, 34, 38–41, 45, 47, 123, 131, 203–5, 207, 214, 225, 226; student associations and, 27, 105, 120, 134–35; student fees, 34, 45–46, 54, 60; student activism/protests, 78, 85–86, 104–5, 143–44, 151–56, 170, 189, 198, 221; student Regents, 37, 62–63, 67, 77, 105, 119, 120, 134–35; targeted outreach, 79, 81–82, 84, 114, 125, 128–30 (passim), 153, 170, 203, 205–6, 229; Wilson, Pete, involvement, 2, 42–43, 54–55, 77, 95, 106–7, 138, 139–41. *See also* SP-1; SP-2

Brass v. California, 185
Bravin, Jess, 53–54
Brophy, Roy, 37, 38, 53, 70, 110–11, 117, 151, 187–88, 189, 192–93, 195, 215, 225
Brown, Edmund, 16
Brown, Willie, 27, 64, 123, 146, 165–66, 169, 178–79
Brown Act, 189
Brown v. Board of Education, 25, 26, 208
budgetary considerations: academic development programs, 189; and state's overall budget, 11; Regents' control, 45, 46, 64, 81–82; state senate control, 184, 208, 222–23
bureaucracy: decision-making rationale, 3, 211, 212; Regents on salaries of, 54; UC academic senate and, 14
Burgener, Clair, 48, 49, 51–55, 57, 58, 62, 125, 151, 187, 189, 190, 195, 211
Bustamante, Cruz, 208

California Civil Rights Initiative (*Proposition 209*; CCRI): Connerly and, 43, 44, 54, 66–67, 69, 71–72, 77, 79, 84–85, 114, 136, 200; cost factors, 43, 84; general, 41, 43–44, 54, 66–67, 69, 71–72, 77, 79, 84–85, 110, 114, 131, 133, 136, 160, 167, 198, 200–1, 203, 205, 206, 207–8, 209; SP-1/SP-2 and, 44, 179, 200; State Assembly, 44, 54, 69
California Master Plan for Higher Education, 13, 23–24, 28, 88, 89
California Postsecondary Education Commission (CPEC), 81, 86–87, 88, 206
Campbell, Glenn, 37, 40, 136, 187, 189, 195
Campbell, Tom, 137, 138
Carmona, Ralph, 34, 37, 55, 60, 63, 76, 114, 118, 122, 127–28, 130–31, 133, 168, 170, 171, 172–73, 179, 187, 189, 195

caucasians: academic admissions criteria, general, 95–96; admissions applicants, overview, 86–87; graduation rates, UC, 92; medical school admissions, 59, 60, 61; midterm (1994) elections, 42; *Proposition 187*, 43, 66

CCRI. *See* California Civil Rights Initiative

chancellors: affirmative action, general, 1, 62, 132–33, 164–65, 192–94; Chancellor Atkinson, 198–99, 207; Chancellor Pister, 62, 115–16, 117, 132–33, 199, 217, 226–27; Chancellor Tien, 75, 138, 162, 170–77, 198; Chancellor Young, 63, 85, 102, 119, 192–93, 198; Regents' relations with, 47, 62, 63, 162, 164–65, 170–77, 192–94, 198–99; resignations, 198–99; UC president, relations with, 14, 132–33, 172, 198–99; within UC governance structure, 14, 62

Chicanos and Chicanas, 81, 86, 87, 88, 93, 95, 98, 99, 103, 109, 111, 172, 202–3

Civil Rights Act, 26, 27–28, 30, 51

Clark, Frank, 37, 187, 189, 195

class size, law school admissions, 100

class status. *See* socioeconomic status

Clinton Administration: affirmative action, 2, 83–84, 141–42, 175, 197, 213, 222; general, 109

Coalition to Defend Affirmative Action by Any Means Necessary, 104, 105, 189, 209

collegiality, 3, 4, 78

color-blind: admissions criteria, 60, 61, 62, 157; faculty/staff hiring, 116; general, 148–49, 168–69, 181, 183; state employment/contracts, 106, 107–8, 130

Colvin, Terry, 110

confirmation, Regents, 4, 13–14, 16–17, 36–41, 45, 46–47, 63, 203–5, 213–14, 226

Connerly, Ward: affirmative action, admissions, 37, 38, 44, 45, 46–48, 52–55, 60–61, 65–76, 91, 94–95, 96, 102, 110, 111, 113–14, 115–17 (passim), 123–35 (passim), 141, 135, 147–48, 153, 154–55, 157–58, 162, 163–65, 171, 172–75, 177, 183, 184–85, 211–12, 212, 213, 215, 220 (*see "SP-1" infra*); affirmative action, admissions quotas, 63–64; affirmative action, faculty/staff hiring, 115–17 (passim), 128–29, 130, 162, 183, 212, 215, 220 (*see "SP-2" infra*); affirmative action, quotas, 85, 126, 127; California Civil Rights Initiative (CCRI), 43, 44, 54, 66–67, 69, 71–72, 77, 79, 84–85, 114, 136, 200; outreach programs, 128, 129, 153, 170; Peltason, Jack, relations with, 46–48, 53, 67, 68–69, 72, 111, 115, 126–27, 129, 130–34, 135, 160, 167, 171; *Proposition 187*, 43, 66, 172–73; shared governance, 225–26; SP-1, 130, 136, 164–65, 170, 179, 183, 184–85, 187, 189, 195, 199, 208–9; SP-2, 130, 136, 158, 163, 164–65, 167–68, 170, 179, 183, 187, 189, 199, 208–9; Wilson, Pete, relations with, 65–66, 77, 106, 141, 163, 171, 215

constitutional law, federal: affirmative action, general, 26, 27, 28, 93, 126, 162 (*see also* Supreme Court, U.S.); California Civil Rights Initiative (CCRI), 44. *See also* Fourteenth Amendment; Supreme Court, U.S.

constitutional law, state: affirmative action, 27, 28, 30, 146; California Civil Rights Initiative (CCRI), 41, 43–44, 54, 66–67, 69, 71–72, 77, 79, 84–85, 110, 114, 131, 133, 136, 160, 167, 198, 200–1, 203, 205, 206, 207–8, 209; *Measure 5*, 16; sex and gender, admissions criteria, 16; UC governance, 11–17, 19, 30, 214, 225–26. *See also* Supreme Court, California contractors and contracting: access principle, 112, 231; *Adarand Constructors v. Pena*, 108–10, 112–13; California Civil Rights Initiative (CCRI), 41, 43–44; color-blind selection of, 106, 107–8, 130; federal affirmative action, 26–27, 108–10, 112–13, 124–25; gender factors, 113, 128, 195, 200; race/ethnicity of, 27, 108–10 (*see also* SP-2); Regents on, 25, 27, 107–10, 111–12, 114–17, 124–25, 128, 222; UC affirmative action, 25, 112–13, 124, 128; *See also* SP-2

Cook, Jerry and Ellen, 48–54, 63, 89–90, 103, 110, 123, 125, 128, 211–12, 213

cost and cost-benefit factors: California Civil Rights Initiative (CCRI), 43, 84; institutional politics, 7–8; socioeconomic diversity in admissions, 30, 81–82, 84; targeted outreach, 81–82, 84; university fees, 34, 45–46, 54, 60, 83

court decisions, federal courts, appellate, 10, 18, 21, 58, 185; student activism, 198. *See also* Supreme Court, California; Supreme Court, U.S.

cultural factors: capital, 31; diversity in admissions, 56, 80; institutional, general, 3, 8, 16, 96, 217–18; Regents' institutional culture, 125, 128, 211–12, 213; symbolic, 3, 4, 65, 71, 72, 73, 75, 94, 105, 120, 168, 179, 208, 211, 215, 217–18. *See also* political factors, general; political parties

cultural theories of organization, 3, 8, 16, 217–18

curricula: academic freedom, general, 21; as admissions criterion, 93; advanced placement/honors courses as admissions criteria, 91, 92–93; Regents, 13, 23; senate, UC academic, 13, 23

Curtis, Philip, 91, 92–93

Custred, Glynn, 43, 44, 69, 84

Davies, John, 46, 55, 61, 62, 69–70, 114–15, 175–76, 187, 189, 195, 204–5, 208

Davis, Angela, 127

Davis, Gray, 37, 39, 78, 133, 166–68, 169, 187, 189, 199–200, 204–5, 206–7

Davis, University of California at: affirmative action admissions, 11, 26–28, 48–51, 58–59, 159; affirmative action, need for, 169; and Office of Civil Rights, 57

decision making: general, 3, 4, 5, 7, 227. *See also* governance; governance structure

del Junco, Tirso, 37, 61, 62, 64–65, 96, 101, 118, 136, 163, 164, 187, 189, 192, 195, 203–4, 219, 224

Democratic Party: California Civil Rights Initiative (CCRI), 200–1, 207; Clinton Administration, 2, 83–84, 109, 141–42, 175, 197, 213, 222; Davis, Gray, as, 166, 205, 207, 216; Kennedy Administration, 25; national mid-term (1994) elections, 41–42; Regents' composition, 37–41, 46, 75, 203–4, 205, 206–7; State Assembly, 2, 85, 201; state government, general, 2, 37, 39–41, 85, 199–200, 201; State Senate, 2, 85, 201, 203, 207, 214, 225, 226; U.S. presidential campaign, 109

Department of Labor, 27

Deukmejian, George, 37, 39, 182, 188

disabled persons, 99, 112, 113

diversity issue: admission considerations, 28, 56, 57, 59, 60, 75–76, 78–79, 89, 92–93, 95, 97–98, 100, 114, 115, 125, 126, 159, 160, 164–65, 179, 171, 173, 174–75, 176, 192–93, 230; admissions, after revocation of affirmative action, 201; admissions matrix, 92–93, 95, 115, 126, 170, 171, 173, 174–75; Regents, diversity of, 17, 30–31, 45–46, 55, 62–63, 79–80, 146, 163, 177, 179–80, 186–87, 223; faculty and staff

diversity issue *(continued)*
  hiring, 111–12, 116–17, 232;
  graduate program admissions/degrees,
  97–98, 100–1; president, UC Office
  of, 59, 62–63, 67–69, 79–81; quotas,
  62, 63; race/ethnicity, general, 11,
  28, 34, 56, 60, 62–63, 78–79, 89, 92,
  97–98, 125, 159, 160, 164–65, 176,
  209; socioeconomic, 30–31, 32–33,
  45–46, 56, 59, 79, 89, 219
Doby, Winston, 91
Dole, Robert, 84, 108, 109
Donahue Higher Education Act. *See*
  California Master Plan for Higher
  Education
Drake, Michael, 59–60

Eastin, Delaine, 37, 75, 116, 130, 133,
  169–70, 187, 189, 195
economic factors: general, 1, 2–5, 6,
  11; UC governance structure, private
  sector control of, 14–15, 16, 17, 30.
  See also budgetary considerations;
  contractors and contracting; cost and
  cost-benefit factors; employment;
  funding; income; socioeconomic
  status; taxation; wealth
educational attainment: disadvantage,
  93, 94, 95. *See also* high school
  graduates; test scores
elementary education. *See* primary and
  secondary education
employment: faculty and staff hiring,
  19, 27, 107–10, 111–12, 114–17,
  197–98, 199 *(see also* SP-2); faculty
  salaries, 34, 45–46; gender discrimination, 25, 26, 106; racial discrimination, 25, 26, 106; Regents on
  affirmative action, 25, 27, 107–10,
  111–12, 114–17, 124–25, 128, 222;
  university staff organizations, 1;
  wage discrimination, 25; Wilson
  executive order, 106. *See also* SP-2
Equal Employment Opportunity
  Commission, 25
Equal Pay Act, 25

ethnic groups. *See* Race/ethnicity
Executive Order 10925, 25
ex officio Regents: affirmative action
  debate, 63, 209; constitutional law,
  13–14, 15, 16, 37

faculty: Academic Council of the
  University of California, 20, 122,
  125, 126, 159, 189; academic
  development programs, 111;
  academic freedom, 21; affirmative
  action, admissions, 73–74, 81, 91,
  119, 121–22, 123, 162, 197–98, 199;
  affirmative action, hiring, 27, 107–
  10, 111–12, 114–17, 197–98, 199
  (see also SP-2); expertise, 83; law
  school admissions, 100; loyalty oath,
  19; Regents, relations with, 1, 14,
  19, 20, 22–23, 37, 73–74, 81, 107–
  10, 111–12, 114, 115, 121, 122,
  183–84, 197–98; salaries, 34, 45–46.
  See also senate, UC academic; SP-2
fairness, 50, 64, 70–71, 76, 77, 88, 90–
  91
federal court decisions: affirmative
  action, general, 10, 18, 21, 58, 185;
  Brass v. California, 185. *See also*
  Supreme Court, U.S.
federal government, other: affirmative
  action plans, 25–27, 30, 108–10,
  112, 124–25, 221; affirmative action,
  1994 mid-term elections, 41–42;
  Clinton administration, 2, 83–84,
  109, 141–42, 175, 197, 213, 222;
  employment/contractor discrimination, 25, 26–27, 30, 108–10, 112,
  124–25; Department of Labor, 27;
  Kennedy administration, 25; land
  grant funding, 13, 15; Office of Civil
  Rights, 30, 51; Reagan administration, 20, 106, 137; Regents' vote,
  reaction to, 197; UC admissions
  policies, 30, 221; UC governance,
  13, 15, 18. *See also* legislation;
  Supreme Court, U.S.
Fletcher, Arthur, 26–27, 221

Flinn, David, 61–62, 76, 79, 110, 124–25
foreign counties. *See* international perspectives
Fourteenth Amendment, 26, 28, 58, 93, 126, 162
funding: academic development, general, 131, 189, 205–6; constitutional law, 13, 16, 21; land grant funding, 13, 15; *Proposition 13*, 33; Regents' vote, reaction to, 197, 222–23; set asides, 107, 113; SP-2, 197, 222–23, 231; student fees and, 34, 45–46; targeted outreach, 81–82, 84, 125, 203, 205–6

Galligani, Dennis, 81, 87–91
Gardner, David, 67
gender factors: Academic Council resolution, 125; admissions requirements, 1, 16, 17, 25, 28, 42, 84, 106, 107, 128, 146, 201, 223–24 (*see also* SP-1); *Bakke*, 28; California Civil Rights Initiative (CCRI), 41, 43–44, 54, 66–67, 69, 71–72, 77, 79, 84–85, 110, 114, 131, 133, 136, 160, 167, 198, 200–1, 203, 205, 206, 207–8, 209; California Master Plan, 28; Civil Rights Act, 26; contractors and contracting, 113, 128, 195, 200; diversity in admissions, 28, 97, 98; employment discrimination, 25, 26, 128, 129, 130, 195, 200, 223–24; faculty and staff hiring, 111–12, 114–17, 200 (*see also* SP-2); general, 2, 3; graduate admissions/degrees, 99, 100; medical school admissions, 59; mid-term (1994) elections, 42; Peltason on, 131; Regents' considerations/vote 1, 42, 89, 115, 116, 127, 131, 148, 149, 151, 153, 154, 156, 181, 183, 188, 193, 185, 201, 223–24, 228; student activism, 151, 153; Wilson on, 84, 106, 107, 146
General Declaration of Principles, 18
Gingrich, Newt, 42, 66, 83, 84
Gomez, Ed, 37, 67, 77, 105, 119, 120, 134–35, 144, 153, 155, 156, 157, 170, 187, 189, 191, 192, 195
Gonzales, Alice, 69, 74, 183, 187, 195, 215
governance: academic freedom, 9–10, 18, 19–20, 21; autonomy and, 16, 17–21, 225–27; constitutional law, California, 11–17, 19, 30, 214, 225–26; federal government and UC, 13, 15, 18; general, 1, 11, 72–73, 160, 211; interest articulation, 45–82, 212; models, 5, 6, 7, 8–10, 211–12; primary and secondary education, 6, 188; state legislation, 13–24. *See also* shared governance
governance structure: Academic Council of the University of California, 20, 122, 125, 126, 159, 189; alumni, general, 16, 76; Berkeley Revolution of 1920, 18–19, 20; California Master Plan for Higher Education, 13, 23–24; chancellors, 14, 62; constitutional law, state, and, 11–17, 30, 214, 225–26; historical and legal context, 13–24; positive theory of institutions (PTI), 6, 7–8, 213–15; private sector influence, 14–15, 16, 17, 30; state government, general, 13–18, 51, 226; trusteeship, 22, 157, 188, 211, 214. *See also* administration, University of California Office of the President; Board of Regents; chancellors; provost; senates, UC academic; shared governance
governors, California: Davis, Gray, 204–5, 206–7; Deukmejian, George, 37, 39, 182, 188; general, 4, 216; gubernatorial appointments, 4, 13–14, 16–17, 36–41, 45, 46–47, 63, 203–5, 213–14, 226. *See also* Wilson, Pete
GPA. *See* grade-point average
graduate admissions/degrees: after revocation of affirmative action, 201–3; law school, 30, 97–103, 201–2; medical school admissions, 1, 26, 27–30, 33, 49, 50–57, 58, 59, 61, 62–65; Regents' control over, 24

grade-point average (GPA), 30, 49, 50, 57, 60, 75, 81, 91, 92, 95, 98, 102

Hayden, Tom, 34, 219–20
Hertzberg, Bob, 208
high school. *See* primary and secondary education
high school graduates: minority, 33, 170, 184; socioeconomic status and aspirations, 31; UC admission requirements, 33–34, 88, 92, 169–70, 206, 229
hiring, affirmative action: academic development programs, 111; faculty, 27, 107–10, 111–12, 114–17, 197–98, 199 (*see also* SP-2); federal law, 25, 124–25, 221; Regents on hiring/contracting, 25, 27, 107–10, 111–12, 114–17, 124–25, 128, 222; UC Black Caucus, 27. *See also* employment; SP-2
Hispanics. *See* Chicanos and Chicanas; Latinos\Latinas
Hitch, Charles, 27
Holst, James, 56–57, 58, 135, 159, 163, 190, 191–92
Hopkins, Judith, 208
Hopper, Cornelius, 59, 63
Hopwood et al. v. State of Texas, 57, 58
Hughes, Teresa, 205

immigrants: California constitutional law, 30; *Proposition 187*, 42, 65–66
income: inequality, 24, 30–36, 76, 87–89 (passim), 117, 120, 138–39, 150–51, 156, 220; outreach, 153, 206. *See also* socioeconomic status
inequality: as basis for affirmative action, 26, 150–51, 155, 221; Connerly on, 71, 126; general, 2, 3 income, 24, 30–36, 76, 87–89 (passim), 117, 120, 138–39, 150–51, 156, 220; State theoretical view, 8–9
institutional factors: affirmative action, general, 1, 26, 212, 213, 225–27; collegiality, 3, 4, 78; culture, general, 3, 8, 16, 96, 217–18; culture,

Regents' institutional, 96, 217–18; interest groups, 6, 7–8, 212, 213–15; positive theory of institutions (PTI), 6, 7–8, 213–15. *See also* autonomy; decision making; political factors; organizational factors
instrumental value of policy, 3, 211, 215–16, 225, 227
interest articulation: general, 45–82, 212; organizational models, 5, 211–12; Regents, 45–46, 52–57, 60–65
interest groups: administration as, 212; general, 4, 5, 83, 122–24, 211, 217; institutional theory, 6, 7–8, 212, 213–15; Regents, 26, 83, 122–24
international perspectives, 3, 98
Irvine, University of California at: medical school admissions, 59, 109; student protests, 198

Jackson, Reverend Jesse, 2, 120–21, 133, 138–39, 141, 142, 147–51, 169, 189, 190, 192, 202, 221, 224
Johnson, S. Sue, 37, 40, 156, 176–77, 187, 189, 195, 208
del Junco, Tirso, 37, 61, 62, 64–65, 96, 101, 118, 136, 163, 164, 187, 189, 192, 195, 203–4, 219, 224
jurisprudence. *See* court decisions; Supreme Court, U.S.

Karabel, Jerome, 91, 102, 126
Kay, Herma Hill, 99–103, 203
Kennedy Administration, 25
Kennedy, Wayne, 115
Kerr, Clark, 20, 226
Khachigian, Meredith, 37, 75, 101, 180–82, 187, 189, 195, 223
King, Martin Luther, 55, 107, 120, 141, 147, 168, 169
Kolligian, Leo, 37, 61, 62, 63, 94, 136, 181–82, 185–86, 187, 189, 195

Laird, Robert, 172
Latinos/Latinas: admissions applicants, overview, 86–87, 88; admissions

disparities, 47, 48, 52; affirmative action, admissions, 33, 47, 48, 52, 80, 81, 96, 115–17, 128, 130, 202–3; affirmative action, faculty and staff hiring, 111, 115; graduate admissions/degrees received, 98, 99, 102, 109; socioeconomic status and race. *See also* Chicanos/Chicanas

law. *See* constitutional law, federal; constitutional law, state; court decisions; legislation

law school admissions: class size and, 100; general, 30, 97–103, 201–2; LSAT scores, 30, 100

Law School Admission Test. *See* LSAT

Leach, Howard, 37, 38, 39–40, 106, 115, 116, 149, 168–69, 176, 187, 189, 195

Lee, Lester, 47–48, 136, 175, 180, 186–87, 189, 195

legal factors. *See* constitutional law, federal; constitutional law, state; court decisions; legislation; referenda

legislation: Civil Rights Act, 26, 27–28, 30, 51; Donahue Higher Education Act (*see* California Master Plan for Higher Education); Equal Pay Act, 25; Morrill Act, 13; Organic Act, 13–14, 16; UC governance structure, 13–24. *See also* constitutional law, federal; constitutional law, state; referenda

Leiman, Arnold, 73–74, 81

Levin, Judith, 8, 9, 37, 127, 170, 178–79, 187, 189, 190, 195, 224

Levin, Lubbe, 112, 116–17

Lockyer, Bill, 214

loyalty oaths, 18, 19–20

LSAT (Law School Admission Test), 30, 100

Massey, Walter, 1, 67, 105, 115, 117, 138, 160, 192, 193–95

mass media: affirmative action at UC, general, 85, 108, 110, 120–21, 135–41 (passim), 143, 170, 171, 196, 200, 213; California Civil Rights Initiative (CCRI), 85; general, 130; Internet, 197; post-Bakke Berkeley admissions, 29; preferential admissions, 181–82; *Proposition 187*, 43, 66–67; Regents/U.S. president relations, 47–48; university funding and fees, 34

MCAT (Medical College Admissions Test), 57, 59, 61

Measure 5, 16

media coverage. *See* mass media

medical school: admissions criteria, 1, 26, 27–30, 49, 50–65

Mikva, Abner, 197

Minnesota State Board for Community Colleges v. Knight, 22

Mitchell-Kernan, Claudia, 98, 111, 114

models and modeling: cultural theories of organization, 3, 8, 16, 217–18; general, 211–15 governance, 5, 6, 7, 8–10, 211–12; interest articulation, 5, 211–12; organizational, 3–8, 16, 211–12, 227; positive theory of institutions (PTI), 6, 7–8, 213–15; social choice theory, 6; State theory, 2, 8–10, 72, 211, 219–20, 222

Montoya, Velma, 37, 93–94, 164, 182–83, 187, 189, 195

Morrill Act, 13

Morrison, Gary, 49–52, 56–59

multidimensional models, 4–5, 7. *See also* positive theory of institutions

NAACP, 2, 168–69, 208

Nakashima, S. Stephen, 37, 74, 149, 169, 179–80, 181, 184, 187, 189, 195, 223

Native Americans. *See* American Indians

news media. *See* mass media

Office of Civil Rights, 30, 51, 57

Open Meeting law. *See* Bagley-Keene Open Meeting law

Organic Act, 13–14, 16

organizational factors: crisis management, 83; general, 2–8, 211; models, 3–8, 16, 211–12, 227; UC, general, 11. *See also* institutional factors
outreach. *See* targeted outreach

Panetta, Leon, 2, 197
peer effects: collegiality, 3, 4, 78 general, 80, 97, 154
Peltason, Jack: chancellors and, 132–33, 172, 198–99; Connerly and, 46–48, 53, 67, 68–69, 72, 111, 115, 126–27, 129, 130–34, 135, 160, 167, 171; other, 37, 56, 78–79, 81, 118, 119, 126–27, 129, 130–37, 146, 159–62, 167, 170–71, 187, 188–89, 191, 195
Philadelphia Plan, 26–27
Pister, Karl, 62, 115–16, 117, 132–33, 199, 217, 226–27
political factors, general: affirmative action, general, 1–2, 3, 37–44, 73, 111, 133–34, 136–37, 143–96 (passim), 197–98, 203–6, 211, 213–14 (*see also* "national politics" *infra*); agendas and agenda control, 5, 7, 40, 77, 194, 200, 201, 203, 214–15, 216; California Civil Rights Initiative (CCRI), 43–44, 83, 84–85, 165, 203; Civil Rights Movement, 2, 55, 72, 107–8, 120–21, 127, 129, 138–39, 141, 142, 147–51, 168–69, 208 (*see also* "Jackson, Jesse" *infra*); Clinton administration, 2, 83–84, 141–42, 175, 197, 213, 222; constitutional law, UC governance, 15–16, 19, 30, 214, 225–26; immigration, 30, 42, 65–66; instrumental value of policy, 3, 211, 215–16, 225, 227; interest articulation, 5, 45–82, 84–85; Jackson, Jesse, 2, 120–21, 133, 138–39, 141, 142, 147–51, 169, 189, 190, 192, 202, 221, 224; Kennedy Administration, 25; loyalty oaths, 18, 19–20; national politics, 2–3, 29, 42, 53, 55, 65–67, 72, 73, 77, 83–84, 108–10, 120–21,
133, 138–42, 147–50, 201 (*see also* "*Jackson, Jesse*" *supra*); Regents' composition, 37–41, 46, 75, 135, 149–50, 188, 203–7; theory, 4, 6, 7–10; U.S. Congress, 41–42, 66, 83, 84; Wilson as U.S. presidential candidate, 65–66, 77. *See also* federal government; interest articulation; interest groups; mass media; state government; student activism/protests
political parties: Communist, 19; loyalty oaths, 19, 186; UC governance, constitutional law, 15; Wilson, Pete, presidential aspirations, 65–66. *See also* Democratic Party; Republican Party
positive theory of institutions (PTI), 6, 7–8, 213–15
president, UC: academic senate, consultation, 18–19, 91; affirmative action debate, 1, 46–47, 53, 55–56, 60–61, 67, 68, 72, 78–79, 111, 118, 130–37, 159–62; chancellors' relations with, 14, 132–33, 172, 198–99; diversity issue, 59, 62–63, 67–69, 79–81; Gardner, David, 67; Hitch, Charles, 27; Kerr, Clark, 20, 226; Regents' relations with, 14, 20, 45–48, 53, 55–56, 60–61, 67, 68, 72–73, 74, 78–79, 86, 111, 118, 130–37, 229, 230; UC president, appointment of, 20. *See also* administration, University of California Office of the President; Peltason, Jack
Preuss, Peter, 102, 116
primary and secondary education: academic development programs, 129, 132, 169, 205–6; applicants from same school considered equally, 92; funding, 150; governance, 6, 188; interest groups and, 217; minority representation in, 81, 101, 150. *See also* high school graduates
principle-agent problem, 6, 47
Proposition 9, 133

Proposition 13, 33–34, 133
Proposition 187, 41, 42–43, 65–66, 172–73
Proposition 209. See California Civil Rights Initiative
provost (Walter Massey), 1, 67, 105, 115, 117, 138, 160, 192, 193–95
PTI. *See* positive theory of institutions
public opinion: affirmative action, general, 2–3; *Proposition 187*, 42–43, 65–66; Regents' meetings, public comment, 74–75, 78, 79, 86, 114, 122–24, 144, 151–56, 189–92, 208, 223, 224–25. *See also* mass media; political factors; student activism/protests
Puerto Ricans, 52, 109
Purdy, Ralph, 59, 61

quotas: Connerly, 85, 126, 127; general, perception of, 85, 124–25, 163, 185, 193, 202; perception of quotas in medical school admissions, 50, 58, 59, 61, 62–65; Wilson, Pete, 107

race/ethnicity: admissions after revocation of affirmative action, 201–3; admissions applicants, overview, 96–87; admissions criteria, 1, 16, 17, 24, 25, 27–36, 34–35, 49–64, 70–77, 88–89, 91–96, 107, 114, 125–40 (passim), 145–96 (passim) (*see also* SP-1); Board of Regents' vote, 1; *Brown v. Board of Education*, 25, 26, 208; critical mass diversity, 99–103 (passim), 127; diversity, general, 11, 28, 34, 56, 60, 62–63, 78–79, 89, 92, 97–98, 125, 159, 160, 164–65, 176, 209; employment discrimination, 25; faculty and staff hiring, 111–12, 114–15; federal contracts, affirmative action, 27, 108–10; general, 3, 48, 47–51; graduate program admissions/degrees, general, 97–103; graduation rates, UC, 92, 98; high school graduates, minority, 33, 170, 184;

immigrants, 30, 42, 65–66; primary and secondary education, minority representation in, 81, 101, 150; socioeconomic status and, 27, 30–36, 93, 103–4, 137–38, 185–86, 219–23; underrepresented groups, 2, 29–30, 49, 52, 57, 60–62, 79, 81, 85–94 (passim), 98, 109, 112, 116, 126, 205; UC admissions by race, 33, 47–51. *See also* color-blind; immigrants; *specific groups*
racism: affirmative action characterized as, 26, 75, 76, 84, 155; public comments to Regents on, 124, 147, 148–49, 150, 152, 154, 155, 156, 223; Regents' reflections on, 168–69, 178, 183, 178–80, 183, 186–88
Rainbow Coalition, 2, 143
referenda: California Civil Rights Initiative (CCRI; *Proposition 209*), 41, 43–44, 54, 66–67, 69, 71–72, 77, 79, 84–85, 110, 114, 131, 133, 136, 160, 167, 198, 200–1, 203, 205, 206, 207–8, 209; *Proposition 9*, 133; *Proposition 13*, 33–34, 133; *Proposition 187*, 41, 42–43, 65–66, 172–73
Reagan, Ronald, 20, 106, 137
Regents. *See* Board of Regents
religion: admissions requirements and, 17, 25, 130, 230; hiring requirements and, 231
Republican Party: California Civil Rights Initiative (CCRI), 43, 127, 200–1; general, 2, 15, 62; mid-term (1994) elections, 41–42; *Proposition 187*, 42–43, 65–66, 127; Regents' composition, 37–41, 62, 135, 149–50, 188, 204; State Assembly, 2, 85, 216; state government, general, 2, 34, 38–41, 85, 216; State Senate, 2, 85; student activism, 104, 143–45; U.S. Congress, 41–42, 66, 83, 84; Wilson, Pete, as U.S. presidential candidate, 65–66, 83, 108
retention and graduation rates, 92, 95–96, 101

Richter, Bernie, 44, 69, 123, 184, 198
Riverside, University of California at, 11, 77, 155–56, 180
Russell, Richard, 34, 55, 163, 163–64, 165, 168

San Diego, University of California at: academic admission requirements, 35–36; academic admissions, 48–49; Chancellor Atkinson, 198–99, 207
San Francisco, University of California at, 60
Santa Barbara, University of California at, 11, 124, 198
Santa Cruz, University of California at: academic admission requirements, 35–36; Chancellor Pister, 62, 115–16, 117, 132–33, 199, 217, 226–27; faculty/staff hiring, 115–16
SAT (Scholastic Aptitude Test): general, 31, 91, 96; socioeconomic status and race, 103
Save Our State Initiative. *See* Proposition 187
Saxon, David, 133
Sayles, Tom, 37, 116, 117, 177–78, 187, 189, 195
Schwartz, Charles, 199
secondary education. *See* primary and secondary education
senates, UC academic: academic freedom, 18–19; admissions criteria, senate on, 13, 14, 18–19, 23, 91–92; affirmative action, general, 1, 19, 47, 80, 102. 123, 129, 131; bureaucracy, 14; constitution of, 14; president, UC, relations with, 18–19, 91; Regents' relations with, 13, 14, 18–19, 20, 22, 91–92, 129, 131, 134, 147, 176, 185, 187, 188–89, 199, 230; shared governance, 20, 22, 47, 230
shared governance: autonomy, legal and historical contest, 16, 17–21, 225–27; Berkeley Revolution of 1920, 18–19, 20; Connerly on, 225–26; crisis management, 83; general, 17–20, 22–23, 160, 188–89, 199–200; loyalty oaths, 18, 19–20; Regents, 18, 19–20, 22–23, 24, 55, 62, 64, 160, 188–89, 197–98; Supreme Court, U.S., 22
Simmons, Daniel, 115, 121, 122, 125, 183–84, 197
social choice theory, 6
socioeconomic status: access and, general, 2, 30–31, 33–34, 150, 189; affirmative action based on, 27, 30–36, 56, 59, 93, 94, 95, 103–4, 137–38, 219–23; affirmative action, cost of, 30, 81–82, 84; Asian Americans, 103, 205; caucasians, 103, 205; diversity, 30–31, 32–33, 45–46, 56, 59, 79, 89, 219; race/ethnicity and, 27, 30–36, 93, 103–4, 137–38, 185–86, 219–23; Regents, diversity of, 17, 30, 31, 45–46; SAT scores, 103. *See also* cultural factors; gender factors; income; race/ethnicity; wealth
SP-1: aftermath, 197–210, 219; Brophy amendment, 187–89, 192–93, 195; California Civil Rights Initiative (CCRI) and, 44, 179, 200; Connerly on, 130, 136, 164–65, 170, 179, 183, 184–85, 187, 189, 195, 199, 208–9; gender-specific impacts, 223–24; *Proposition 187* and, 42; Regents' debate, 1, 37, 54, 55, 72, 77, 130, 136, 158, 163–65, 168, 170, 176, 178, 180, 182–83, 187–89, 203–4, 205, 222; RE-28, 207–9; State Assembly, aftermath of, 201, 205, 216; State Senate, aftermath of, 201–7 (passim), 225; text of, 229–30; UCOP, 119; voting on, 37, 189, 195, 197, 201, 203, 205, 206–9, 215, 219
SP-2: aftermath, 197–210, 219; Board of Regents' debate, 1, 37, 54, 55, 72, 77, 130, 136, 158, 163–65, 167–68, 170, 176, 180, 182–83, 203–4, 205, 222; California Civil Rights Initiative (CCRI) and, 44, 179, 200; Connerly on, 130, 136, 158, 163, 164–65, 167–68, 170, 179, 183, 187, 189, 199, 208–9; gender-specific impacts, 223–

24; *Proposition 187*, 42; public opinion, 187; RE-28, 207–9; State Assembly, aftermath of, 201, 205, 216; State Senate, aftermath of, 201–7 (passim), 225; text of, 231–32; UCOP, 119; voting on, 37, 187, 195, 197, 201, 203–4, 205, 206–9, 215, 219

Special Committee on Affirmative Action Policies, 55, 68, 70–76, 79, 87–88, 110

State Assembly: affirmative action, general, 27, 65, 205; *Bakke*, admissions after, 28; California Civil Rights Initiative (CCRI), 44, 54, 69; Democratic Party, 2, 85, 201; loyalty oath, 19; Regents' appointments/composition, 13, 37; Regents' relations with, 61, 65, 70–71, 123, 146, 169, 184; Republican Party, 2, 85, 216; SP-1/SP-2, aftermath, 201, 205, 216

state government: California Master Plan for Higher Education, 13, 23–24, 28, 88, 89; California Postsecondary Education Commission (CPEC), 81, 86–87, 88, 206; Democratic Party, 2, 37, 39–41, 85, 199–200, 201; officials, overview, 1, 13–14; national mid-term (1994) elections, 41–42; Republican Party, 2, 34, 38–41, 85, 216; UC governance, 13–18, 51, 226. *See also* constitutional law, state; governor, California; referenda; State Assembly; State Senate

Statement of Principles on Academic Freedom and Tenure, 21

Statement on the Relationship of Faculty Governance to Academic Freedom, 23

State Senate: *Bakke*, admissions after, 28, 206; Democratic Party, 2, 85, 201, 203, 207, 214, 225, 226; Regents' appointments/composition, 13, 15–16, 34, 38–41, 45, 47, 203–5, 225, 226; Regents' relations with, 123, 131, 203–4, 207, 214, 225; Republican Party, 2, 85; SP-1/SP-2, aftermath, 201–7 (passim), 225

State theory, 2, 8–10, 72, 211, 219–20, 222

stigma: affirmative action characterized as, 71, 130, 148, 161, 162, 177, 180–81, 191, 193–94

student activism/protests: affirmative action, 78, 85–86, 104–5, 119–20, 126–27, 138, 139, 143–45, 151–56, 170, 189, 198; campus protests, climate, 20; organizational models, 5; university fees, 34

student associations: affirmative action, general, 1, 27, 105, 120, 134–35, 153

student attitudes, general: affirmative action, 126–27; socioeconomic status and aspirations, 31

Student Regents: Bravin, Jess, 53–54; Gomez, Ed, 37, 67, 77, 105, 119, 120, 134–35, 144, 153, 155, 156, 157, 170, 187, 189, 191, 192, 195; Wooten, Terrence, 62–63, 77

Supreme Court, California: *Bakke v. Regents of the University of California*, 27; Regents' loyalty oath, 18, 19; *Tolman v. Underhill*, 19

Supreme Court, U.S.: academic freedom, 21; affirmative action, general, 25, 26, 27–29, 159; *Adarand Constructors v. Pena*, 108–10, 112–13; *Brown v. Board of Education*, 25, 26, 208; institutional autonomy, 21, 22; *Minnesota State Board for Community Colleges v. Knight*, 22; shared governance, 22; *UC Regents v. Bakke*, 1, 26, 27–30, 49, 50–51, 56–58, 61, 126, 127, 136, 162–63, 206

Takasugi, Nao, 223

targeted outreach: Connerly on, 128, 129, 153, 170; cost-effectiveness, 81–82, 84; other, 79, 81–82, 84, 114, 125, 128–30 (passim), 153, 170, 203, 205–6, 229

taxation: *Proposition 13*, 33–34, 133; Wilson on affirmative action impacts, 145–46
test scores, 50, 51, 92, 98. *See also* SAT; LSAT; MCAT
Tien, Chang-Lin, 75, 138, 162, 170–73, 162, 170–77, 198
Tolman v. Underhill, 19
trusteeship, 22, 157, 188, 211, 214

UCLA: admissions criteria, Regents' control, 95–96; affirmative action policies, general, 91, 91–95, 96, 98, 126, 159, 180, 202–3; Chancellor Young, 63, 85, 101, 119, 192, 193. 198; graduate admissions/degrees, general, 98–99; law admissions, 30; medical admissions, 51, 58, 65
UCOP. *See* administration, University of California Office of the President
UC Regents v. Bakke, 1, 26, 27–30, 49, 50–51, 56–58, 61, 126, 127, 136, 162–63, 206
Umscheid, Rod, 112–13

Vasconcellos, John, 222–23

Watkins, Dean, 37, 62, 102, 187, 189, 195

wealth: Regents, 17, 103; affirmative action beneficiaries among wealthy, 94; race and, 150, 151, 156. *See also* socioeconomic status
white. *See* caucasians
Wilson, Pete: affirmative action debate, general, 2, 42–43, 54–55, 77, 95, 106–7, 110, 119, 120–21, 127, 128, 133, 134, 135, 136, 138–39, 142, 144, 145–46, 151, 153, 158, 160–62, 163, 165, 169, 170–77, 187, 188, 189, 196, 200–1, 214–15; Connerly, relations with, 65–66, 77, 106, 141, 163, 171, 215; *Proposition 187*, 42–43, 127; Regents' appointments, 37, 39, 41, 45, 177, 203–5, 214–15; Regents, letter to, 106; SP-1, 136, 187, 195, 229; Regents' meetings open to public, 190, 191; SP-2, 136, 187, 195, 231; U.S. presidential candidacy, 65–66, 77, 83, 84, 106–7, 110, 145–46, 166–67, 169, 196, 200, 216, 223
Winans, Joseph, 15
women. *See* Gender factors
Wood, Thomas, 44, 69, 84
Wooten, Terrence, 62–63, 77

Young, Charles, 63, 85, 102, 119, 192–93, 198

SUNY series: Frontiers in Education
Philip G. Altbach, Editor

LIST OF TITLES

Excellence and Equality: A Qualitatively Different Perspective on Gifted and Talented Education—David M. Fetterman
Class, Race, and Gender in American Education—Lois Weis (ed.)
Change and Effectiveness in Schools: A Cultural Perspective—Gretchen B. Rossman, H. Dickson Corbett, and William A. Firestone (eds.)
The Curriculum: Problems, Politics, and Possibilities—Landon E. Beyer and Michael W. Apple (eds.)
Crisis in Teaching: Perspectives on Current Reforms—Lois Weis, Philip G. Altbach, Gail P. Kelly, Hugh G. Petrie, and Sheila Slaughter (eds.)
The Character of American Higher Education and Intercollegiate Sport—Donald Chu
Dropouts from Schools: Issues, Dilemmas, and Solutions—Lois Weis, Eleanor Farrar, and Hugh G. Petrie (eds.)
The Higher Learning and High Technology: Dynamics of Higher Education Policy Formation—Sheila Slaughter
Religious Fundamentalism and American Education: The Battle for the Public Schools—Eugene F. Provenzo, Jr.
The High Status Track: Studies of Elite Schools and Stratification—Paul W. Kingston and Lionel S. Lewis (eds.)
The Economics of American Universities: Management, Operations, and Fiscal Environment—Stephen A. Hoenack and Eileen L. Collins (eds.)
Going to School: The African-American Experience—Kofi Lomotey (ed.)
Curriculum Differentiation: Interpretive Studies in U.S. Secondary Schools—Reba Page and Linda Valli (eds.)
The Racial Crisis in American Higher Education—Philip G. Altbach and Kofi Lomotey (eds.)
The Great Transformation in Higher Education, 1960-1980—Clark Kerr
College in Black and White: African American Students in Predominantly White and in Historically Black Public Universities—Walter R. Allen, Edgar G. Epps, and Nesha Z. Haniff (eds.)
Critical Perspectives on Early Childhood Education—Lois Weis, Philip G. Altbach, Gail P. Kelly, and Hugh G. Petrie (eds.)
Textbooks in American Society: Politics, Policy, and Pedagogy—Philip G. Altbach, Gail P. Kelly, Hugh G. Petrie, and Lois Weis (eds.)
Black Resistance in High School: Forging a Separatist Culture—R. Patrick Solomon
Emergent Issues in Education: Comparative Perspectives—Robert F. Arnove, Philip G. Altbach, and Gail P. Kelly (eds.)
Creating Community on College Campuses—Irving J. Spitzberg, Jr. and Virginia V. Thorndike
Teacher Education Policy: Narratives, Stories, and Cases—Hendrik D. Gideonse (ed.)

Beyond Silenced Voices: Class, Race, and Gender in United States Schools—Lois Weis and Michelle Fine (eds.)
The Cold War and Academic Governance: The Lattimore Case at Johns Hopkins—Lionel S. Lewis
Troubled Times for American Higher Education: The 1990s and Beyond—Clark Kerr
Higher Education Cannot Escape History: Issues for the Twenty-first Century—Clark Kerr
Multiculturalism and Education: Diversity and Its Impact on Schools and Society—Thomas J. LaBelle and Christopher R. Ward
The Contradictory College: The Conflicting Origins, Impacts, and Futures of the Community College—Kevin J. Dougherty
Race and Educational Reform in the American Metropolis: A Study of School Decentralization—Dan A. Lewis and Kathryn Nakagawa
Professionalization, Partnership, and Power: Building Professional Development Schools—Hugh G. Petrie (ed.)
Ethnic Studies and Multiculturalism—Thomas J. LaBelle and Christopher R. Ward
Promotion and Tenure: Community and Socialization in Academe—William G. Tierney and Estela Mara Bensimon
Sailing Against the Wind: African Americans and Women in U.S. Education—Kofi Lomotey (ed.)
The Challenge of Eastern Asian Education: Implications for America—William K. Cummings and Philip G. Altbach (eds.)
Conversations with Educational Leaders: Contemporary Viewpoints on Education in America—Anne Turnbaugh Lockwood
Managed Professionals: Unionized Faculty and Restructuring Academic Labor—Gary Rhoades
The Curriculum (Second Edition): Problems, Politics, and Possibilities—Landon E. Beyer and Michael W. Apple (eds.)
Education / Technology / Power: Educational Computing as a Social Practice—Hank Bromley and Michael W. Apple (eds.)
Capitalizing Knowledge: New Intersections of Industry and Academia—Henry Etzkowitz, Andrew Webster, and Peter Healey (eds.)
The Academic Kitchen: A Social History of Gender Stratification at the University of California, Berkeley—Maresi Nerad
Grass Roots and Glass Ceilings: African American Administrators in Predominantly White Colleges and Universities—William B. Harvey (ed.)
Community Colleges as Cultural Texts: Qualitative Explorations of Organizational and Student Culture—Kathleen M. Shaw, James R. Valadez, and Robert A. Rhoads (eds.)
Educational Knowledge: Changing Relationships between the State, Civil Society, and the Educational Community—Thomas S. Popkewitz (ed.)
Transnational Competence: Rethinking the U.S.-Japan Educational Relationship—John N. Hawkins and William K. Cummings (eds.)
Women Administrators in Higher Education: Historical and Contemporary Perspectives—Jana Nidiffer and Carolyn Terry Bashaw (eds.)
Faculty Work in Schools of Education: Rethinking Roles and Rewards for the Twenty-first Century—William G. Tierney (ed.)

The Quest for Equity in Higher Education: Towards New Paradigms in an Evolving Affirmative Action Era—Beverly Lindsay and Manuel J. Justiz (eds.)

The Racial Crisis in American Higher Education (Revised Edition): Continuing Challenges for the Twenty-first Century—William A. Smith, Philip G. Altbach, and Kofi Lomotey (eds.)

Increasing Access to College: Extending Possibilities for All Students—William G. Tierney and Linda Serra Hagedorn (eds.)

Burning Down the House: Politics, Governance, and Affirmative Action at the University of California—Brian Pusser